Programming Interviews Exposed

Secrets to Landing Your Next Job

Second Edition

Programming Interviews Exposed

Secrets to Landing Your Next Job
Second Edition

John Mongan

Noah Suojanen

Eric Giguère

BICENTENNIAL 1807 WILEY 2007 BICENTENNIAL

Wiley Publishing, Inc.

Programming Interviews Exposed: Secrets to Landing Your Next Job Second Edition

Published by
Wiley Publishing, Inc.
10475 Crosspoint Boulevard
Indianapolis, IN 46256
www.wiley.com

Published simultaneously in Canada

ISBN: 978-0-470-12167-2

Manufactured in the United States of America

10 9 8 7 6 5 4 3

Library of Congress Cataloging-in-Publication Data:

Mongan, John, 1976-
Programming interviews exposed : secrets to landing your next job / John Mongan, Noah Suojanen, Eric Giguère. — 2nd ed.
p. cm.
Includes index.
ISBN 978-0-470-12167-2 (pbk.)
1. Employment interviewing. 2. Computer programming — Vocational guidance. I. Suojanen, Noah, 1978- II. Giguère, Eric, 1967- III. Title.
HF5549.5.I6M664 2007
650.14'4 — dc22

2007003315

For general information on our other products and services please contact our Customer Care Department within the United States at (800) 762-2974, outside the United States at (317) 572-3993 or fax (317) 572-4002.

Wiley also publishes its books in a variety of electronic formats. Some content that appears in print may not be available in electronic books.

To my family

—Noah Suojanen

To those who encouraged me, living and dead

—John Mongan

To my parents, Jean-Claude and Marie-Joelle, who encouraged and supported my love of programming

—Eric Giguère

Credits

Acquisitions Editor
Carol Long

Development Editor
Maureen Spears

Production Editor
William A. Barton

Copy Editor
Luann Rouff

Editorial Manager
Mary Beth Wakefield

Production Manager
Tim Tate

Vice President and Executive Group Publisher
Richard Swadley

Vice President and Executive Publisher
Joseph B. Wikert

Graphics and Production Specialists
Sean Decker
Carrie A. Foster
Jennifer Mayberry
Alicia B. South

Quality Control Technicians
John Greenough
Brian H. Walls

Project Coordinator
Erin Smith

Proofreading and Indexing
Aptara

Anniversary Logo Design
Richard Pacifico

Acknowledgments

Putting out any book, even a second edition, requires a lot of work from many people. John and Eric would first of all like to thank Maureen Spears, our editor, for her patience throughout this process and the work she did in switching the book over to the WROX format. We'd also like to thank Carol Long for spearheading the updating of the original book, and everyone else at Wiley who worked on the production, marketing, and distribution of this book.

No second edition would have been possible without the first edition, however, and the many people who contributed to it. For this reason, we also thank our original editors, Margaret Hendrey and Marjorie Spencer, for their patience and helpfulness. We are also grateful to our original reviewers and advisors, Dan Hill, Elise Lipkowitz, Charity Lu, Rob Maguire, and Tom Mongan. Dan's contributions in particular were tremendous — the quality of the first edition was vastly improved by his careful and meticulous reviews.

Contents

Contents

Preface to the Second Edition

John and Noah probably didn't think they were writing a long-lived book, but that's what *Programming Interviews Exposed* has become. So how do you update a book that's a classic in its field? Very carefully!

Fans of the first edition will be pleased to know that the second edition is mostly an update, not a complete rewrite. The programming examples have been updated, obviously, to reflect the changes that have occurred in the nearly ten years that have passed since the first edition was written. Examples that were almost entirely in C and C++ are now in C++, Java, and C#—although the language hardly matters in most cases, as algorithms generally only require minor syntactical changes to switch from one language to another. All the examples are easily understandable to an experienced programmer.

Some new material has been added, but most of the old problems are intact, with some clarifications and corrections where necessary. In addition, inclusive language is now used to reflect the fact that programmers—including the interviewers—aren't all male. More headings have also been added for organizational purposes.

The approachable style of the first edition has not changed. You'll find this book to be an easy read and a great way to prepare yourself for the entire programming interview process. Kudos to John and Noah for their excellent book. We all hope you enjoy this revised edition. Please feel free to mail us at `authors@piexposed.com` if you have questions or comments about the book. Visit the official *Programming Interviews Exposed* site at `http://www.piexposed.com` for updates and more information.

Eric Giguère

Preface to the First Edition

If you're like us, you don't usually read prefaces. This one has some useful information in it, though, so we hope you'll make an exception. If you're still tempted to skip the preface, here's what you really need to know: You'll get as much out of this book as you put into it. If you read this book cover to cover, you'll learn something, but not nearly as much as you would if you take some time trying to work through the problems on your own before you read the answers.

This book will help prepare you for the interviews you will face when seeking a job in programming, development, technical consulting, or any other field that warrants a programming interview. Programming interviews bear little resemblance to those described in traditional job-hunting and interview books. They consist almost entirely of programming problems, puzzles, and technical questions about computers. This book discusses each of the kinds of problems you are likely to encounter and illustrates how they are best approached using questions from real interviews as examples.

At this point you may be wondering who we are and what gives us the authority to write this book. We're both recent graduates who've been through a lot of interviews in the past few years. We've interviewed for jobs ranging from technical consulting with large established companies to writing device drivers for start-ups. This book is based on the experiences and observations we've taken from those interviews — what yielded offers and what didn't. We believe that this is the best possible basis for a book like this. Rather than give you some HR exec's idea of how interviewing should be done or a head hunter's impression of how it might be done, we will tell you what interviews are really like at America's top software and computer companies and what you need to do to get the job you want.

> *For the record, we don't think that the way interviewing is done today is necessarily the way it should be done. The current paradigm puts too much emphasis on ability to solve puzzles and familiarity with a relatively limited body of knowledge, and it generally fails to measure a lot of the skills that are critical to success in industry.*

To that end, we haven't made up any of the questions in this book. Every last one of them has been lifted from a recent interview. The distributions of problem type and difficulty are similar to what you should expect to encounter in your interviews. We must emphasize that the problems presented in this book are a *representative* sample of the questions asked in interviews, not a comprehensive compilation. Reading this book straight through and memorizing the answers would completely miss the point. You may be asked some of the questions that appear in this book, but you should not expect that. A large and constantly changing body of questions is asked, and any intelligent interviewer who has seen this book will never again use any of the questions that appear here. On the other hand, interview questions encompass relatively few topic areas and types of questions, and these rarely change. If you work on learning to solve not just the specific problems we present, but the *types* of problems we present, you'll be able to handle anything they throw at you in an interview.

We've taken a couple of steps to facilitate the objective of improving your problem-solving skills. First, where appropriate, we provide reviews of important topics before we present questions on those topics. Second, instead of merely giving answers to the problems, we illustrate the problem-solving process from beginning to solution. We've found that most textbooks and nearly all puzzle books take a different approach to examples: They begin with a problem, go immediately to the answer, and then explain why the answer is correct. In our experience, the result is that the reader may understand the particular answer and why it's right, but is left with no clue as to how the author came up with that solution or how a similar problem might be solved. We hope that our step-by-step approach to solutions will address this issue, helping you to understand not only the answers but also how you arrive at the answers.

Learning by watching is never as effective as learning by doing. If you want to get the most out of this book, you will have to work out the problems yourself. We suggest the following method. After you read a problem, put the book down and try to work out the solution. If you get stuck, start reading the solution. We never blurt out the answer at the beginning, so you don't have to worry that we're going to give away the entire solution. Read just far enough to get the hint you need, and then put down the book and keep working. Repeat this as necessary. The more of the solution you work out yourself, the better your understanding will be. In addition, this method closely resembles the actual interview experience, where you will have to solve the problems yourself, but the interviewer will give you hints when you get stuck.

Programming is a difficult and technical art. It would be impossible to teach everything you need to know about computers and programming in one book. Therefore, we've had to make some assumptions about who you are. We assume that you have a background in computers equivalent to at least the first year or two of a computer science degree. Specifically, we expect that you are comfortable with programming in C, that you've had some experience with object-oriented programming in C++ or perhaps Java, and that you know the fundamentals of computer architecture and computer science theory. These are effectively the minimum requirements for a general development job, so most interviewers will have similar expectations. If you find yourself lacking in any of these areas, you should seriously consider seeking more education before starting your job search and interviews.

It's also possible that you have a great deal more computer knowledge and experience than what we've described as the minimum requirements. If so, you may be particularly interested in some of the more advanced topics we include, such as databases, graphics, concurrency, and Perl. However, don't ignore the basic topics and questions, no matter how much experience you have. Interviewers tend to start with the fundamentals regardless of what's on your resume.

We have made every effort to ensure that all of the information in this book is correct. All of the code has been compiled and tested. Nevertheless, as you probably know all too well from your own programs, a few bugs and errors are inevitable. As we become aware of such problems, we will post corrections at `http://www.piexposed.com`.

We're confident that you'll find this book useful in getting the job you want. We hope that you may also find it an entertaining exploration of some clever puzzles in your chosen profession. If you'd like to tell us about your reaction to our book, share your thoughts on any particular problem or topic, or provide a problem from one of your recent interviews, we'd love to hear from you. Please e-mail us at `authors@piexposed.com`.

Go find a killer job!

John and Noah

Before the Search

Before starting your job search, there are some preliminary tasks to perform. There's no point applying for jobs without knowing what you like, for example. Just being a good coder isn't enough — you have to understand what the market wants and how you can adapt your own skills to find the right job for yourself.

Know Yourself

Stereotypes to the contrary, all programmers are *not* alike. Knowing what kind of programmer you are is crucial to finding the right kind of job. While you can probably do many different kinds of programming tasks, they won't all turn your crank in the same manner. Doing something you don't really enjoy is fine on a short-term basis, but you need to be interested in and excited by what you're doing to sustain you over the long term. The best programmers are passionate about their work, and you can't truly be passionate about something that's only moderately interesting to you.

If you're not sure what you like or dislike, ask yourself some questions:

- **Are you a systems programmer or an application developer?** Systems programmers work on the code that keeps computer systems running: frameworks, tools, compilers, drivers, servers, and so on. Other programmers are their primary audience, and there's little interaction with nonprogrammers. Application developers, on the other hand, work on the pieces that those nonprogrammers use to do their own work, and there's often more interaction with nontechnical people.
- **Do you like coding user interfaces?** If so, and if you're skilled at it, consider yourself lucky. User interface design is finicky work, easy to criticize, and hard to do well, especially when internationalization and accessibility issues are taken into account.
- **Are you a good debugger?** If you think finding problems in your own code is bad enough, imagine what it's like to fix problems with someone else's code. It requires strong analytical and problem-solving skills. Finding and fixing bugs can be extremely rewarding in its own right, but it's definitely *not* for everyone.

- ❑ **Do you like testing?** Testing — also referred to as *quality assurance*, or QA for short — is often maligned by inexperienced programmers, but those who've been around the block once or twice value independent testing. Skilled testers are hard to find, and programming skills are usually required to write tools and automated test cases.
- ❑ **Are you an architect or a coder?** Every coding job includes some kind of design aspect, but certain jobs lean more one way than the other. If you enjoy the designing more than the coding, a position as a software architect might be more appealing. That said, architecture positions can involve *a lot* of interaction with others and little or no coding, though you need a good understanding of how to code in order to be an effective architect. Unless you take formal training in software architecture, the usual route to becoming an architect is to code first and then display an aptitude for designing and fitting together different pieces of a project.

While the preceding questions deal with the different kinds of programming that might interest you, there are also nonprogramming questions to consider:

- ❑ **Does management interest you?** Some coders have a long-term goal of becoming a manager, but others shiver at the very thought. If management is your goal, however, you'll need to develop leadership skills and demonstrate that you can manage the human parts of the software development equation as well as the technical pieces. If management is *not* your goal, look for companies with good *technical* career paths so you're not forced to manage people in order to be promoted.
- ❑ **Do you want to work for a big company?** There are advantages and disadvantages to working at big companies. For example, a large company usually offers more job stability and some kind of career path. It may also have a name brand that nontechies recognize. On the other hand, you may feel stifled by the bureaucracy, rigidness, and intercompany rivalry that is often found within bigger companies.
- ❑ **Do you want to work for a small company?** The pay may be less, but getting in on the ground floor at a new company can ensure future advancement (and possibly substantial remuneration) as the company grows and succeeds. The downside, of course, is that most new ventures fail and you may be out of a job within a year or two.
- ❑ **Are open-source projects preferable?** The vast majority of programming jobs have usually involved proprietary, closed-source projects, which some programmers find objectionable. There's been a small shift in favor of more open software development, which provides more opportunities for people like yourself to participate in open-source projects and still be paid for that participation.
- ❑ **Do you want long-term or short-term projects?** Some programmers crave change, spending a few months at most on each project. If you like short-term projects and don't mind traveling, a gig with a consulting company might make more sense than a more conventional corporate job.

It's important to realize that there are no universal answers to these questions, no right or wrong way to answer them. The more truthful you can be with yourself in answering them, however, the more likely you'll be able to find the kind of programming job you truly enjoy.

Know the Market

Knowing what you'd like to do is great, but don't box yourself in too narrowly. You also need to understand the current job market and how it constrains your search for the "ideal" job, especially during an economic downturn like the one that burst the original Internet bubble of the late '90s.

Basic Market Information

There are a number of sources of information about what's hot and what's not in the developer job market, including the following:

- **Online job listings** — Large job sites such as Dice (which specializes in technology-related career listings), Monster, and HotJobs are your first line of research into what companies want.
- **Bookstores** — Even though more and more programmer documentation is available online, printed books are still a significant market for technical publishers. The number of books published on any given topic is a good indication of the degree to which skills related to that topic are valued by potential employers. Look out especially for niche topics that are suddenly going mainstream.
- **Social networking and bookmarking sites** — Some of these sites enable you to find potential employers, or enable them to find you. Others provide an indirect "pulse" of the market by the bookmarks and comments other programmers leave about various technologies and employers.
- **Professional development courses** — Colleges and universities try to keep abreast of what companies want, and create professional development courses around those needs.

If you're not in college or university anymore, find out what languages and technologies the local institutions and/or your alma mater are requiring of their computer science students; although academic needs don't always coincide with what employers want, educational institutions on the whole try to graduate students with practical skills that employers can use.

What About Outsourcing?

The rise of *outsourcing* — having an outside company handle tasks that aren't central to a company's lines of business — is always a topic of heated discussion within the development community. Outsourcing is not new, of course — companies have long outsourced tasks such as payroll administration and property maintenance — but the growing number of well-educated people in developing nations and the fact that software development can be done anywhere there's Internet access have made it possible for companies to *offshore* tasks that would normally have required a *local* workforce, whether or not the jobs were outsourced. The disparity in wages between offshore and local talent can result in large savings for companies that offshore their software development — at least that's the promise that the outsourcing companies make in their sales pitches.

Many software developers find themselves worrying whether outsourcing (and offshoring in particular) is going to put them out of a job, especially those who work in information technology (IT) departments within a larger company looking to cut costs wherever they can. These fears are not unfounded, unfortunately, so when you're looking for a job consider taking steps to avoid landing a job that will be outsourced at some point in the future. Following are some suggestions:

- **Work for software development firms** — A software firm's *raison d'être* is the intellectual property it develops. While medium and large firms may open development centers in other parts of the world, the smart ones are unlikely to move their entire operations to other countries or entrust their future to outside firms. That said, some companies will outsource all or substantial parts of a project to the developing world for cost reasons, so it pays to research a company's behaviors and policies in this regard.
- **Work for an outsourcer** — For various reasons, many outsourcing firms end up hiring personnel in the developed world, including the United States.
- **Move up the programmer food chain** — Design-oriented jobs are less likely to be outsourced. Good coders are cheap and plentiful, but good designers are much harder to find. (This assumes, of course, that good design skills are separate from good coding skills, and not everyone takes that view, although many companies do.)
- **Take a management job** — Management can be a refuge from outsourcing, so a management-oriented career path is one option to consider.

Of all these options, moving up the food chain is usually the best approach. The more nonprogramming knowledge your job requires, or the more interaction with customers, the less likely you are to be outsourced. There's no *guarantee* you'll never be outsourced, of course, or that you'll always keep your job. Your company may shutter or downsize the project you're working on at any point, after all, and put you back on the street. This is why developing reusable and marketable skills throughout your career is extremely important.

Develop Marketable Skills

The appendix covers how your résumé is primarily a *marketing tool* to get you job interviews. This assumes, of course, that you have *marketable skills* to offer a prospective employer. You can only stretch the truth so far, and if even you exaggerate or outright lie about your skills and what you've accomplished in the past, you probably won't make it through technical interviews designed specifically to weed out the liars and exaggerators of this world. What you need to do, then, is develop skills and accomplishments that will make you stand out from the crowd both on paper and in the interviews, especially if you're entering the job market for the first time. Here are some approaches you can take:

- **Upgrade your credentials** — Companies such as Google are well known for favoring job applicants with graduate degrees. Getting a master's or doctorate degree is one way to upgrade your credentials. Although pursuing a graduate degree is a large commitment on your part, you can upgrade your credentials in other ways, such as taking university or professional development courses or participating in programming contests.
- **Get certified** — Certification is a touchy issue in the software development profession, but there's no doubt that some jobs either prefer or require candidates to be certified in specific technologies, especially IT jobs.
- **Work on a side project** — A great way to expand your skill set is to work on a project that is not directly related to your primary work or study focus. Starting or joining an open-source development project is one way to go. Or if you're working at a company, see if they'll let you spend time on an ancillary project.

- **Do well in school** — Although grades aren't everything, they are one measure that companies use in order to rank new graduates with little job experience. The better your grades, especially in computer science and mathematics courses, the more you'll impress a potential employer.
- **Keep learning** — The end of formal education doesn't mean you should stop learning, especially when there's so much information about programming available from a wide variety of sources. Whether it's books or blogs, there's always a way to keep yourself current, no matter what type of programming you do. It's also a great way to expand your horizons and discover other areas of interest.
- **Be an intern** — New graduates who've managed to secure employment during their nonschool terms — especially those that participate in cooperative education programs — have a huge leg up over their peers who haven't yet ventured into the real world. Software development in the field is often very different from software development in an academic setting, and potential employers are very cognizant of this.

The key is to *keep learning*, no matter what stage of your career you're at. Marketable skills don't develop overnight; they take some effort and initiative on your part, but they'll have long-lasting effects on your career.

Note that one of the best ways to develop marketable skills is to *accomplish something*, whether it's in your current job, something you did as a side project, or something you worked on as an intern or for a class project. Being able to talk intelligently and confidently about a project for which you played a primary role in its success is incredibly important. Make sure you can describe the problem clearly and succinctly and how your project solved the problem, even to a nontechnical person. Displaying a passion for programming is always positive and one way to make yourself stand out from the other candidates.

Sanitize Your Online Profile

Once you've applied for a job, the first step in landing an interview is to make it past the screeners. Screeners are the humans who examine prospective job applicants after their résumés have made it through the company's automated filtering system. Their task is to trim the applicant pool to manageable levels. They comb through the remaining résumés, looking for anomalies and discrepancies in each job application, or any indication that the prospective employee would be a poor fit for the company. Even if your résumé is perfectly tailored to make it past the filtering system, the screeners can stop your application dead in its tracks based on what they find out about you, which is why your online profile is so important.

Many screeners now look online to learn more about prospective employees. The impression they get from your online profile can affect your chances of being hired. If your résumé lists extensive experience with C# but they find a forum posting you made only six months ago asking how to open a file in C#, they'll probably conclude that you're exaggerating your experience level, putting your whole résumé into doubt. Or if they see disturbing and/or inflammatory material that they think you've authored, they may decide to pass you over for an interview, no matter how well your résumé reads or how long ago you wrote those things. No one's proud of everything they ever did in high school or college, but those who have grown up in the post-Internet era will see things follow them that they'd rather forget about, something the older generations rarely had to contend with.

At some point before you apply for a job, take a good look at your online profile. Put yourself in a company's shoes and see how much information — good or bad — they can find about you, or link to you. If your online profile is possibly going to prevent you from being hired, take some steps to sanitize your profile. Remove questionable material from the Web and from the search engines. Abandon old e-mail addresses and online identities.

Develop a newer, better online profile for yourself that doesn't throw any red flags in front of the screeners. Finding a good job is hard enough as it is — why make it harder?

Summary

What you do *before* a formal job search is critical to finding the right kind of job. With that in mind, you should consider the following things:

- ❑ Know your likes and dislikes as a programmer and a prospective employee.
- ❑ Understand the market in order to find and apply for the best jobs.
- ❑ Develop the marketable skills that employers look for and that will enhance your career.
- ❑ Don't forget to check your public profile to make sure there are no surprises that can turn off potential employers.

When you have a good grasp of all of these points, you're ready to begin your job search.

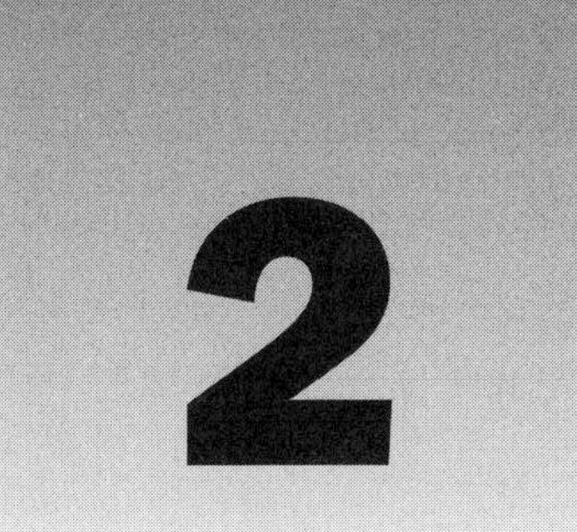

The Job Application Process

Interviewing and recruiting procedures are similar at most tech companies. The more prepared you are for what you will encounter, the more successful you will be. This chapter familiarizes you with the entire job-search process, from contacting companies to starting your new job, so you won't have to write off your first few application attempts as learning experiences. Hiring procedures at technical companies are often substantially different from those followed by more traditional firms, so you may find this information useful even if you've spent some time in the working world.

Finding and Contacting Companies

The first step in getting a job is finding and making contact with companies you're interested in working for. Although networking through a contact with a company provides the highest probability of success, there are a number of other possibilities, including working with a headhunter or contacting the company directly.

Networking

Networking (the social kind) is the best way to find jobs. Tell all your friends about what kind of job you're looking for. Even if they don't work for the kinds of companies that might hire you, they probably know people who do. Coming from "Susan's friend" or "Bill's neighbor," your résumé is sure to receive more careful consideration than the hundreds of anonymous résumés that come flooding in from strangers. Companies often reward employees for successful referrals, so don't think there's nothing in it for them. Social networking sites such as LinkedIn are another way to find additional contacts, both directly and indirectly.

Once you have a contact at a company, it's up to you to make the most of it. If the contact is not a close friend, it's tempting to call him or her and say, "Hi, I'd like to speak with you about getting a job." Presumably, your contact already knows that this is the ultimate reason why you're calling, so cutting to the chase may seem reasonable. This approach, though, is tactless and likely to be unsuccessful. Your contact may find it arrogant or presumptive that you would assume his or her company needs you before you've even heard about the company or its current needs. For best results, you need to be more circumspect:

- ❑ Start by setting up a time to speak. You don't want to annoy your contact by trying to talk with him or her at an inconvenient time.
- ❑ When you do speak to your contact, begin by asking about the company and finding out what it does. If it sounds like a good place to work, ask about openings. If an opening sounds ideal for you, explain why you believe that you would be a good match. Don't be surprised if the contact doesn't know which jobs are currently open, especially in larger companies. You can often find this information online from the company's Web site or via job sites such as Dice. (That said, not all job openings are posted, so it doesn't hurt to ask.)
- ❑ Finally, thank the person for his or her time and ask if you can send a résumé or if there's another person you can speak with about any openings.

Working with Headhunters

Especially when labor markets are tight, many firms use outside recruiters known as *headhunters* to help them find candidates. If you list yourself with a headhunter, she will assist you with your job search and call you when she learns of an opening that matches your skill set. Some headhunters are more helpful than others, so ask around to see if anyone you know has recommendations. If you can't locate a headhunter this way, you can search the Web for headhunters, recruiters, or staffing services. You can check out a prospective headhunter by asking for references, but be aware that headhunters deal with so many people that even those who frequently do a poor job will have 5 or 10 satisfied clients who serve as references.

The term "headhunter" is used universally by applicants and employers, but many of those to whom the term is applied find it insulting. Therefore, it's probably best not to use the word "headhunter" when talking to one. Avoid headhunters who want to act as your sole agent or want you to pay them fees — reputable headhunters understand that they are only a part of your job search and that their compensation comes from employers, not applicants.

When you work with a headhunter, it's important to understand his or her motivation. Headhunters are paid only when an applicant they've referred is hired. It is therefore in a headhunter's best interest to put as many people as possible into as many jobs as possible as quickly as possible. A headhunter has no financial incentive to find you the best possible job — or to find a company the best possible applicant, for that matter. If you recognize that a headhunter is in business for the purpose of making a living, not for the purpose of helping you, you are less likely to be surprised or disappointed by your experiences. This is not to suggest that headhunters are bad people or that as a rule they take advantage of applicants or companies. Headhunters can be very helpful and useful, but you must not expect them to look out for your interests above their own.

Contacting the Company Directly

You can also try contacting companies directly. The Internet is the best medium for this approach. You may know of some companies you'd like to work for, or you can search the Web to find companies in your area. Most companies' Web pages have instructions for submitting résumés. If the Web site lists specific openings, read through them and submit your résumé specifically for the openings you're interested in. If you don't have a contact within the company, it's best to look for specific job openings: In many companies, résumés targeted at a specific job opportunity are forwarded directly to the hiring manager, while those that don't mention a specific opening languish in the human resources database. A tech-oriented job site such as Dice is a good place to start your search if you don't have a specific company already in mind. Nontechnical recruiting and networking sites such as Monster and LinkedIn are also worth exploring.

If a site doesn't provide any directions for submitting your résumé, look for an e-mail address to which you can send it. Send your résumé as both plain text in the body of the e-mail (so the recipient can read it without having to do any work) and, unless there are instructions to the contrary, as an attached file (so the recipient can print a copy). A PDF file is ideal (easily created with OpenOffice or free converters such as PrimoPDF); otherwise, attach a Microsoft Word file. Do not send a file in any other format unless specifically requested. Be sure to convert the file so that it can be read by older versions of Word, and be *absolutely certain* that your résumé isn't carrying any macro viruses.

Approaching a company directly like this is a bit of a long shot, especially when the résumé is sent to a generic human resources e-mail address. Many companies use automated screening software to filter incoming résumés, so if your résumé lacks the right buzzwords a human probably won't even see it — consult the appendix for tips on getting your résumé past the automated screeners. With a good resume in hand, however, it takes so little time and effort to apply that you have nothing to lose.

Job Fairs and Classified Ads

Job fairs are an easy way to learn about and make contact with a lot of companies without much effort. Your chances of success with any one particular company at a job fair are low because each company sees so many applicants, but given the number of companies at a job fair, your overall odds may still be favorable. If you collect business cards at the job fair and follow up with people afterward, you can distinguish yourself from the rest of the job fair crowd.

You can also try more traditional job-search methods such as newspaper classified ads. In addition, if they are available to you, college career centers, alumni organizations, and professional associations can also be helpful in finding jobs.

The Interview Process

If someone is sufficiently impressed by your résumé to want to talk to you, the next step is one or more screening interviews, usually followed by an on-site interview. This section discusses the various stages of the interview process and how to dress for success.

Screening Interviews

Screening interviews are usually conducted by phone and last anywhere from 15 minutes to an hour. You should take the interview in a quiet room with no distractions and keep pen and paper handy to take notes. Screening interviews may also take place on the spot at a job fair or on campus as part of a college recruiting process.

The initial screening interview is with a company recruiter or human resources representative. The recruiter wants to make sure that you're interested in doing the job the company is hiring for, that you have the skills needed for the position, and that you're willing to accept any logistical requirements of the position, such as relocation or travel. If you make it past the recruiter, there's normally a second screening interview in which a technical person will ask you a few knowledge-based questions. These questions are designed to eliminate applicants who have inflated their résumés or are weak in skills that are key to the position. If the feedback from the technical interviewer(s) is positive, the recruiter will get back to you, usually within a week, to schedule an on-site interview at the company's office.

On-Site Interviews

Your performance in on-site interviews is the biggest factor in determining whether you get an offer. These interviews consist mostly of a variety of technical questions: problems requiring you to implement a simple program or function; questions that test your knowledge of computers, languages, and programming; and mathematics and logic puzzles. The majority of this book focuses on helping you answer these questions and succeed in your interviews.

Your on-site interviews usually last either a half day or a full day, and they typically consist of three to six interviews of 30 to 60 minutes each. Arrive early and well-rested at the company's office and take a washroom break if at all possible before any of the interviewing starts. You'll likely be greeted by either the recruiter you've been dealing with or the hiring manager. You may get an informal tour before the actual interviewing starts, which is a good way to see what the working conditions are like at that location.

Your interviewers are often the members of the team you would be working with if you were hired. Most companies have a rule that any interviewer can block an applicant from being hired, so all of your interviews are important. Sometimes you may interview with two separate teams on the same day. Usually each group you interview with will make a separate decision about giving you an offer.

The company usually takes you out for lunch midway through your interview day. A free lunch at a nice restaurant or even at the company cafeteria is certainly something to be enjoyed, but don't let your guard down completely. If you make a negative impression at lunch, you may lose your offer. Be polite, and avoid alcohol and messy foods like ribs. These general guidelines apply to all company outings, including evening recruiting activities. Moderate drinking is acceptable during evening outings, but show restraint. Getting drunk isn't likely to improve your chances of getting an offer.

At the end of the day, you will usually meet with the boss; if he spends a lot of time trying to sell you on working for the company, it's a pretty strong indication that you've done well in your interviews and an offer will follow.

Dress

Job applicants traditionally wear suits to interviews. Most tech companies, though, are strictly business casual these days. The running joke at some of these companies is that the only people who wear suits are interview candidates and salespeople.

This is one area where it's critical to do some research. It's probably not to your advantage to wear a suit if nobody else at the company is wearing them, not even the salespeople. On the other hand, if you wear jeans and a T-shirt, interviewers may feel you're not showing sufficient respect or seriousness, even though they may be wearing jeans themselves. Ask around to see what's appropriate for the company. The location of the company and the nature of its business are important factors to consider: a suit is *de rigueur* when interviewing at a bank or brokerage, unless of course you're interviewing on the West Coast.

In general, though, a suit is overkill for a technical job interview. A standard technical interviewing outfit for men consists of nondenim cotton pants, a collared shirt, and loafers (no sneakers or sandals). Unless the job you're interviewing for has a significant business or consulting aspect whereby formal dress will be required, you generally don't need to wear a jacket or a tie. Women can dress similarly to men. No matter what your sex, go light on the perfume or cologne.

Be sure to turn off or mute all electronic devices before the interview starts. If you forget to do this and a device starts ringing, buzzing, or vibrating during the interview, apologize to the interviewer and immediately disable the device. Whatever you do, don't answer a call or read any messages during the interview — if you can't give the interviewer your undivided attention, he or she won't be inclined to recommend you for the job.

A Recruiter's Role

Your interviews and offer may be coordinated by a company recruiter or human resources representative. If so, the recruiter is usually responsible for the scheduling and logistical aspects of your interview, including reimbursing you for travel or lodging expenses. Recruiters aren't usually involved in the hiring decision, but they may pass on information about you to those who are. They are also usually the ones who will call you back about your offer and handle negotiations.

Recruiters are often very good at what they do. The vast majority of recruiters are honorable people deserving of your respect and courtesy. Nevertheless, don't let their friendliness fool you into thinking that their job is to help you; their job is to get you to sign with their company as quickly as possible for as little money as possible. As with headhunters, it's important to understand the position recruiters are in so you can understand how they behave:

- **Recruiters may focus on a job's benefits or perks to draw attention away from negative aspects of a job offer.** They generally tell you to come to them with any questions about your offer. This is fine for benefit and salary questions, but ill advised when you have questions about the job itself. The recruiter usually doesn't know very much about the job you're being hired to do. When you ask a specific question about the job, the recruiter has little incentive to do the work to find the answer, especially if that answer might cause you to turn down the offer. Instead, the recruiter is likely to give you a vague response along the lines of what he or she thinks you want to hear. When you want straight answers to your questions, it's best to go directly to the people you'll be working for. You can also try going directly to your potential manager if you feel the recruiter is being unreasonable with you. This is a somewhat risky strategy — it certainly won't win you the recruiter's love — but often the hiring manager has the authority to overrule decisions or restrictions made by the recruiter. Hiring managers are often more willing to be flexible than recruiters. You're just another applicant to the recruiter, but to the hiring manager, you're the person he chose to work with.

- **Once the decision is made to give you an offer, the recruiter's job is to do anything necessary to get you to accept the offer at the lowest possible salary.** A recruiter's pay is often tied to how many candidates he or she signs. To maneuver you, recruiters sometimes try to play career counselor or advisor by asking you about each of your offers and leading you through a supposedly objective analysis to determine which is the best offer. Not surprisingly, this exercise always leads to the conclusion that the offer from the recruiter's company is clearly the best choice.
- **Some recruiters are territorial enough about their candidates that they won't give you your prospective team's contact information.** To protect against this possibility, collect business cards from your interviewers during your interviews, particularly from your prospective managers. Then you'll have the necessary information without having to go through the recruiter.

Offers and Negotiation

When you get an offer, you've made it through the hardest part: You now have a job, if you want it. However, the game isn't over yet. You're looking for a job because you need to make money; how you play the end game largely determines how much you get.

When your recruiter or hiring manager makes you an offer, he or she may also tell you how much the company is planning to pay you. Perhaps a more-common practice, though, is for the recruiter or hiring manager to tell you that the company would like to hire you and ask you how much you want to make. Answering this question is covered in detail in Chapter 15, "Nontechnical Questions."

Once you've been given a specific offer that includes details about salary, signing bonus, and stock options, you need to decide whether you're satisfied with it. This shouldn't be a snap decision — never accept an offer on the spot. Always spend at least a day thinking about important decisions like this; it's surprising how much can change in a day.

Dealing with Recruiter Pressures

Recruiters often employ a variety of high-pressure tactics to get you to accept offers quickly. They may tell you that you must accept the offer within a few days if you want the job, or they may offer you an exploding signing bonus, a signing bonus that decreases by a fixed amount each day. Don't let this bullying rush your decision. If the company really wants you (and it probably does if it made you an offer), then these limits and terms are negotiable, even when a recruiter claims they aren't. You may have to go over the recruiter's head and talk to your hiring manager if the recruiter refuses to be flexible. If these conditions really are non-negotiable, you probably don't want to work for a rigid company full of bullies anyway.

Negotiating Your Salary

If, after careful consideration, the offer meets or exceeds your expectations, you're all set. On the other hand, if you're not completely happy with your offer, you should try to negotiate. All too often, applicants assume that offers are non-negotiable and reject offers without negotiation or accept offers they're not pleased with. In fact, almost every offer is negotiable to some extent.

You should never reject an offer for monetary reasons without trying to negotiate. When you're negotiating an offer that you would otherwise reject, you hold the ultimate high card. You're ready to walk, so you have nothing to lose.

Even when an offer is in the range you were expecting, it's often worthwhile to try negotiating. As long as you are respectful and truthful in your negotiations and your requests are reasonable, you'll never lose an offer just because you tried to negotiate it. In the worst case, the company refuses to change the offer and you're no worse off than before you tried to negotiate.

In determining what is reasonable, the authors frequently apply the maxim "Pigs get fat, but hogs get slaughtered."

If you decide to negotiate your compensation package, here's how you do it:

- **Figure out exactly what you want.** You may want a signing bonus, better pay, or more stock options.
- **Arrange a phone call with the appropriate negotiator**. Your negotiator is usually the same person who gave you the terms of your offer. Don't call the negotiator blind because you may catch him or her at an inconvenient time.
- **Explain your case.** Say you appreciate receiving the offer and explain why you're not completely happy with it. For example, you could say, "I'm very pleased to have received the offer, but I'm having a hard time accepting it because it's not competitive with my other offers." Or you could say, "Thank you again for the offer, but I'm having trouble accepting it because I know from discussions with my peers and from talking with other companies that this offer is below market rates." If the negotiator asks you to go into greater detail about which other companies have offered you more money and how much, or where your peers work, you're under no obligation to do so. You can easily say, "I keep all my offers confidential, including yours, and feel that it's unprofessional to give out that sort of information."
- **Thank the negotiator for his time and help and say that you're looking forward to hearing from him again.** Negotiators rarely change an offer on the spot. The company's negotiator may ask you what you had in mind or, conversely, tell you that the offer is non-negotiable. Claiming that the offer is non-negotiable is often merely a hardball negotiation tactic, so in either case you should respond by politely and respectfully spelling out exactly what you expect in an offer and giving the negotiator a chance to consider what you've said.

Many people find negotiation uncomfortable, especially when dealing with professional recruiters who do it every day. It's not uncommon for someone to accept an offer as close enough just to avoid having to negotiate. If you feel this way about negotiation, try looking at it this way: You rarely have anything to lose, and even modest success in negotiation can be very rewarding. If it takes you a 30-minute phone call to get your offer increased by $3,000, you've made $6,000 per hour. Even lawyers aren't paid that much.

Accepting and Rejecting Offers

At some point, your negotiations will be complete, and you will be ready to accept an offer. After you inform a company you're accepting its offer, be sure to keep in touch to coordinate start dates and paperwork.

It's also important to be professional about declining your other offers. Contacts are very important, especially in the computer business where people change jobs frequently. You've no doubt built contacts at all the companies that made you offers. It's foolish to squander your contacts at other companies by failing to inform them of your decision. If you had a recruiter at the company, you should e-mail him or her with your decision. (Don't expect them to be overjoyed, however.) You should also personally call the hiring managers who made you an offer to thank them and let them know what you decided. For example, you can say, "I want to thank you again for extending me the offer. I was very impressed with your company, but I've decided it's not the best choice for me right now. Thank you again, and I appreciate your confidence in me." Besides simply being classy, this approach will often get a response such as, "I was pleased to meet you, and I'm sorry that you won't be joining us. If things don't work out at that company, give me a call and maybe we can work something out. Best of luck."

This gives you a great place to start the next time you need to play the game.

Summary

There are various ways to find prospective jobs, but networking through friends and acquaintances is usually the best method. If that's not possible, find and contact companies directly. You may also engage the services of a headhunter, though be aware that the headhunter's motivations aren't always aligned with yours.

The interviews are the most important part of the job application process. There will be one or two screening interviews, usually done by phone, to ensure that you're applying for the right job and that you are actually qualified. After the screening interviews, there are usually a series of on-site technical interviews that will ultimately determine whether or not a job offer comes your way. Be sure to dress appropriately for the interviews and turn off any electronic gadgets you might have with you.

During the interview process you'll frequently interact with one of the company's recruiters, especially if a job offer is made. Be sure to understand the recruiter's role during this process.

When an offer is made, don't accept it immediately. Give yourself time to consider it. Look over the offer and try to negotiate a better deal, as most offers aren't fixed in stone, no matter what the recruiter says. After accepting a job offer, be sure to contact anyone else who has made you an offer and thank them for considering you.

Approaches to Programming Problems

Coding questions are generally the meat of an interview. They are your opportunity to demonstrate that you can do the job. These questions are a large component of the process that most computer and software companies use to decide who to hire and who not to hire. Many companies make offers to less than 10 percent of the people who interview with them. The questions are generally rather difficult. If everyone (or even most people) were able to answer a particular question quickly, the company would stop asking it because it wouldn't tell them anything about the applicants. Many of the questions are designed to take up to an hour to solve, so don't get frustrated if you don't see the answer right away. Almost no one does.

These problems are hard! Some of the questions are designed to see how you handle a problem when you don't immediately see the solution.

The Process

The point of the coding questions is to determine if and how well you can code. It's the most important part of the interview, because the code you write and the answers you give to the interviewer will largely determine whether or not he or she recommends you for the job.

The Scenario

You will usually be working one-on-one with your interviewer. He or she will give you a marker and a whiteboard (or pen and paper) and ask you to write some code. The interviewer will probably want you to talk through the question before you start writing. Generally, you will be asked to code a function or method, but sometimes you will need to write a class definition or a sequence of related code modules. In any case, you will be writing code, either in an actual programming language or in some form of pseudo-code.

The Problems

The problems the interviewers ask have very specific requirements. They have to be short enough to be explained and solved reasonably quickly, yet complex enough that not everyone can solve them. Therefore, it's unlikely that you'll be asked any real-world problems. Almost any worthy real-world problem would take too long to explain, let alone solve. That isn't an option in an interview. Instead, many of these problems require tricks or uncommonly used features of a language.

The problems often prohibit you from using the most-common way to do something or from using the ideal data structure. For example, you might be given a problem like this: "Write a function that determines whether two integers are equal without using any comparative operators."

This is an outright silly and contrived problem. Almost every language that ever existed has some way to compare two integers. However, you're not off the hook if you respond, "This is a stupid question; I'd always use the equality operator. I'd never have this problem." In fact, you flunk if you answer this way. The interviewer is looking for a different way to compare two integers. (Hint: Try using bit operators.)

Describe the better way to solve the problem, but solve the question as it was asked. For example, if you are asked to solve a certain problem with a hash table, you might say, "This would be easy with a binary search tree because it's much easier to extract the largest element, but let's see how I can solve this with a hash table . . ."

Many questions involve ridiculous restrictions, use obscure features of languages, and seem silly and contrived. Play within the rules. Real-world programming is rarely done in a vacuum. The ability to work within the particular constraints of a situation is an important skill to develop.

Problems are generally asked in ascending order of difficulty. This is not a hard-and-fast rule, but you can expect them to get more difficult as you answer more of them correctly. Often, different interviewers will communicate with each other about what they asked you, what you could answer, and what you couldn't answer. If you answer all the problems in your early interviews but find yourself stumped by harder problems later, this may indicate that earlier interviewers were impressed with your responses.

Which Languages to Use

If you are applying for a job with specific language requirements, you should know those languages and expect to use them to solve the questions you are given. If you are applying for a general programming or development position, a thorough knowledge of a mainstream language such as C#, Java, and/or C++ is enough to get by, although familiarity with the C language is also useful in many situations. Your interviewer may permit you to use other popular languages, such as JavaScript, PHP, or Perl. If you are given a choice, select the language you know best, but expect to be required to solve some problems in a specific language. Interviewers are less likely to be amenable to you using less-mainstream languages such as Lisp, Python, Tcl, Prolog, COBOL, or Fortran, but if you are particularly expert in one of these, there's no harm in asking.

Before you go to your interview, make sure you are completely comfortable with the use and syntax of any language you plan to use. If it's been a few years since you've done any C++ programming, for example, you should at the very least thumb through a good C++ reference guide and refamiliarize yourself with the language.

One final note about language selection: Whether rightly or wrongly, many people consider Visual Basic to be a lesser language. Unless you are applying for a job in which you will be using this language, it's probably best to avoid it in your interviews. Things change, however, so be aware of current language trends. A few years ago, for example, the same could be said of JavaScript, but the rise of AJAX (an acronym for *Asynchronous JavaScript and XML*) as a core technology for developing responsive browser-based applications has changed the industry's view about JavaScript.

Interactivity Is Key

The code you write in the interview is probably the only example of your code that your interviewer will see. If you write ugly code, your interviewer will assume you always write ugly code. This is your chance to shine and show your best code. Take the time to make your code solid and pretty.

Brush up on the languages you expect to use, and write your best code.

Programming questions are designed to see both how well you can code and how you solve problems. If all the interviewer wanted to do were measure your coding ability, he could give you a piece of paper with problems and come back an hour later to evaluate how you did, just as they do in programming contests. What the interviewer wants is to see your thought processes as you work through each stage of the programming problem.

The problem-solving process in these interviews is very interactive, and if you're having difficulty, the interviewer will generally guide you to the correct answer via a series of hints. Of course, the less help you need to solve the problem, the better you look, but showing an intelligent thought process and responding well to the hints you are given is also very important.

Even when you immediately know the answer to a problem, because it's something you've already done before, don't just blurt it out. Break the answer down into discrete steps and explain the thought processes behind each step. The point is to show the interviewer that you understand the underlying concepts, not that you've managed to memorize the answer to a programming puzzle.

If you know any additional information pertaining to the problem, you may want to mention it during the process to show your general knowledge of programming, even if it's not directly applicable to the problem at hand. In answering these problems, show that you're not just a propeller-head coder. Demonstrate that you have logical thought processes, are generally knowledgeable about computers, and can communicate well.

Keep talking! Always explain what you are doing! Otherwise, the interviewer has no way of knowing how you tackle complex programming problems.

Solving the Questions

Now it's time to solve the questions, but don't just jump in. Instead, remember you want to fully understand the problem. You should try an example, and then focus on the algorithm that will solve the problem. You then want to explain your solution and code for the solution. The following steps walk you through the process:

The Basic Steps

The best way to solve an interview problem is to approach it methodically. Here are the suggested steps:

1. **Make sure you understand the problem.** Your initial assumptions about the problem may be wrong, or the interviewer's explanation may be very brief or difficult to follow. You can't demonstrate your skills if you don't understand the problem. Don't hesitate to ask your interviewer questions about the problem, and don't start solving it until you understand it. The interviewer may be deliberately obscuring things in order to determine whether you can find and understand the real problem.

2. **Once you understand the question, try an example.** This example may lead to insights about how to solve the problem or bring to light any remaining misunderstandings that you have. Starting with an example also demonstrates a methodical, logical thought process. Examples are especially useful if you don't see the solution right away.

Make sure you understand the problem before you start solving it, and then start with an example to solidify your understanding.

3. **Focus on the algorithm you will use to solve the problem.** Often, this will take a long time and require additional examples. This is to be expected. Interactivity is important during this process. If you stand quietly staring at the whiteboard, the interviewer has no way of knowing whether you're making productive headway or are simply clueless. Talk to your interviewer and tell him or her what you are doing. For example, you might say something like, "I'm wondering whether I can store the values in an array and then sort them, but I don't think that will work because I can't quickly look up elements in an array by value." This demonstrates your skill, which is the point of the interview, and may also lead to hints from the interviewer, who might respond, "You're very close to the solution. Do you really need to look up elements by value, or could you . . ."

   It may take a long time to solve the problem, and you may be tempted to begin coding before you figure out an exact solution. Resist this temptation. Consider who you would rather work with: someone who thinks about a problem for a long time and then codes it correctly the first time or someone who hastily jumps into a problem, makes several errors while coding, and doesn't have any idea where he or she is going. Not a difficult decision, is it?

4. **After you've figured out your algorithm and how you will implement it, explain your solution to the interviewer.** This gives him or her an opportunity to evaluate your solution before you begin coding. Your interviewer may say, "Sounds great, go ahead and code it," or something like, "That's not quite right because you can't look up elements in a hash table that way." In either case, you gain valuable information.

5. **While you code, it's important to explain what you're doing.** For example, you might say, "Here, I'm initializing the array to all zeroes." This narrative enables the interviewer to follow your code more easily.

Explain what you are doing to your interviewer before and while coding the solution. Keep talking!

6. **Ask questions when necessary.** You generally won't be penalized for asking factual questions that you might otherwise look up in a reference. You obviously can't ask a question like, "How do I solve this problem?" but it is acceptable to ask a question like, "I can't remember — what format string do I use to print out a localized date?" While it's better to know these things, it's okay to ask this sort of question.

7. **After you've written the code for a problem, immediately verify that the code is correct by tracing through it with an example.** This step demonstrates very clearly that your code works in at least one case. It also illustrates a logical thought process and your desire to check your work and search for bugs. The example may also help you flush out minor bugs in your solution.

8. **Make sure you check your code for *all* error and special cases, especially boundary conditions.** Many error and special cases are overlooked by programmers; forgetting these cases in an interview indicates you may forget them on the job. For example, if you allocate memory dynamically, make sure you check that the allocation did not fail. (If time does not allow for extensive checking, at the very least explain that you *should* check for such failures.) Covering error and special cases will impress your interviewer and help you correctly solve the problem.

Try an example, and check all error and special cases.

Once you try an example and feel comfortable that your code is correct, the interviewer may ask you questions about what you wrote. Commonly, these questions focus on running time, alternative implementations, and complexity. If your interviewer does not ask you these questions, you should volunteer the information to show that you are cognizant of these issues. For example, you could say, "This implementation has linear running time, which is the best possible because I have to check all the input values. The dynamic memory allocation will slow it down a little, as will the overhead of using recursion."

When You Get Stuck

Getting stuck on a problem is expected and an important part of the interviewing process. Interviewers want to see how you respond when you don't recognize the answer to a question immediately. Giving up or getting frustrated is the worst thing to do if this happens to you. Instead, show interest in the problem and keep trying to solve it:

- **Go back to an example**. Try performing the task and analyzing what you are doing. Try extending from your specific example to the general case. You may have to use very detailed examples. This is okay, because it shows the interviewer your persistence in finding the correct solution.

When all else fails, return to a specific example. Try to move from the specific example to the general case and from there to the solution.

- **Try a different data structure.** Perhaps a linked list, an array, a hash table, or a binary search tree will help. If you're given an unusual data structure, look for similarities between it and more-familiar data structures. Using the right data structure often makes a problem much easier.
- **Consider the less-commonly used or more-advanced aspects of a language.** Sometimes the key to a problem involves one of these features.

Sometimes a different data structure or advanced language feature is key to the solution.

Even when you don't feel stuck, you may be having problems. You may be missing an elegant or obvious way to implement something and writing too much code. Almost all interview coding questions have short answers. You rarely need to write more than 15 lines of code and almost never more than 30. If you start writing a lot of code, you may be heading in the wrong direction.

Analyzing Your Solution

Once you've answered the problem, you may be asked about the efficiency of your implementation. Often, you have to compare trade-offs between your implementation and another possible solution and identify the conditions that make each option more favorable. Common questions focus on memory or space usage, especially when recursion is involved.

A good understanding of *big-O analysis* is critical to making a good impression with the interviewer. Big-O analysis is a form of run-time analysis that measures the efficiency of an algorithm in terms of the time it takes for the algorithm to run as a function of the input size. It's not a formal benchmark, just a simple way to classify algorithms by relative efficiency.

Most coding problem solutions in this book include a run-time analysis to help you solidify your understanding of the algorithms.

Analyzing Two Examples

Let's start with an example of big-O analysis in action. Consider a simple function that returns the maximum value stored in an array of non-negative numbers. The size of the array is n. There are at least two easy ways to implement the function. In the first alternative, you keep track of the current largest number as the function iterates through the array and return that value when you are done iterating. This implementation, called CompareToMax, looks like this:

```
/* Returns the largest integer in the array */
int CompareToMax(int array[], int n)
{
    int curMax, i;

    /* Make sure that there is at least one element in the array. */
    if (n <= 0)
        return -1;

    /* Set the largest number so far to the first array value. */
    curMax = array[0];

    /* Compare every number with the largest number so far. */
    for (i = 1; i < n; i++) {
        if (array[i] > curMax) {
            curMax = array[i];
        }
    }
    return curMax;
}
```

The second alternative compares each value to all the other values. If all other values are less than or equal to a given value, that value must be the maximum value. This implementation, called CompareToAll, looks like this:

```
/* Returns the largest integer in the array */
int CompareToAll(int array[], int n)
```

```
{
    int  i, j;
    bool isMax;

    /* Make sure that there is at least one element in the array. */
    if (n <= 0)
        return -1;

    for (i = n-1; i > 0; i--) {
        isMax = true;
        for (j = 0; j < n; j++) {
            /* See if any value is greater. */
            if (array[j] > array[i])
                isMax = false; /* array[i] is not the largest value. */
        }
        /* If isMax is true, no larger value exists; array[i] is max. */
        if (isMax) break;
    }

   return array[i];
}
```

Both of these functions correctly return the maximum value. Which one is more efficient? You could try benchmarking them, but it's usually impractical (and inefficient) to implement and benchmark every possible alternative. You need to be able to predict an algorithm's performance without having to implement it. Big-O analysis enables you to do exactly that: compare the predicted relative performance of different algorithms.

How Big-O Analysis Works

In big-O analysis, input size is assumed to be n. In this case, n simply represents the number of elements in an array. In other problems, n may represent the number of nodes in a linked list, or the number of bits in a data type, or the number of entries in a hash table, and so on. After figuring out what n means in terms of the input, you have to determine how many times the n input items are examined in terms of n. "Examined" is a fuzzy word because algorithms differ greatly. Commonly, an examination might be something like adding an input value to a constant, creating a new input item, or deleting an input value. In big-O analysis, these operations are all considered equivalent. In both CompareToMax and CompareToAll, "examine" means comparing an array value to another value.

In CompareToMax, each array element was compared once to a maximum value. Thus, the n input items are each examined once, resulting in n examinations. This is considered $O(n)$, usually referred to as *linear time*: The time required to run the algorithm increases linearly with the number of input items.

You may notice that in addition to examining each element once, there is a check to ensure that the array is not empty and a step that initializes the curMax variable. It may seem more accurate to call this an $O(n + 2)$ function to reflect these extra operations. Big-O analysis, however, yields the *asymptotic* running time, the limit of the running time as n gets very large. As n approaches infinity, the difference between n and $n + 2$ is insignificant, so the constant term can be ignored. Similarly, for an algorithm running in $n + n^2$ time, the difference between n^2 and $n + n^2$ is negligible for very large n. Thus, in big-O analysis you eliminate all but the highest-order term, the term that is largest as n gets very large. In this case, n is the highest-order term. Therefore, the CompareToMax function is $O(n)$.

The analysis of CompareToAll is a little more difficult. First, you have to make an assumption about where the largest number occurs in the array. For now, assume that the maximum element is at the end of the array. In this case, this function may compare each of n elements to n other elements. Thus, there are $n(n$ examinations, and this is an $O(n^2)$ algorithm.

The analysis so far has shown that CompareToMax is $O(n)$ and CompareToAll is $O(n^2)$. This means that as the array grows, the number of comparisons in CompareToAll will become much larger than in CompareToMax. Consider an array with 30,000 elements. CompareToMax compares on the order of 30,000 elements, whereas CompareToAll compares on the order of 900,000,000 elements. You would expect CompareToMax to be much faster because it examines 30,000 times fewer elements. In fact, one benchmark timed CompareToMax at less than .01 seconds, while CompareToAll took 23.99 seconds.

The fastest-possible running time for any run-time analysis is `O(1)`, commonly referred to as *constant running time*. An algorithm with constant running time always takes the same amount of time to execute, regardless of the input size.

Best, Average, and Worst Cases

You may think this comparison was stacked against CompareToAll because the maximum value was at the end. This is true, and it raises the important issues of *best case*, *average case*, and *worst case* running times. The analysis of CompareToAll was a worst-case scenario: The maximum value was at the end of the array. Consider, however, the average case, where the largest value is in the middle. You end up checking only half the values n times because the maximum value is in the middle. This results in checking $n\ (n\ /\ 2) = n^2/\ 2$ times. This would appear to be an $O(n^2/\ 2)$ running time. Consider, though, what the 1/2 factor means. The actual time to check each value is highly dependent on the machine instructions that the code translates to and then on the speed at which the CPU can execute the instructions. Therefore, the 1/2 doesn't mean very much. You could even come up with an $O(n^2)$ algorithm that was faster than an $O(n^2/\ 2)$ algorithm. In big-O analysis, you drop all constant factors, so the average case for CompareToAll is no better than the worst case. It is still $O(n^2)$.

The best-case running time for CompareToAll is better than $O(n^2)$. In this case, the maximum value is at the beginning of the array. The maximum value is compared to all other values only once, so the result is an $O(n)$ running time.

Note that in CompareToMax, the best-case, average-case, and worst-case running times are identical. Regardless of the arrangement of the values in the array, the algorithm is always $O(n)$.

Ask the interviewer which scenario they're most interested in. Sometimes there are clues to this in the problem itself. Some sorting algorithms with terrible worst cases for unsorted data may nonetheless be well suited for a problem if the input is already sorted.

How to Do Big-O Analysis

The general procedure for big-O run-time analysis is as follows:

1. Figure out what the input is and what n represents.
2. Express the number of operations the algorithm performs in terms of n.

3. Eliminate all but the highest-order terms.
4. Remove all constant factors.

For the algorithms you'll be tested on, big-O analysis should be straightforward as long as you correctly identify the operations that are dependent on the input size.

Optimizations and Big-O Analysis

Algorithm optimizations do not always yield the expected changes in their overall running times. Consider the following optimization to CompareToAll: Instead of comparing each number to every other number, compare each number only with the numbers that follow it in the array. In essence, every number before the current number has already been compared to the current number. Thus, the algorithm is still correct if you compare only to numbers occurring after the current number.

What's the worst-case running time for this implementation? The first number is compared to n numbers, the second number to $n - 1$ numbers, the third number to $n - 2$, resulting in a number of comparisons equal to $n + (n - 1) + (n - 2) + (n - 3) + \ldots + 1$. This is a very common result, a mathematical series whose answer is expressed as $n^2/2 + n/2$. n^2 is the highest-order term, so this version of the algorithm still has an $O(n^2)$ running time in the worst case. For large input values, the change you make to the algorithm has no real effect on its running time.

Summary

How you solve the programming problems you'll be presented with during your interviews will determine whether or not you get a job offer, so it's important to answer them as correctly and completely as you can. The problems usually get progressively harder as the day progresses, so don't be surprised if you end up needing an occasional hint from the interviewer. You'll normally code in a mainstream programming language, but the choice of language is ultimately dictated by the requirements of the job for which you're applying, so be sure you're familiar with the right languages.

Interact with your interviewer as much as possible as you attempt each problem. Let him or her know what you're thinking at each point in your analysis of the problem and your attempts at coding an answer. Start by making sure you understand the problem, and then try some examples to reinforce that understanding. Choose the algorithm and make sure it works for those examples. Don't forget to test for special cases. If you're stuck, try more examples and/or choose a different algorithm. Keep obscure or advanced language features in mind when looking for alternate answers.

If asked to comment on the performance of a solution, a big-O run-time analysis is usually sufficient. Algorithms that run in linear or constant time are usually preferred.

Linked Lists

The deceptively simple linked list is the basis for a surprising number of problems regarding the handling of dynamic data. Problems about efficient list traversal, list sorting, and the insertion or removal of data from either end of a list are good tests of basic data-structure concepts, which is why we devote an entire chapter to linked lists. Their simplicity appeals to interviewers, who want to present at least two or three problems over the course of an hour-long interview. This means that they have to give you problems that you can be reasonably expected to answer in 20 to 30 minutes. You can write a relatively complete implementation of a linked list in less than 10 minutes, leaving you plenty of time to solve the problem. In contrast, it might take you most of the interview period to implement a more complex data structure such as a hash table. In addition, there is little variation in the way linked lists are implemented, which means that an interviewer can simply say "linked list" and not waste time discussing and clarifying implementation details.

Linked list problems are typically posed for jobs requiring C or C++ experience because they're an easy way to determine whether a candidate understands how pointers work, so most of the examples in this chapter are in C++, but without any use of C++'s object-oriented programming facilities. It's assumed that you're using a C++ compiler so that you can use the C++ new and delete operators in your code.

If you're not experienced with C or C++, you may find the linked lists problems in this chapter quite challenging, especially because languages such as Java and C# provide linked list implementations as standard library routines. Still, linked lists are so basic that we suggest you familiarize yourself with them before moving on to the more-complicated data structures found in the following chapters.

Kinds of Linked List

There are three basic kinds of linked list: singly-linked lists, doubly-linked lists and circularly-linked lists. Although most problems involve singly-linked lists, which are the simplest to implement — an example is shown in Figure 4-1 — it's important to understand the other two kinds as well.

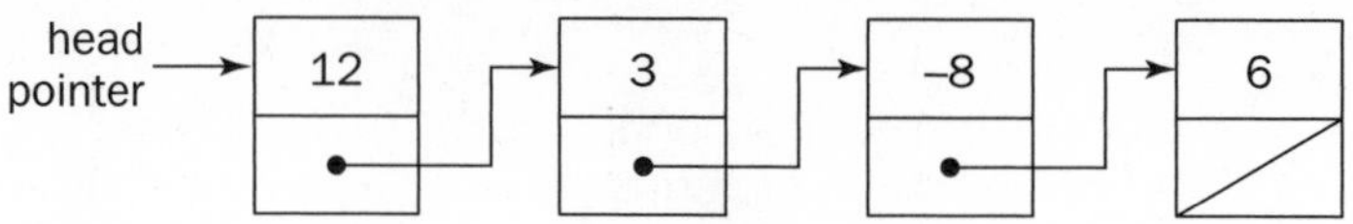

Figure 4-1

When an interviewer says "linked list" he or she generally means a linear singly-linked list. This list consists of a number of data elements in which each data element has a *next* pointer or *next* reference (the link) to the element that follows. The last element in the list has an empty or null link.

In C or C++, an element's next pointer and the data the element holds are usually bound together as a single unit, as shown in the following example:

```
typedef struct IntElement {
    struct IntElement *next;
    int               data;
} IntElement;
```

Placing the next pointer at the beginning of the structure or class makes it easy to write generic list-handling routines that work no matter what data the element holds.

In other languages it's more common to create generic linked list routines whose elements store *references* to arbitrary objects. In Java or C# it might be a simple class like this:

```
public class ListElement {
    ListElement next;
    Object      data;

    public ListElement( Object data ){
        this.data = data;
    }
}
```

Although there's more overhead in this scenario, it works well in languages where unused objects are automatically found and destroyed via garbage collection. Otherwise, careful attention must be paid to the allocation and deallocation of any referenced objects.

Whatever language they are implemented in, singly-linked lists have a host of special cases and potential programming traps. Because the links in a singly-linked list consist only of next pointers (or references), the list can be traversed only in the forward direction, so a complete traversal of the list must begin with the first element. In other words, you need a pointer or reference to the first element of a list in order to locate all the elements in the list. Consequently, the term *linked list* is often used as shorthand for the first element of a linked list. If an interviewer says that a function takes a linked list as an argument, he or she probably means that it takes a pointer/reference to the first element of a linked list as an argument.

The first element of a singly-linked list is referred to as the *head* of the list; the last element is referred to as the *tail* element.

Doubly-Linked Lists

A doubly-linked list, shown in Figure 4-2, eliminates many difficulties inherent in a singly-linked list. A doubly-linked list differs from a singly-linked list in that each element has a link to the previous element in the list in addition to the link to the next element. (The first element in the list has an empty or null previous link.) This additional link makes it possible to traverse the list in either direction. The entire list can be traversed starting from any element. A doubly-linked list has head and tail elements just like a singly-linked list.

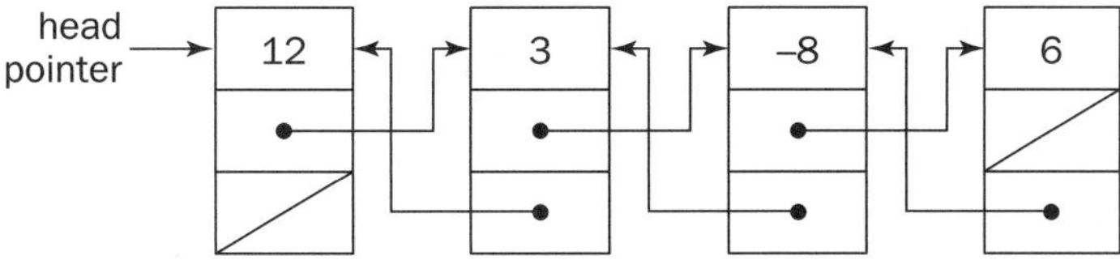

Figure 4-2

Because many list operations that are difficult with singly-linked lists are trivial when bidirectional links are available, doubly-linked lists are rarely seen in interview problems; and if the problem isn't any easier with a doubly-linked list, there's no point in adding the overhead of bidirectional links.

Circularly-Linked Lists

The final variation on the linked list theme is the circularly-linked list, which comes in singly- and doubly-linked varieties. Circularly-linked lists have no ends — no head or tail. The primary traversal problem is cycle avoidance — if you don't track where you start, you'll cycle infinitely through the list. Although they have some interesting properties, circularly-linked lists rarely appear in interview problems.

Basic Linked List Operations

Most linked list problems require a thorough understanding of basic operations on singly-linked lists. These operations include tracking the head element so the list doesn't get lost, traversing the list, and inserting or deleting list elements. Again, these operations are trivial with a doubly-linked list, so the problems will almost always use singly-linked lists.

Tracking the Head Element

The head element of a singly-linked list must always be tracked; otherwise, the list will be lost in memory. This means that the pointer or reference to the head of the list must be updated when a new element is inserted ahead of the first element or when the existing first element is removed from the list. Tracking the head element becomes a problem when you alter the list inside a function or method, because the caller must be made aware of the new head element. For example, the following Java/C# code is incorrect because it fails to update the reference to the head of the list:

```
public void insertInFront( ListElement list, Object data ){
    ListElement l = new ListElement( data );
    l.next = list;
}
```

The correct solution is to return the new head element from the method:

```
public ListElement insertInFront( ListElement list, Object data ){
    ListElement l = new ListElement( data );
    l.next = list;
    return l;
}
```

The caller simply updates its reference to the head element accordingly:

```
Object data = ....; // data to insert
ListElement head = ....; // reference to head

head = insertInFront( head, data );
```

In C/C++ it's easier to make mistakes with pointer misuse. Consider this C/C++ code for inserting an element at the front of a list:

```
bool insertInFront( IntElement *head, int data ){
    IntElement *newElem = new IntElement;
    if( !newElem ) return false;

    newElem->data = data;
    head = newElem; // Incorrect!
    return true;
}
```

The preceding code is incorrect because it only updates the *local copy* of the head pointer. The correct version passes in a pointer to the head pointer:

```
bool insertInFront (IntElement **head, int data) {
    IntElement *newElem = new IntElement;
    if(!newElem) return false;
    newElem->data = data;

    newElem->next = *head;

    *head = newElem;
    return true;
}
```

In C++, the head pointer could also be passed in by reference.

Traversing

Often, you need to work with list elements other than the head element. Operations on any but the first element of a linked list require traversal of some elements of the list, and you must always check for the end of the list. The following traversal is wrong:

```
public ListElement find( ListElement head, Object data ){
    while( head.data != data ){
        head = head.next;
    }

    return head;
}
```

The preceding search method works fine as long as the object to find is actually in the list. If it isn't, an error occurs when you travel past the last element. A simple change to the loop fixes the problem:

```
public ListElement find( ListElement head, Object data ){
    while( head != null && head.data != data ){
        head = head.next;
    }

    return head;
}
```

The onus is on the caller to check for a non-null return value. It may make more sense to throw an exception once the end of the list is reached.

Always test for the end of a linked list as you traverse it.

Inserting and Deleting Elements

Because elements in a singly-linked list are maintained exclusively with links to the next element, any insertion or deletion of elements in the middle of a list requires modification of the previous element's link. This may require a traversal of the list, because there's no other way to find a preceding element. Special care must be taken when dealing with the head of the list. Here's a C/C++ example showing how to delete an element:

```
bool deleteElement( IntElement **head, IntElement *deleteMe )
{
    IntElement *elem = *head;

    if( deleteMe == *head ){ /* special case for head */
        *head = elem->next;
        delete deleteMe;
        return true;
    }

    while( elem ){
        if( elem->next == deleteMe ){
            /* elem is element preceding deleteMe */
            elem->next = deleteMe->next;
            delete deleteMe;
            return true;
        }
        elem = elem->next;
    }
    /* deleteMe not found */
    return false;
}
```

Deletion and insertion require a pointer or reference to the element immediately preceding the deletion or insertion location.

Performing deletions raises another issue in C/C++. Suppose you want to remove all the elements from a linked list. The natural inclination is to use a single pointer to traverse the list, freeing elements as you go. A problem arises, however, when this is implemented. Do you advance the pointer or free the element first? If you advance the pointer first, then the freeing is impossible because you overwrote the pointer to the element to be freed. If you free the element first, advancing the pointer is impossible because it involves reading the next pointer in the element that was just freed. The solution is to use two pointers, as in the following example:

```
void deleteList( IntElement **head )
{
    IntElement *deleteMe = *head;

    while( deleteMe ){
        IntElement *next = deleteMe->next;
        delete deleteMe;
        deleteMe = next;
    }

    *head = NULL;
}
```

Deletion of an element always requires at least two pointer variables. In fact, insertion requires two pointer variables as well, but because one of them is used for an element in the list and the other for the pointer returned by the memory allocation call, there's little danger of forgetting this in the insertion case.

Linked List Problems

What follows are some typical problems about linked lists that you might encounter during an interview.

Stack Implementation

Discuss the stack data structure. Implement a stack in C using either a linked list or a dynamic array, and justify your decision. Design the interface to your stack to be complete, consistent, and easy to use.

This problem is aimed at determining three things:

1. Your knowledge of basic data structures
2. Your ability to write routines to manipulate these structures
3. Your ability to design consistent interfaces to a group of routines

A stack is a last-in-first-out (LIFO) data structure: Elements are always removed in the reverse order in which they were added. The add element and remove element operations are conventionally called *push* and *pop*, respectively. Stacks are useful data structures for tasks that are divided into multiple subtasks. Tracking return addresses, parameters, and local variables for subroutines is one example of stack use; tracking tokens when parsing a programming language is another.

One of the ways to implement a stack is by using a *dynamic array*, an array that changes size as needed when elements are added. (See Chapter 6, "Arrays and Strings," for a more complete discussion of arrays.) The main advantage of dynamic arrays over linked lists is that arrays offer random access to the array elements — you can immediately access any element in the array simply by knowing its index. However, operations on a stack always work on one end of the data structure (the top of the stack), so the random accessibility of a dynamic array gains you little. In addition, as a dynamic array grows, it must occasionally be resized, which can be a time-consuming operation as elements are copied from the old array to the new array.

Conversely, linked lists usually allocate memory dynamically for each element, and that overhead can be significant when dealing with small-sized elements, especially if heuristics are used to minimize the number of times the array has to be resized. For these reasons, a stack based on a dynamic array is usually faster than one based on a linked list. In the context of an interview, though, the primary concern is ease and speed of implementation: Implementing a linked list is far less complicated than implementing a dynamic array, so a linked list is probably the best choice for your solution. Be sure to explain the pros and cons of both approaches to your interviewer, of course.

After explaining your choice, you can design the routines and their interfaces. If you take a moment to design your code before writing it, you can avoid mistakes and inconsistencies in implementation. More important, this shows you won't skip right to coding on a larger project where good planning is essential to success. As always, talk to the interviewer about what you're doing.

Your stack will need `push` and `pop` routines. What will the prototype for these functions be? Assuming you're not encapsulating the routines within a class, each function must be passed the stack it operates on. The `push` operation will be passed the data it is to push, and `pop` will return a piece of data from the stack.

The simplest way to pass the stack is to pass a pointer to the stack. Because the stack will be implemented as a linked list, the pointer to the stack will be a pointer to the head of the list. In addition to the pointer to the stack, you could pass the data as a second parameter to `push`. The `pop` could take only the pointer to the stack as an argument and return the value of the data it popped from the stack.

To write the prototypes, you need to know the type of the data that will be stored on the stack. You should declare a `struct` for a linked list element with the appropriate data type. If the interviewer doesn't make any suggestion, storing void pointers is a good general-purpose solution. Void pointer storage yields a `struct` and prototypes that look like the following:

```
typedef struct Element {
    struct Element *next;
    void *data;
} Element;

void push( Element *stack, void *data );
void *pop( Element *stack );
```

Now consider what will happen in these routines in terms of proper functionality and error handling. Both operations change the first element of the list. The calling routine's stack pointer must be modified to reflect this change, but any change you make to the pointer that is passed to these functions won't be propagated back to the calling routine. You can solve this problem by having both routines take a pointer to a pointer to the stack. This way, you can change the calling routine's pointer so that it continues to point at the first element of the list. Implementing this change results in the following:

```
void push( Element **stack, void *data );
void *pop( Element **stack );
```

What about error handling? The `push` operation needs to dynamically allocate memory for a new element. Memory allocation is always an operation that can fail, so remember to ensure that the allocation succeeded when you write this routine. You also need some way to indicate to the calling routine whether the `push` succeeded or failed. In C, it's generally most convenient to have a routine indicate success or failure by its return value. This way, the routine can be called from the condition of an `if` statement with error handling in the body. Have `push` return true for success and false for failure. (Throwing an exception is also an option in C++ and other languages with exception support.)

Can `pop` fail? It doesn't have to allocate memory, but what if it's asked to pop an empty stack? It should indicate that the operation was unsuccessful, but it still has to be able to return data when it is successful. A C function has a single return value, but `pop` really needs to return two values: the data it popped and an error code.

There are a number of possible solutions to this problem, none of which are entirely satisfactory. One approach is to use the single return value for both purposes. If `pop` is successful, have it return the data; if it is unsuccessful, return `NULL`. As long as your data is a pointer type and you never need to store null pointers on the stack, this works fine. If you have to store null pointers, however, there's no easy way to determine whether the null pointer returned by `pop` represents a legitimate element that you stored or an empty stack. Although restricting the stack to storing non-null pointers might be acceptable in some cases, we will assume that for this problem it is not.

Another option is to return a special value that can never represent a legal piece of data — a pointer to a reserved memory block, for example, or (for stacks dealing with non-negative numbers only) a negative value.

Suppose, however, that you can't use the return value for both the data and the error code. You must therefore return two distinct values. How else can a function return data? The same way the stack parameter is handled: by passing a pointer to a variable. The routine can return data by using the pointer to change the variable's value, which the caller will then check after popping the stack.

There are two possibilities for the interface to `pop`. You can have `pop` take a pointer to an error code variable as an argument and return the data, or you can have it take a pointer to a data variable and return an error code. Intuitively, most programmers would expect `pop` to return data. However, using `pop` is awkward if the error code is not its return value: Instead of simply calling `pop` in the condition of an `if` or `while` statement, you have to explicitly declare a variable for the error code and check its value in a separate statement after you call `pop`. Furthermore, `push` would take a data argument and return an error code, whereas `pop` would take an error code argument and return data. This may offend your sense of symmetry (it does ours). On the other hand, most programmers intuitively expect `pop` to return data. Neither alternative is clearly correct; there are problems with either approach. In an interview, it wouldn't matter too much which alternative you choose as long as you are able to identify the pros and cons of each and justify your choice. We think error code arguments are particularly irksome, so we continue this discussion by assuming you chose to have pop return an error code. This results in the following prototypes:

```
bool push( Element **stack, void *data );
bool pop( Element **stack, void **data );
```

You will also want to write createStack and deleteStack functions, even though neither of these is absolutely necessary in a linked list stack implementation. You could delete the stack by calling pop until the stack is empty and create a stack by passing push a null pointer as the stack argument. However, writing these functions provides a complete, implementation-independent interface to the stack. A stack implemented as a dynamic array would probably need createStack and deleteStack functions. By including these functions in your implementation you create the possibility that someone could change the underlying implementation of the stack without having to change the programs that use the stack — always a good thing.

With the goals of implementation independence and consistency in mind, it's a good idea to have these functions return error codes, too. Even though in a linked list implementation neither createStack nor deleteStack can fail, they might fail under a different implementation, such as if createStack couldn't allocate memory for a dynamic array. If you design the interface with no way for these functions to indicate failure, you severely handicap anyone who might want to change your implementation. Again, you face the same problem as with pop: createStack must return both the empty stack and an error code. You can't use a null pointer to indicate failure because a null pointer is the empty stack for a linked list implementation. In keeping with our previous decision, we write an implementation with an error code as the return value. Because createStack won't be able to return the stack as its value, it will have to take a pointer to a pointer to the stack. Because all the other functions take a pointer to the stack pointer, it makes sense to have deleteStack take its stack parameter in the same way. This way you don't have to remember which functions require only a pointer to a stack and which take a pointer to a pointer to a stack — they all work the same way. This reasoning gives you the following prototypes:

```
bool createStack( Element **stack );
bool deleteStack( Element **stack );
```

Once everything is designed properly, the coding is fairly simple. The createStack routine sets the stack pointer to NULL and returns success, as follows:

```
bool createStack( Element **stack ){
    *stack = NULL;
    return true;
}
```

The push operation allocates the new element, checks for failure, sets the data of the new element, places it at the top of the stack, and adjusts the stack pointer, as follows:

```
bool push( Element **stack, void *data ){
    Element *elem = new Element;
    if(!elem) return false;

    elem->data = data;
    elem->next = *stack;
    *stack = elem;
    return true;
}
```

The pop operation checks that the stack isn't empty, fetches the data from the top element, adjusts the stack pointer, and frees the element that is no longer on the stack, as follows:

```
bool pop( Element **stack, void **data ){
    Element *elem;
    if (!(elem = *stack)) return false;

    *data = elem->data;
    *stack = elem->next;
    delete elem;
    return true;
}
```

While deleteStack could call pop repeatedly, it's more efficient to simply traverse the data structure, freeing as you go. Don't forget that you need a temporary pointer to hold the address of the next element while you free the current one:

```
bool deleteStack( Element **stack ){
    Element *next;
    while( *stack ){
        next = (*stack)->next;
        delete *stack;
        *stack = next;
    }
    return true;
}
```

Before the discussion of this problem is complete, it is worth noting (and probably worth mentioning to the interviewer) that the interface design would be much more straightforward in an object-oriented language. The createStack and deleteStack operations become the constructor and destructor, respectively. The push and pop routines are bound to the stack object, so they don't need to have the stack explicitly passed to them, and the need for pointers to pointers evaporates. An exception can be thrown when a memory allocation fails, which enables you to use the return value of pop for data instead of an error code. A C++ version looks like the following:

```
class Stack
{
public:
    Stack();
    ~Stack();
    void push( void *data );
    void *pop();
protected:
    // Element struct needed only internally
    typedef struct Element {
        struct Element *next;
        void *data;
    } Element;

    Element *head;
};

Stack::Stack() {
    head = NULL;
    return;
```

```
}

Stack::~Stack() {
    while( head ){
        Element *next = head->next;
        delete head;
        head = next;
    }
    return;
}

void Stack::push( void *data ){
    //Allocation error will throw exception
    Element *element = new Element;
    element->data = data;
    element->next = head;
    head = element;
    return;
}

void *Stack::pop() {
    Element *popElement = head;
    void *data;

    /* Assume StackError exception class is defined elsewhere */
    if( head == NULL )
        throw StackError( E_EMPTY );

    data = head->data;
    head = head->next;
    delete popElement;
    return data;
}
```

You could eliminate this implementation's reliance on exceptions by adding explicit C-style error handling along the lines of that used in the first implementation.

Maintain Linked List Tail Pointer

`head` and `tail` are global pointers to the first and last element, respectively, of a singly-linked list of integers. Implement C functions for the following prototypes:

```
bool remove( Element *elem );

bool insertAfter( Element *elem, int data );
```

The argument to `remove` is the element to be deleted. The two arguments to `insertAfter` give the data for the new element and the element after which the new element is to be inserted. It should be possible to insert at the beginning of the list by calling `insertAfter` with `NULL` as the element argument. These functions should return true if successful and false if unsuccessful.

Your functions must keep the `head` and `tail` pointers current.

This problem seems relatively straightforward. Deletion and insertion are common operations for a linked list, and you should be accustomed to using a head pointer for the list. The requirement of maintaining a tail pointer is the only unusual aspect of this problem. This requirement doesn't seem to fundamentally change anything about the list or the way you operate on it, so it doesn't look as if you need to design any new algorithms. Just be sure to update the head and tail pointers when necessary.

When will you need to update these pointers? Obviously, operations in the middle of a long list will not affect either the head or tail. You need to update the pointers only when you change the list such that a different element appears at the beginning or end. More specifically, when you insert a new element at either end of the list, that element becomes the new beginning or end of the list. When you delete an element at the beginning or end of the list, the next-to-first or next-to-last element becomes the new first or last element.

For each operation you will have a general case for operations in the middle of the list and special cases for operations at either end. When you are dealing with many special cases, it can be easy to miss some of them, especially if some of the special cases have more specific special cases of their own. One technique for identifying special cases is to consider what circumstances are likely to lead to special cases being invoked. Then, you can check whether your proposed implementation works in each of these circumstances. If you discover a circumstance that creates a problem, you have discovered a new special case.

The circumstance where you are instructed to operate on the ends of the list has already been discussed. Another problem-prone circumstance is a `NULL` pointer argument. The only other thing that can change is the list on which you are operating — specifically, its length. What lengths of lists might create problematic circumstances? You can expect somewhat different cases for the beginning, middle, and end of the list. Any list that doesn't have these three distinct classes of elements could lead to additional special cases. An empty list has no elements, so it obviously has no beginning, middle, or end elements. A one-element list has no middle elements and one element that is both the beginning and end element. A two-element list has distinct beginning and end elements, but no middle element. Any list longer than this has all three classes of elements and is effectively the general case of lists — unlikely to lead to additional special cases. Based on this reasoning, you should explicitly confirm that your implementation works correctly for lists of length 0, 1, and 2.

At this point in the problem, you can begin writing `remove`. As mentioned earlier, you need a special case for deleting the first element of the list. You can compare the element to be deleted to `head` to determine whether you need to invoke this case:

```
bool remove( Element *elem ){
    if (elem == head) {
        head = elem->next;
        delete elem;
        return true;
    }
    ...
```

Now write the general middle case. You'll need an element pointer to keep track of your position in the list (we'll call the pointer `curPos`). Recall that to delete an element from a linked list, you need a pointer to the preceding element so you can change its next pointer. The easiest way to find the preceding element is to compare `curPos->next` to `elem`, so `curPos` points to the preceding element when you find `elem`. You also need to construct your loop so as not to miss any elements. If you initialize `curPos` to `head`, then `curPos->next` starts as the second element of the list. Starting at the second item is fine because you treat the first element as a special case, but make your first check before advancing `curPos` or you'll miss the second element. If `curPos` becomes `NULL`, you have reached the end of the list without finding the element you were supposed to delete, so you should return failure. The middle case yields the following (added code is emphasized):

```
bool remove( Element *elem ){
    Element *curPos = head;

    if (elem == head) {
        head = elem->next;
        delete elem;
        return true;
    }

    while( curPos ){
        if( curPos->next == elem ){
            curPos->next = elem->next;
            delete elem;
            return true;
        }
        curPos = curPos->next;
    }

    return false;
    ...
```

Next, consider the last element case. The last element's next pointer is `NULL`. To remove it from the list, you need to make the next-to-last element's next pointer `NULL` and free the last element. If you examine the loop constructed for middle elements, you will see that it can delete the last element as well as middle elements. The only difference is that you need to update the tail pointer when you delete the last element. If you set `curPos->next` to `NULL`, you know you changed the end of the list and must update the tail pointer. Adding this to complete the function, you get the following:

```
bool remove( Element *elem ){
    Element *curPos = head;

    if( elem == head ){
        head = elem->next;
        delete elem;
    }

    while( curPos ){
        if( curPos->next == elem ){
            curPos->next = elem->next;
            delete elem;
            if( curPos->next == NULL )
                tail = curPos;
            return true;
        }
```

```
            curPos = curPos->next;
        }

        return false;
    }
```

This solution covers the three discussed special cases. Before you present the interviewer with this solution, you should check behavior for `NULL` pointer arguments and the three potentially problematic list length circumstances. What happens if `elem` is `NULL`? The `while` loop traverses the list until `curPos->next` is `NULL` (when `curPos` is the last element). Then, on the next line, evaluating `elem->next` dereferences a `NULL` pointer. Because it's never possible to delete `NULL` from the list, the easiest way to fix this problem is to return false if `elem` is `NULL`.

If the list has zero elements, then `head` and `tail` are both `NULL`. Because you'll be checking that `elem` isn't `NULL`, `elem == head` will always be false. Further, because `head` is `NULL`, `curPos` will be `NULL`, and the body of the `while` loop won't be executed. There doesn't seem to be any problem with zero-element lists. The function simply returns false because nothing can be deleted from an empty list.

Now try a one-element list. In this case, `head` and `tail` both point to the one element, which is the only element you can delete. Again, `elem == head` is true. `elem->next` is `NULL`, so you correctly set `head` to `NULL` and free the element; however, `tail` still points to the element you just freed. As you can see, you need another special case to set `tail` to `NULL` for one-element lists.

What about two-element lists? Deleting the first element causes `head` to point to the remaining element, as it should. Similarly, deleting the last element causes `tail` to be correctly updated. The lack of middle elements doesn't seem to be a problem. You can add the two additional special cases and then move on to `insertAfter`:

```
bool remove( Element *elem ){
    Element *curPos = head;

    if( !elem )
        return false;

    if( elem == head ){
        head = elem->next;
        delete elem;
        /* special case for 1 element list */
        if( !head )
            tail = NULL;
        return true;
    }

    while( curPos ){
        if( curPos->next == elem ){
            curPos->next = elem->next;
            delete elem;
            if( curPos->next == NULL )
                tail = curPos;
            return true;
        }
```

```
            curPos = curPos->next;
        }

        return false;
    }
```

You can apply similar reasoning to writing `insertAfter`. Because you are allocating a new element in this function, you must take care to check that the allocation was successful and that you don't leak any memory. Many of the special cases encountered in `delete` are relevant in `insertAfter`, however, and the code is structurally very similar:

```
    bool insertAfter( Element *elem, int data ){
        Element *newElem, *curPos = head;

        newElem = new Element;
        if( !newElem )
            return false;
        newElem->data = data;

        /* Insert at beginning of list */
        if( !elem ){
            newElem->next = head;
            head = newElem;

            /* Special case for empty list */
            if( !tail )
                tail = newElem;
            return true;
        }

        while( curPos ){
            if( curPos == elem ){
                newElem->next = curPos->next;
                curPos->next = newElem;

                /* Special case for inserting at end of list */
                if( !(newElem->next) )
                    tail = newElem;
                return true;
            }
            curPos = curPos->next;
        }

        /* Insert position not found; free element and return failure */
        delete newElem;
        return false;
    }
```

This problem turns out to be an exercise in special cases. It's not particularly interesting or satisfying to solve, but it's very good practice. Many interview problems have special cases, so you should expect to encounter them frequently. In the real world of programming, unhandled special cases represent bugs that may be difficult to find, reproduce, and fix. Programmers who identify special cases as they are coding are likely to be more productive than those who find special cases through debugging. Intelligent interviewers recognize this and pay attention to whether a candidate identifies special cases as part of the coding process or needs to be prompted to recognize special cases.

Bugs in removeHead

Find and fix the bugs in the following C/C++ function that is supposed to remove the head element from a singly-linked list:

```
void removeHead( Node *head ){
    delete head;          /* Line 1 */
    head = head->next;    /* Line 2 */
}
```

These bug-finding problems occur with some frequency, so it's worthwhile to discuss a generic strategy that you can apply to this and other problems.

Because you will generally be given only a small amount of code to analyze, your bug-finding strategy will be a little different from real-world programming. You don't need to worry about interactions with other modules or other parts of the program. Instead, you must do a systematic analysis of every line of the function without the help of a debugger. Consider four common problem areas for any function you are given:

1. **Check that the data comes into the function properly.** Make sure you aren't accessing a variable that you don't have, you aren't reading something as an `int` that should be a `long`, and you have all the values you need to perform the task.
2. **Check that each line of the function works correctly.** The function is undoubtedly performing a task. Verify that the task is executed correctly at each line and that the desired result is produced at the end.
3. **Check that the data comes out of the function correctly**. The return value should be what you expect. In addition, if the function is expected to update any caller variables, make sure this occurs.
4. **Check the common error conditions.** Error conditions vary depending on the specifics of a problem. They tend to involve unusual argument values. For instance, functions that operate on data structures may have trouble with empty or nearly empty data structures; functions that take a pointer as an argument may fail if passed a `NULL` pointer.

Starting with the first step, verify that data comes into the function properly. In a linked list, you can access every node given only the head. Because you are passed the list head, you have access to all the data you require—no bugs so far.

Now do a line-by-line analysis of the function. The first line frees `head`—okay so far. Line 2 then assigns a new value to `head` but uses the old value of `head` to do this. That's a problem. You have already freed `head`, and you are now dereferencing freed memory. You could try reversing the lines, but this would cause the element after `head` to be freed. You need to free `head`, but you also need its `next` value after it has been freed. You can solve this problem by using a temporary variable to store `head`'s `next` value. Then you can free `head` and use the temporary variable to update `head`. These steps make the function look like the following:

```
void removeHead( Node *head ){
    Node *temp = head->next;   /* Line 1 */
    delete head;               /* Line 2 */
    head = temp;               /* Line 3 */
}
```

Now, move to step 3 of the strategy and make sure the function returns values properly. Though there is no explicit return value, there is an implicit one. This function is supposed to update the caller's `head` value. In C, all function parameters are passed by value, so functions get a local copy of each argument, and any changes made to that local copy are not reflected outside the function. Any new value you assign to `head` on line 3 has no effect — another bug. To correct this, you need a way to change the value of `head` in the calling code. Variables cannot be passed by reference in C, so the solution is to pass a pointer to the variable you want to change — in this case, a pointer to the head pointer. After the change, the function should look like this:

```
void removeHead( Node **head ){
    Node *temp = (*head)->next;   /* Line 1 */
    delete *head;                 /* Line 2 */
    *head = temp;                 /* Line 3 */
}
```

Now you can move on to the fourth case and check error conditions. Check a one-element and a zero-element list. In a one-element list, this function works properly. It removes the one element and sets the `head` to `NULL`, indicating that the head was removed. Now take a look at the zero-element case. A zero-element list is simply a `NULL` pointer. If `head` is a `NULL` pointer, you would dereference a `NULL` pointer on line 1. To correct this, check whether `head` is a `NULL` pointer and be sure not to dereference it in this case. This check makes the function look like the following:

```
void removeHead( Node **head ){
    Node *temp;
    if( !(*head) ){
        temp = (*head)->next;
        delete *head;
        *head = temp;
    }
}
```

You have checked that the body of the function works properly, that the function is called correctly and returns values correctly, and that you have dealt with the error cases. You can declare your debugging effort complete and present this version of `removeHead` to the interviewer as your solution.

Mth-to-Last Element of a Linked List

Given a singly-linked list, devise a time- and space-efficient algorithm to find the *m*th-to-last element of the list. Implement your algorithm, taking care to handle relevant error conditions. Define *m*th to last such that when *m* = 0, the last element of the list is returned.

Why is this a difficult problem? Finding the *m*th element from the beginning of a linked list would be an extremely trivial task, because singly-linked lists can only be traversed in the forward direction. For this problem you are asked to find a given element based on its position relative to the *end* of the list. While you traverse the list, however, you don't know where the end is, and when you find the end there is no easy way to backtrack the required number of elements.

You may want to tell your interviewer that a singly-linked list is a particularly poor choice for a data structure when you frequently need to find the *m*th-to-last element. If you were to encounter such a problem while implementing a real program, the correct and most-efficient solution would probably be to substitute a more-suitable data structure (such as a doubly-linked list) to replace the singly-linked list. Although this comment shows that you understand good design, the interviewer will still want you to solve the problem as it was originally phrased.

How, then, can you get around the problem that there is no way to traverse backward through this data structure? You know that the element you want is m elements from the end of the list. Therefore, if you traverse m elements forward from an element and that places you exactly at the end of the list, you have found the element you were searching for. One approach is to simply test each element in this manner until you find the one you're searching for. Intuitively, this feels like an inefficient solution because you will be traversing over the same elements many times. If you analyze this potential solution more closely, you will see that you would be traversing m elements for most of the elements in the list. If the length of the list is n, the algorithm would be approximately $O(mn)$. You need to find a solution more efficient than $O(mn)$.

What if you stored some of the elements (or, more likely, pointers or references to the elements) as you traversed the list? Then, when you reach the end of the list, you could look back m elements in your storage data structure to find the appropriate element. If you use an appropriate temporary storage data structure, this algorithm would be $O(n)$ because it requires only one traversal through the list. Yet this approach is far from perfect. As m becomes large, the temporary data structure would become large as well. In the worst-case scenario, this approach might require almost as much storage space as the list itself—not a particularly space-efficient algorithm.

Perhaps working back from the end of the list is not the best approach. Because counting from the beginning of the list is trivial, is there any way to count from the beginning to find the desired element? The desired element is m from the end of the list, and you know the value of m. It must also be l elements from the beginning of the list, although you don't know l. However, $l + m = n$, the length of the list. It's easy to count all the elements in the list. Then you can calculate $l = n - m$, and traverse l elements from the beginning of the list. Although this process involves two passes through the list, it's still $O(n)$. It requires only a few variables' worth of storage, so this method is a significant improvement over the previous attempt. If you could change the functions that modify the list such that they would increment a count variable for every element added and decrement it for every element removed, you could eliminate the count pass, making this a relatively efficient algorithm. Again, though this point is worth mentioning to the interviewer, he or she is probably looking for a solution that doesn't modify the data structure or place any restrictions on the methods used to access it.

Assuming you must explicitly count the elements in the current algorithm, you will have to make almost two complete traversals of the linked list. A very large list on a memory-constrained system might exist mostly in paged-out virtual memory (on disk). In such a case, each complete traversal of the list would require a large amount of disk access to swap the relevant portions of the list in and out of memory. Under these conditions, an algorithm that made only one complete traversal of the list might be significantly faster than an algorithm that made two traversals, even though they would both be O(n). Is there a way to find the target element with a single traversal?

The counting-from-the-beginning algorithm obviously demands that you know the length of the list. If you can't track the length so that you know it ahead of time, you can determine the length only by a full-list traversal. There doesn't seem to be much hope for getting this algorithm down to a single traversal.

Try reconsidering the previous linear time algorithm, which required only one traversal but was rejected for requiring too much storage. Is it possible to reduce the storage requirements of this approach?

When you reach the end of the list, you are really interested in only one of the m elements you've been tracking — the element that is m elements behind your current position. You are tracking the rest of the m elements merely because the element m behind your current position changes every time your position advances. Keeping a queue m elements long whereby you add the current element to the head and remove an element from the end every time you advance your current position ensures that the last element in the queue is always m elements behind your current position.

In effect, you are using this m element data structure to make it easy to implicitly advance an m-behind pointer in lock step with your current position pointer. However, this data structure is unnecessary — you can explicitly advance the m-behind pointer by following each element's next pointer just as you do for your current position pointer. This is as easy as (or perhaps easier than) implicitly advancing by shifting through a queue, and it eliminates the need to track all the elements between your current position pointer and your m-behind pointer. This algorithm seems to be the one you've been looking for: linear time, a single traversal, and negligible storage requirements. Now you just need to work out the details.

You'll use two pointers: a current position pointer and an m-behind pointer. You will have to ensure that the two pointers are actually spaced m elements apart; then you can advance them at the same rate. When your current position is the end of the list, m-behind will point to the mth-to-last element. How can you get the pointers spaced properly? If you count elements as you traverse the list, you can move the current position pointer to the mth element of the list. If you then start the m-behind pointer at the beginning of the list, they will be spaced m elements apart.

Are there any error conditions you need to watch for? If the list is less than m elements long, then there is no mth-to-last element. In such a case, you would run off the end of the list as you tried to advance the current position pointer to the mth element, possibly dereferencing a null pointer in the process. Therefore, check that you don't hit the end of the list while doing this initial advance.

With this caveat in mind, you can implement the algorithm. Note that it's easy to introduce off-by-one errors in any code that spaces any two things m items apart or counts m items from a given point. You may want to refer to the exact definition of "mth to last" given in the problem and try a little example on paper to make sure you get your counts right, particularly in the initial advancement of the `current` pointer.

```
Element *findMToLastElement( Element *head, int m ){
    Element *current, *mBehind;
    int i;

    /* Advance current m elements from beginning,
     * checking for the end of the list
     */
    current = head;
```

```
        for (i = 0; i < m; i++) {
            if (current->next) {
                current = current->next;
            } else {
                return NULL;
            }
        }

        /* Start mBehind at beginning and advance pointers
         * together until current hits last element
         */
        mBehind = head;
        while( current->next ){
            current = current->next;
            mBehind = mBehind->next;
        }

        /* mBehind now points to the element we were
         * searching for, so return it
         */
        return mBehind;
    }
```

List Flattening

Start with a standard doubly-linked list. Now imagine that in addition to next and previous pointers, each element has a child pointer, which may or may not point to a separate doubly-linked list. These child lists may have one or more children of their own, and so on, to produce a multilevel data structure, as shown in Figure 4-3.

Flatten the list so that all the nodes appear in a single-level, doubly-linked list. You are given the head and tail of the first level of the list. Each node is a C struct with the following definition:

```
typedef struct Node {
    struct Node *next;
    struct Node *prev;
    struct Node *child;

    int         value;

} Node;
```

This list-flattening problem gives you plenty of freedom. You have simply been asked to flatten the list. There are many ways to accomplish this task. Each way results in a one-level list with a different node ordering. Start by considering several options for algorithms and the node orders they would yield. Then implement the algorithm that looks easiest and most efficient.

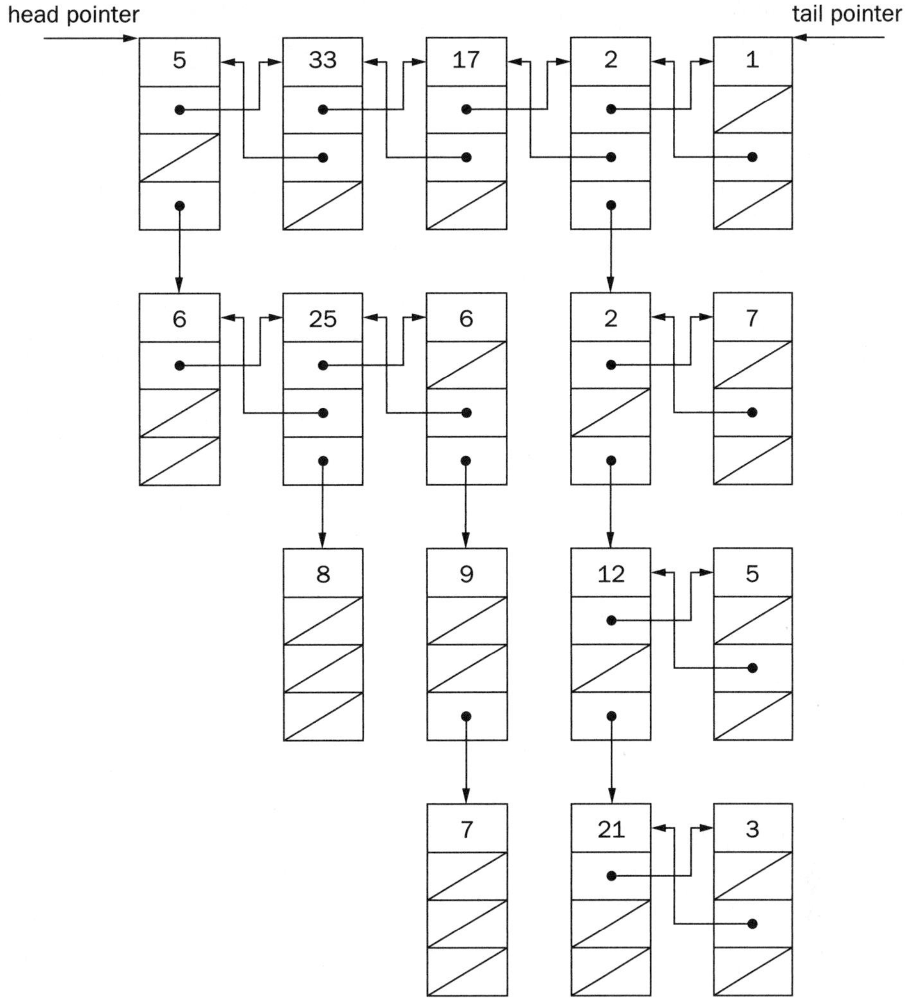

Figure 4-3

Begin by looking at the data structure itself. This data structure is a little unusual for a list. It has levels and children — somewhat like a tree. A tree also has levels and children, but in a tree, no nodes on the same level are connected. You might try to use a common tree-traversal algorithm and copy each node into a new list as you visit it as a simple way to flatten the structure.

The data structure is not exactly a normal tree, so any traversal algorithm you use will have to be modified. From the perspective of a tree, each separate child list in the data structure forms a single extended tree-node. This may not seem too bad: Where a standard traversal algorithm checks the child pointers of each tree-node directly, you just need to do a linked list traversal to check all the child pointers. Every time you check a node, you can copy it to a duplicate list. This duplicate list will be your flattened list.

Before you work out the details of this solution, consider its efficiency. Every node is examined once, so this is an O(n) solution. There is likely to be some overhead for the recursion or data structure required for the traversal. In addition, you are making a duplicate copy of each node to create the new list. This copying is inefficient, especially if the structure is very large. Therefore, you should search for a more-efficient solution that doesn't require so much copying.

So far, the proposed solution has concentrated on an algorithm, letting the ordering follow. Instead, try focusing on an ordering and then try to deduce an algorithm. You can focus on the data structure's levels as a source of ordering. It helps to define the parts of a level as *child lists*. Just as rooms in a hotel are ordered by level, you can order nodes by the level in which they occur. Every node is in a level and appears in an ordering within that level (arranging the child lists from left to right). Therefore, you have a logical ordering just like hotel rooms. You can order by starting with all the first-level nodes, followed by all the second-level nodes, followed by all the third-level nodes, and so on. Applying these rules to the example data structure, you should get the ordering shown in Figure 4-4.

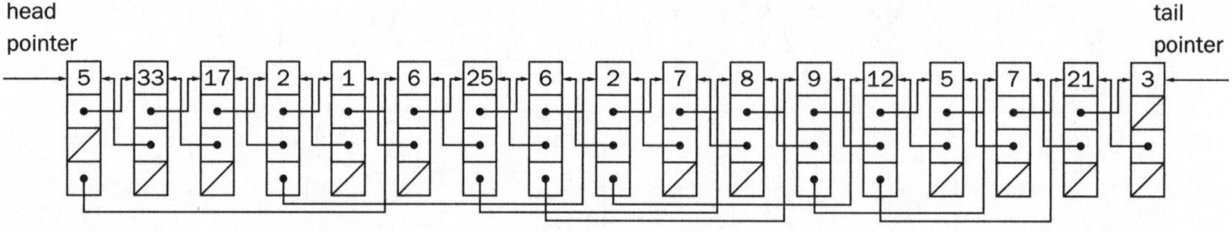

Figure 4-4

Now try to discover an algorithm that yields this ordering. One property of this ordering is that you never rearrange the order of the nodes in their respective levels, so you could connect all the nodes on each level into a list and then join all the connected levels. However, to find all the nodes on a given level so that you can join them, you would have to do a breadth-first search of that level. Breadth-first searching is inefficient, so you should continue to look for a better solution.

In Figure 4-3, the second level is composed of two child lists. Each child list starts with a different child of a first-level node. You could try to append the child lists one at a time to the end of the first level instead of combining the child lists.

To append the child lists one at a time, traverse the first level from the start, following the next pointers. Every time you encounter a node with a child, append the child (and thus the child list) to the end of the first level and update the tail pointer. Eventually, you will append the entire second level to the end of the first level. You can continue traversing the first level and arrive at the start of the old second level. If you continue this process of appending children to the end of the first level, you will eventually append every child list to the end and have a flattened list in the required order. More formally, this algorithm is as follows:

```
Start at the beginning of the first level
While you are not at the end of the first level
    If the current node has a child
        Append the child to the end of the first level
        Update the tail pointer
    Advance to next node
```

This algorithm is easy to implement because it's so simple. In terms of efficiency, every node after the first level is examined twice. Each node is examined once when you update the tail pointer for each child list and once when you examine the node to see if it has a child. The nodes in the first level are examined only once when you examine them for children because you had a first-level tail pointer when you began. Therefore, there are no more than $2n$ comparisons in this algorithm, and it is an $O(n)$ solution. This is the best time order you can achieve because every node must be examined.

There are other equally efficient solutions to this problem. One such solution involves inserting child lists after their parents, rather than at the end of the list.

The code for this algorithm is as follows:

```
void flattenList( Node *head, Node **tail)
    Node *curNode =  head;
    while( curNode ){
        /* The current node has a child */
        if( curNode->child ){
            append( curNode->child, tail );
        }
        curNode = curNode->next;
    }
}

/* Appends the child list to the end of the tail and updates ⮐
 * the tail.
 */
void append( Node *child, Node **tail ){
    Node *curNode;

    /* Append the child child list to the end */
    (*tail)->next = child;
    child->prev = *tail;

    /*Find the new tail, which is the end of the child child ⮐
     *list.
     */
    for( curNode = child; curNode->next;
         curNode = curNode->next )
        ; /* Body intentionally empty */

    /* Update the tail pointer now that curNode is the new
     * tail.
     */
    *tail = curNode;
}
```

Regarding the first line of code in the preceding block, you need a pointer to the tail pointer so that changes to the tail pointer are retained when the function returns.

List Unflattening

Unflatten the list. Restore the data structure to its original condition before it was passed to `FlattenList`.

This problem is the reverse of the previous problem, so you already know a lot about this data structure. One important insight is that you can create the flattened list by combining all of the child lists into one long level. To get back the original list, you must separate the long flattened list back into its original child lists.

Try doing the exact opposite of what you did to create the list. When flattening the list, you traversed down the list from the start and added child lists to the end. To reverse this, you go backward from the tail and break off parts of the first level. You could break off a part when you encounter a node that was the beginning of a child list in the unflattened list. Unfortunately, this is more difficult than it might seem because you can't easily determine whether a particular node is a child (indicating that it started a child list) in the original data structure. The only way to determine whether a node is a child is to scan through the child pointers of all the previous nodes. All this scanning would be inefficient, so you should examine some additional possibilities to find an efficient solution.

One way to get around the child node problem is to go through the list from start to end, storing pointers to all the child nodes in a separate data structure. Then you could go backward through the list and separate every child node. Looking up nodes in this way frees you from repeated scans to determine whether a node is a child or not. This is a good solution, but it still requires an extra data structure. Now try looking for a solution without an extra data structure.

It seems you have exhausted all the possibilities for going backward through the list, so try an algorithm that traverses the list from the start to the end. You still can't immediately determine whether a node is a child. One advantage of going forward, however, is that you can find all the child nodes in the same order that you appended them to the first level. You would also know that every child began a child list in the original list. If you separate each child node from the node before it, you get the unflattened list back.

You can't simply traverse the list from the start, find each node with a child, and separate the child from its previous node. You would get to the end of your list at the break between the first and second level, leaving the rest of the data structure untraversed. This solution is not too bad, though. You can traverse every child list, starting with the first level (which is a child list itself). When you find a child, continue traversing the original child list and also traverse the newly found child list. You can't traverse both at the same time, however. You can save one of these locations in a data structure and traverse it later. However, rather than design and implement a data structure, you can use recursion. Specifically, every time you find a node with a child, separate the child from its previous node, start traversing the new child list, and then continue traversing the original child list.

This is an efficient algorithm because each node is checked at most twice, resulting in an O(n) running time. Again, an O(n) running time is the best you can do because you must check each node at least once to see if it is a child. In the average case, the number of function calls is small in relation to the number of nodes, so the recursive overhead is not too bad. In the worst case, the number of function calls is no more than the number of nodes. This solution is approximately as efficient as the earlier proposal that required an extra data structure, but somewhat simpler and easier to code. Therefore, this recursive solution would probably be the best choice in an interview. In outline form, the algorithm looks like the following:

```
Explore path:
    While not at the end
        If current node has a child
            Separate the child from its previous node
            Explore path beginning with the child
        Go onto the next node
```

The code for this algorithm is as follows:

```
/*This is a wrapper function that also updates the tail pointer.*/
void unflatten( Node *start, Node **tail ){
    Node *curNode;

    exploreAndSeparate( start );

    /* Update the tail pointer */
    for( curNode = start; curNode->next;
         curNode = curNode->next)
        ; /* Body intentionally empty */

    *tail = curNode;
}

/* This is the function that actually does the recursion and
 * the separation
 */
void exploreAndSeparate( Node *childListStart ){
    Node *curNode = childListStart;

    while( curNode ){
        if( curNode->child ){
            /* terminates the child list before the child */
            curNode->child->prev->next = NULL;
            /* starts the child list beginning with the child */
            curNode->child->prev = NULL;
            exploreAndSeparate( curNode->child );
        }
        curNode = curNode->next;
    }
}
```

Null or Cycle

You are given a linked list that is either NULL-terminated (acyclic), as shown in Figure 4-5, or ends in a cycle (cyclic), as shown in Figure 4-6.

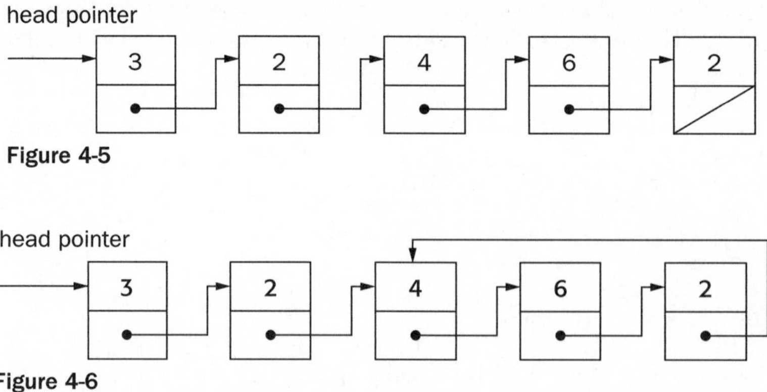

Figure 4-5

Figure 4-6

Write a function that takes a pointer to the head of a list and determines whether the list is cyclic or acyclic. Your function should return false if the list is acyclic and true if it is cyclic. You may not modify the list in any way.

Start by looking at the pictures to see if you can determine an intuitive way to differentiate a cyclic list from an acyclic list.

The difference between the two lists appears at their ends. In the cyclic list, there is an end node that points back to one of the earlier nodes. In the acyclic list, there is an end node that is NULL terminated. Thus, if you can find this end node, you can test whether the list is cyclic or acyclic. In the acyclic list, it is easy to find this end node. You traverse the list until you reach a NULL-terminated node. In the cyclic list, though, it is more difficult. If you just traverse the list, you go in a circle and won't know whether you're in a cyclic list or just a long acyclic list. You need a more-sophisticated approach.

Try looking at the end node a bit more. The end node points to a node that has another node pointing at it. This means that there are two pointers pointing at the same node. This node is the only node with two elements pointing at it. You can design an algorithm around this property. You can traverse the list and check every node to determine whether two other nodes are pointing at it. If you find such a node, the list must be cyclic. Otherwise, the list is acyclic, and you will eventually encounter a NULL pointer.

Unfortunately, it is difficult to check the number of nodes pointing at each element. See if you can find another special property of the end node in a cyclic list. When you traverse the list, the end node's next node is a node that you have previously encountered. Instead of checking for a node with two pointers pointing at it, you can check whether you have already encountered a node. If you find a previously encountered node, you have a cyclic list. If you encounter a NULL pointer, you have an acyclic list. This is only part of the algorithm. You still have to figure out how to determine whether or not you have previously encountered a node.

The easiest way to do this would be to mark each element as you visit it, but you've been told you're not allowed to modify the list. You could keep track of the nodes you've encountered by putting them in a separate, already-encountered list. Then you would compare the current node to all of the nodes in the already-encountered list. If the current node ever points to a node in the already-encountered list, you have a cycle. Otherwise, you'll get to the end of the list and see that it's NULL terminated and thus acyclic. This would work, but in the worst case the already-encountered list would require as much memory as the original list itself. See if you can reduce this memory requirement.

What are you storing in the already-encountered list? The already-encountered list's first node points to the original list's first node, its second node points to the original list's second node, its third node points to the original list's third node, and so on. You're creating a list that mirrors the original list. This is unnecessary — you can just use the original list.

Try this approach: Because you know your current node in the list and the start of the list, you can compare your current node's next pointer to all of its previous nodes directly. For the ith node, compare its next pointer to see if it points to any of nodes 1 to $i - 1$. If any are equal, you have a cycle.

What's the time order of this algorithm? For the first node, 0 previous nodes are examined; for the second node, one previous node is examined; for the third node, two previous nodes are examined, and so on. Thus, the algorithm examines $0 + 1 + 2 + 3 + ... + n$ nodes. As discussed in Chapter 3, such an algorithm is $O(n^2)$.

That's about as far as you can go with this approach. Although it's difficult to discover without some sort of hint, there is a better solution involving two pointers. What can you do with two pointers that you couldn't do with one? You can advance them on top of each other, but then you might as well have one pointer. You could advance them with a fixed interval between them, but this doesn't seem to gain anything. What happens if you advance the pointers at different speeds?

In the acyclic list, the faster pointer will reach the end. In the cyclic list, they will both loop endlessly. The faster pointer will eventually catch up with and pass the slower pointer. If the fast pointer ever passes the slower pointer, you have a cyclic list. If it encounters a NULL pointer, you have an acyclic list. In outline form, this algorithm looks like this:

```
Start two pointers at the head of the list
Loop infinitely
    If the fast pointer reaches a NULL pointer
        Return that the list is NULL terminated
    If the fast pointer moves onto or over the slow pointer
        Return that there is a cycle
    Advance the slow pointer one node
    Advance the fast pointer two nodes
```

You can now implement this solution:

```
/* Takes a pointer to the head of a linked list and determines if
 * the list ends in a cycle or is NULL terminated
 */
bool determineTermination( Node *head ){
    Node *fast, *slow;
    fast = slow = head;
    while( true ){
        if( !fast || !fast->next )
            return false;
        else if( fast == slow || fast->next == slow )
            return true;
```

```
            else {
                slow = slow->next;
                fast = fast->next->next;
            }
        }
    }
```

Is this algorithm faster than the earlier solution? If this list is acyclic, the faster pointer comes to the end after examining n nodes, while the slower pointer traverses $\frac{1}{2}$ n nodes. Thus, you examine $\frac{3}{2}n$ nodes, which is an O(n) algorithm.

What about a cyclic list? The slower pointer will never go around any loop more than once. When the slower pointer has examined n nodes, the faster pointer will have examined $2n$ nodes and have "passed" the slower pointer, regardless of the loop's size. Therefore, in the worst case you examine $3n$ nodes, which is still O(n). Regardless of whether the list is cyclic or acyclic, this two-pointer approach is much better than the one-pointer approach to the problem.

Summary

Although they are simple data structures, problems about linked lists often arise in interviews focusing on C/C++ experience as a way to determine whether a candidate understands basic pointer manipulation. Each element in a singly-linked list contains a pointer to the next element in the list, while each element in a doubly-linked list points to both the previous and the next elements. The first element in both list types is referred to as the *head*, while the last element is referred to as the *tail*. Circularly-linked lists have no head or tail; instead, the elements are linked together to form a cycle.

List operations are much simpler to perform on doubly-linked lists, so most interview problems use singly-linked lists. Typical operations include updating the head of the list, traversing the list to find a specific element from the end of the list, and inserting or removing list elements.

Trees and Graphs

Trees and graphs are common data structures in programming, so they are both fair game in a programming interview. Trees, in particular, appear frequently because they enable an interviewer to test your knowledge of recursion and run-time analysis. Trees are also simple enough that you can implement them within the time constraints of an interview. Although graph problems are interesting, they are usually very complicated and do not lend themselves to interview problems. Therefore, the emphasis of this chapter is on trees.

Unlike Chapter 4's use of C/C++ in the problems, in this and the subsequent chapters you're going to use more modern languages like C# and Java. This means you'll be creating classes to properly encapsulate your code and you generally won't be using pointers anymore.

Trees

A tree is made up of nodes (data elements) with zero, one, or several references to other nodes. Each node has only one other node referencing it. The result is a data structure that looks like Figure 5-1.

As in a linked list, a node is represented by a structure or class, and trees can be implemented in any language that includes pointers or references. In object-oriented languages you usually define a class for the common parts of a node, and one or more subclasses for the data held by a node. For example, these are the C# classes you might use for a tree of integers:

```
public class Node {
    public Node[] children;
}

public class IntNode : Node {
    public int value;
}
```

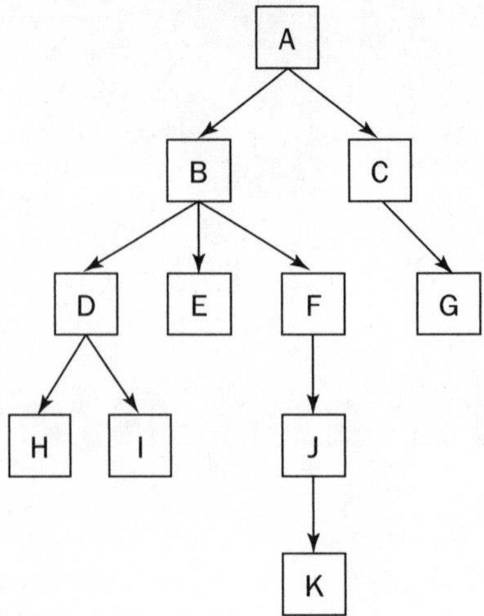

Figure 5-1

In this definition, children is an array that keeps track of all the nodes that this node references. Note that for simplicity we exposed the children as public data members. A proper class definition would make them private and expose methods to manipulate them. A fuller Java equivalent (with methods and constructors) to the preceding classes would be as follows:

```
public abstract class Node {
    private Node[] children;

    public Node( Node[] children ){
        this.children = children;
    }

    public int getNumChildren(){
        return children.length;
    }

    public Node getChild( int index ){
        return children[ index ];
    }
}

public class IntNode extends Node {
    private int value;

    public IntNode( Node[] children, int value ){
        super( children );
        this.value = value;
    }

    public int getValue(){
        return value;
    }
}
```

Even this example is not complete, however, because there is no error handling and no way to dynamically add or remove nodes from a tree. During an interview you may want to keep things simple by using public data members, folding classes together, or by only sketching out the various methods that are needed to manage the tree. For the latter, you could also define an interface instead of a base class and not bother defining the methods. Ask the interviewer how much detail is wanted and design your code accordingly. If the interviewer provides no guidance, be sure to explain your choices as you go along.

Looking at the tree shown in Figure 5-1, you can see that there is only one top-level node. From this node, it is possible to follow pointers and reach every other node. This top-level node is called the *root*. The root is the only node from which you are guaranteed to have a path to every other node. The root node is inherently the start of any tree. Therefore, people will often say "tree" when talking about the root node of the tree.

Following is some additional tree-related vocabulary:

- **Parent** — A node that points to other nodes is the *parent* of those nodes. Every node except the root has one parent. In Figure 5-1, B is the parent of D, E, and F.
- **Child** — A node is the *child* of any node that points to it. In Figure 5-1, each of the nodes D, E, and F is a child of B.
- **Descendant** — All the nodes that can be reached by following a path of child nodes from a particular node are the *descendants* of that node. In Figure 5-1, D, E, F, H, I, J, and K are the descendants of B.
- **Ancestor** — An *ancestor* of a node is any other node for which the node is a descendant. For example, A, B, and D are the ancestors of I.
- **Leaves** — The *leaves* are nodes that do not have any children. G, H, I, and K are leaves.

Binary Trees

So far, you've been using the most general definition of a tree. In practice, when an interviewer says "tree," he or she usually means a special type of tree called a *binary tree*. In a binary tree, each node has no more than two children, commonly referred to as *right* and *left*. Figure 5-2 shows an example of a binary tree.

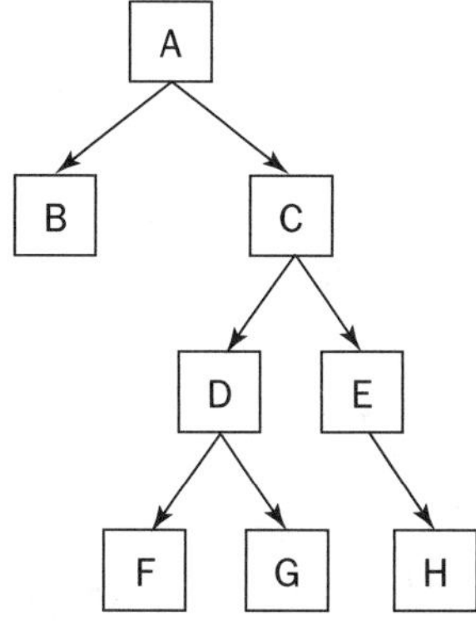

Figure 5-2

Here's a simple implementation of a binary tree. For simplicity, we combine everything into a single class:

```
public class Node {
    private Node left;
    private Node right;
    private int  value;

    public Node( Node left, Node right, int value ){
        this.left = left;
        this.right = right;
        this.value = value;
    }

    public Node getLeft() { return left; }
    public Node getRight() { return right; }
    public int getValue() { return value; }
}
```

When an element has no left or right child, the corresponding reference is null.

Problems involving only binary trees can often be solved more quickly than equivalent problems about generic trees, but they are no less challenging. Because time is at a premium in an interview, most tree problems will be binary tree problems. If an interviewer just says "tree," it's a good idea to clarify whether he or she is referring to a generic tree or a binary tree.

People often say "tree" when they mean "binary tree."

Binary Search Trees

Trees are often used to store sorted or ordered data. By far, the most common way to store data in a tree is using a special tree called a *binary search tree (BST)*. In a BST, the value held by a node's left child is less than or equal to its own value, and the value held by a node's right child is greater than or equal to its value. In effect, the data in a BST is sorted by value: All the descendants to the left of a node are less than or equal to the node and all the descendants to the right of the node are greater than or equal to the node. Figure 5-3 is an example of a BST.

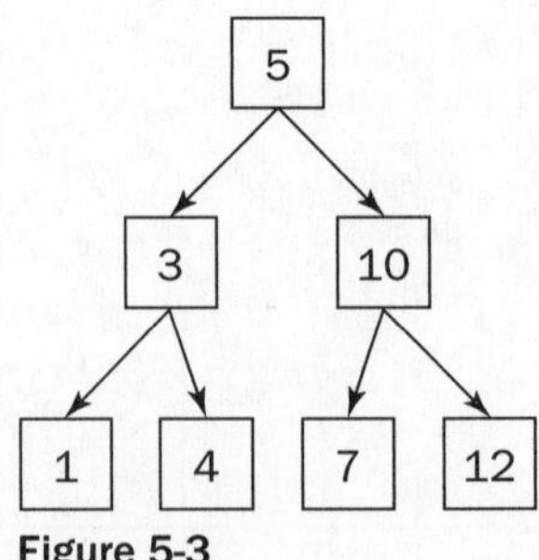

Figure 5-3

BSTs are so common, in fact, that many people mean a BST when they say "tree." Again, ask for clarification before proceeding.

People often say "tree" when they mean "binary search tree."

Lookup

One advantage of a binary search tree is that the lookup operation (locating a particular node in the tree) is fast and simple. This is particularly useful for data storage. In outline form, the algorithm to perform a lookup in a BST is as follows:

```
Start at the root node
Loop while current node is non-null
    If the current node's value is equal to your value
        Return the current node
    If the current node's value is less than your value
        Make the right node your current node
    If the current node's value is greater than your value
        Make the left node your current node
End loop
```

If you fall out of the loop, the node wasn't in the tree.

Here's one way to code the search in C# or Java:

```
Node findNode( Node root, int value ){
    while( root != null ){
        int currval = root.getValue();
        if( currval == value ) break;
        if( currval < value ){
            root = root.getRight();
        } else { // currval > value
            root = root.getLeft();
        }
    }

    return root;
}
```

This lookup is a fast operation because you eliminate half the nodes from your search on each iteration by choosing to follow the left subtree or the right subtree. In the worst case, you will know whether the lookup was successful by the time there is only one node left to search. Therefore, the running time of the lookup is equal to the number of times that you can halve n nodes before you get to 1. This number, x, is the same as the number of times you can double 1 before reaching n, and it can be expressed as $2^x = n$. You can find x using a logarithm. For example, $\log_2 8 = 3$ because $2^3 = 8$, and so the running time of the lookup operation is $O(\log_2(n))$. It is common to omit the base 2 and call this $O(\log(n))$. $\log(n)$ is very fast. Consider that $\log_2 1{,}000{,}000{,}000$ (30. Logarithms with different bases differ by a constant factor, so the base is ignored in big-O notation.

Lookup is an O(log(n)) operation in a binary search tree.

Note one caveat to saying that lookup is $O(\log(n))$ in a BST. Lookup is only $O(\log(n))$ if you can guarantee that the number of nodes remaining to be searched will be halved or nearly halved on each iteration. In the worst case, each node has only one child. In such a case, you have a linked list because each node points to only one other node. Lookup then becomes an $O(n)$ operation just as in a linked list. The good news is that there are ways to guarantee that every node has approximately the same number of nodes on its left side as its right. A tree with approximately the same number of nodes on each side is called a *balanced tree.*

Of the methods to guarantee that every node has approximately the same number of nodes per side, the most common is called a red-black tree.

Without going into too much detail (as the special cases get very nasty), it is also possible to delete and insert into a balanced BST in O(log(n)) time.

Deletion and insertion are O(log(n)) operations in binary search trees.

Binary search trees have other important properties. For example, it is possible to obtain the smallest element by following all the left children, and to obtain the largest element by following all the right children. The nodes can also be printed out, in order, in O(n) time. It is even possible, given a node, to find the next-highest node in O(log(n)) time.

Tree problems are often designed to test your ability to think recursively. Each node in a tree is the root of a subtree beginning at that node. This subtree property is conducive to recursion because recursion generally involves solving a problem in terms of similar subproblems and a base case. In tree recursion you start with a root, perform an action, and then move to the left or right subtree (or both, one after the other). This process continues until you reach a null reference, which is the end of a tree (and a good base case). For example, the preceding lookup operation can be reimplemented recursively as follows:

```
Node findNode( Node root, int value ){
    if( root == null ) return null;
    int currval = root.getValue();
    if( currval == value ) return root;
    if( currval < value ){
        return findNode( root.getRight(), value );
    } else { // currval > value
        return findNode( root.getLeft(), value );
    }
}
```

Most problems with trees have this recursive form. A good way to start thinking about any problem involving a tree is to start thinking recursively.

Many tree operations can be implemented recursively.

Heaps

Another common tree is a *heap*. Heaps are trees (usually binary trees) with a twist: Each child of a node has a value *less than* or *equal to* the node's own value. (The data implementation of a heap, however, can be different from what we discussed previously.) Consequently, the root node always has the largest value in the tree, which means that it's possible to find the maximum value in constant time: Simply return the root value. Insertion and deletion are still O(log(n)), but lookup becomes O(n). It is not possible to find the next-higher node to a given node in O(log(n)) time or to print out the nodes in sorted order in O(n) time as in a BST.

You could model the patients waiting in a hospital emergency room with a heap. As each patient enters, he or she is assigned a priority and put into the heap. A heart attack patient would get a higher priority than a patient with a stubbed toe. When a doctor becomes available, the doctor would want to examine the patient with the highest priority. The doctor can determine the patient with the highest priority by extracting the max value from the heap, which is a constant time operation.

If extracting the max value needs to be fast, then use a heap.

Common Searches

It's nice when you have a tree with ordering properties such as a BST or a heap. Often you're given a tree that isn't a BST or a heap. For example, you may have a tree that is a representation of a family tree or a company job hierarchy. You have to use different techniques to retrieve data from this kind of tree. One common class of problems involves searching for a particular node. Two very common search algorithms are used to accomplish this task.

Breadth-First Search

One way to search a tree is to do a *breadth-first search (BFS)*. In a BFS you start with the root, move left to right across the second level, then move left to right across the third level, and so forth. You continue the search until either you have examined all of the nodes or you find the node you are searching for. The time to find a node is $O(n)$, so this type of search is best avoided for large trees. A BFS also uses a large amount of memory because it is necessary to track the child nodes for all nodes on a given level while searching that level.

Depth-First Search

Another common way to search for a node is by using a *depth-first search (DFS)*. A depth-first search follows one branch of the tree down as many levels as possible until the target node is found or the end is reached. When the search can't go down any farther, it is continued at the nearest ancestor with unexplored children. DFS has much lower memory requirements than BFS because it is not necessary to store all of the child pointers at each level. In addition, DFS has the advantage that it doesn't examine any single level last (BFS examines the lowest level last). This is useful if you suspect that the node you are searching for will be in the lower levels. For example, if you were searching a job hierarchy tree looking for an employee who started less than three months ago, you would suspect that lower-level employees are more likely to have started recently. In this case, if the assumption were true, a DFS would usually find the target node more quickly than a BFS.

There are other types of searches, but these are the two most common that you will encounter in an interview.

Traversals

Another common type of tree problem is called a *traversal*. As opposed to a search, where you look for a particular node and stop when you find it, a traversal visits every node and performs some operation on it. There are many types of traversals, each of which visits nodes in a different order, but you're only likely to be asked about the three most common types of traversal for binary trees:

- **Preorder** traversal of a node performs the operation first on the node itself, then on its left descendants, and finally on its right descendants. In other words, a node is always visited before any of its children.

- **Inorder** traversal performs the operation first on the node's left descendants, then on the node itself, and finally on its right descendants. In other words, the left subtree is visited first, then the node itself, and then the node's right subtree.
- **Postorder** traversal performs the operation first on the node's left descendants, then on the node's right descendants, and finally on the node itself. In other words, all of a node's children are visited before the node itself.

These traversals can also happen with nonbinary trees as long as you have a way to classify whether a child is "less than" (on the left of) or "greater than" (on the right of) its parent node.

Recursion is usually the simplest way to implement a traversal. See the problems in the chapter for some examples.

If you're asked to implement a traversal, recursion is a good way to start thinking about the problem.

Graphs

Graphs are more complicated than trees. Like trees, they consist of nodes with children. (A tree is actually a type of graph.) Unlike trees, a node can have multiple "parents," possibly creating a loop (a cycle). In addition, the links between nodes, as opposed to the nodes themselves, may have values or weights. These links are called *edges* because they may contain more information than just a pointer. In a graph, edges can be one way or two way. A graph with one-way edges is called a *directed graph*. A graph with only two-way pointers is called an *undirected graph*. A directed graph is shown in Figure 5-4, and an undirected graph is shown in Figure 5-5.

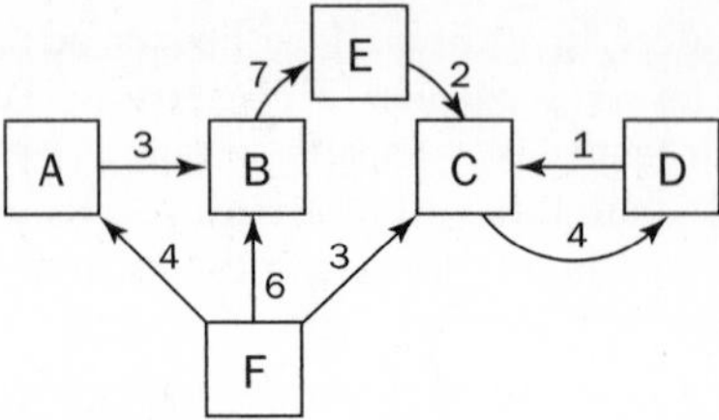

Figure 5-4

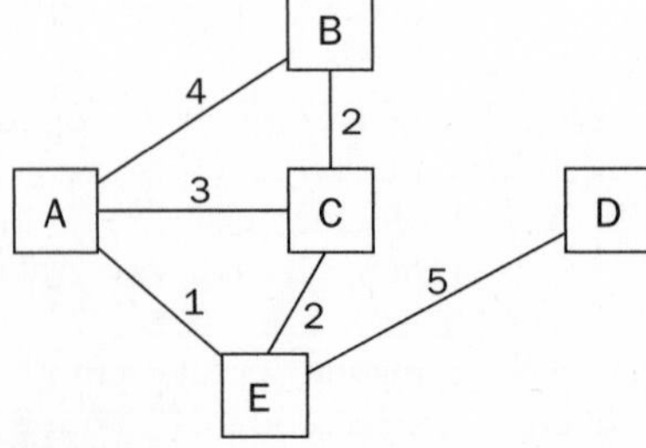

Figure 5-5

Graphs are commonly used to model real-world problems that are difficult to model with other data structures. For example, a directed graph could represent the aqueducts connecting cities (since water only flows one way). You might use such a graph to help you find the fastest way to get water from city A to city D. An undirected graph can represent something complicated, like a series of relays in signal transmission.

Unlike trees, there are many ways to represent graph data structures in code. The choice of representation is often determined by the algorithm being implemented. Graphs are often used in real-world programming, but graph problems are difficult to solve in the time allotted for an interview, so the preceding overview of graph definitions should be sufficient.

Binary Tree Problems

As previously mentioned, binary trees are the mostly commonly used forms of trees. Here are some typical problems regarding binary trees.

Preorder Traversal

Informally, a preorder traversal involves walking around the tree in a counterclockwise manner starting at the root, sticking close to the edges, and printing out the nodes as you encounter them. For the tree shown in Figure 5-6, the result is 100, 50, 25, 75, 150, 125, 110, 175. Perform a preorder traversal of a binary search tree, printing the value of each node.

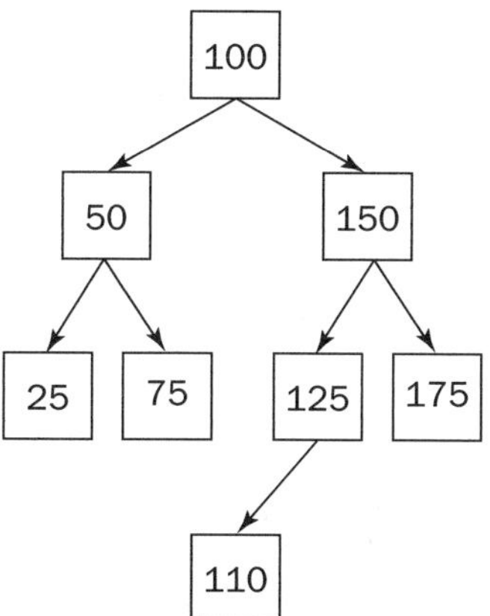

Figure 5-6

To discover an algorithm for printing out the nodes in the correct order, you should examine what happens as you print out the nodes. You go to the left as far as possible, come up the tree, go one node to the right, and then go to the left as far as possible, come up the tree again, and so on. The key is to think in terms of subtrees.

The two largest subtrees are rooted at 50 and 150. Note one very important thing about the nodes in these two subtrees: All of the nodes in the subtree rooted at 50 are printed out before any of the nodes in the subtree rooted at 150. In addition, the root node for each subtree is printed out before the rest of the subtree. Generally, for any node in a preorder traversal, you would print the node itself, followed by the left subtree, and then the right subtree. If you begin the printing process at the root node, you would have a recursive definition as follows:

1. Print out the root (or subtree's root) value.
2. Do a preorder traversal on the left subtree.
3. Do a preorder traversal on the right subtree.
4. Define a `Node` class similar to the one we created for binary search trees and add a `printValue` method to the class to print out the node's value. A preorder traversal is easily coded using recursion:

```
void preorderTraversal( Node root ){
    if( root == null ) return;
    root.printValue();
    preorderTraversal( root.getLeft() );
    preorderTraversal( root.getRight() );
}
```

What's the running time on this algorithm? Every node is examined once, so it's O(n).

Note that `inorder` and `postorder` traversals are almost identical; all you vary is the order in which the node and subtrees are visited:

```
void inorderTraversal( Node root ){
    if( root == null ) return;
    inorderTraversal( root.getLeft() );
    root.printValue();
    inorderTraversal( root.getRight() );
}

void postorderTraversal( Node root ){
    if( root == null ) return;
    postorderTraversal( root.getLeft() );
    postorderTraversal( root.getRight() );
    root.printValue();
}
```

The running time is always O(n) for these traversals.

Preorder Traversal, No Recursion

Perform a preorder traversal of a binary search tree, printing the value of each node, but this time you may *not* use recursion.

Sometimes recursive algorithms can be replaced with iterative algorithms that accomplish the same task in a fundamentally different manner using different data structures. Consider the data structures you know and think about how they could be helpful. For example, you might try using a list, an array, or another binary tree.

Unfortunately, because recursion is so intrinsic to the definition of a preorder traversal, you may have trouble finding an entirely different iterative algorithm to use in place of the recursive algorithm. In such a case, the best course of action is to understand what is happening in the recursion and try to emulate the process iteratively.

Recursion implicitly uses a stack data structure by placing data on the call stack. That means there should be an equivalent solution that avoids recursion by explicitly using a stack. Assume you have a stack class that can store nodes (writing the stack is a separate problem). Here's a skeleton class definition for the stack, ignoring all the error handling and cleanup that would normally be required:

```
public class NodeStack {
    public void push( Node n ){ .... }
    public Node pop() { .... }
}
```

If you're not sure what each of these methods does, revisit the stack implementation in Chapter 4. Although that stack was implemented using C/C++, the concepts are identical.

Reexamine your recursive solution to see exactly what is occurring. If you understand how the recursive implementation implicitly stored data on the stack, you can write an iterative implementation that explicitly stores its data on a stack in a similar fashion.

Let's start with the recursive algorithm:

```
Print out the root (or subtree's root) value.
Do a preorder traversal on the left subtree.
Do a preorder traversal on the right subtree.
```

When you first enter the procedure, you print the root node's value. Next, you recursively call the procedure to traverse the left subtree. When you make this recursive call, the calling procedure's state is saved on the stack. When the recursive call returns, the calling procedure can pick up where it left off.

In this algorithm, the calling procedure picks up where it left off by doing a traversal of the right subtree. Effectively, the recursive call serves to implicitly store the address of the right subtree on the stack so it can be traversed after the left subtree traversal is complete. Each time you print a node and move to its left child, the right child is first stored on an implicit stack. Whenever there is no child, you return from a recursive call, effectively popping a right child node off the implicit stack so you can continue traversing.

To summarize, the algorithm prints the value of the current node, pushes the right child onto an implicit stack, and moves to the left child. The algorithm pops the stack to obtain a new current node when there are no more children (when it reaches a leaf). This continues until the entire tree has been traversed and the stack is empty.

Before implementing this algorithm, first remove any unnecessary special cases that would make the algorithm more difficult to implement. Instead of coding separate cases for the left and right children, why not push pointers to both nodes onto the stack? Then all that matters is the order in which the nodes are pushed onto the stack: You need to find an order that enables you to push both nodes onto the stack so that the left node is always popped before the right node.

Because a stack is a last-in-first-out data structure, push the right node onto the stack first, followed by the left node. Instead of examining the left child explicitly, simply pop the first node from the stack, print its value, and push both of its children onto the stack in the correct order. If you start the procedure by pushing the root node onto the stack and then pop, print, and push as described, you can emulate the recursive preorder traversal. To summarize:

```
Create the stack
Push the root node on the stack
While the stack is not empty
    Pop a node
    If the node is not null
        Print its value
        Push the node's right child on the stack
        Push the node's left child on the stack
```

The code (with no error checking) for this algorithm is as follows:

```
void preorderTraversal( Node root ){
    NodeStack stack = new NodeStack();
    stack.push( root );
    while( true ){
        Node curr = stack.pop();
        if( curr == null ) break;
        curr.printValue();
        Node n = curr.getRight();
        if( n != null ) stack.push( n );
        n = curr.getLeft();
        if( n != null ) stack.push( n );
    }
}
```

What's the running time for this algorithm? Each node is examined only once and pushed on the stack only once. Therefore, this is still an O(n) algorithm. You don't have the overhead of many function calls in this implementation. On the other hand, the stack used in this implementation will probably require dynamic memory allocation, so it's unclear whether the iterative implementation would be more or less efficient than the recursive solution. The point of the problem, however, is to see how well you understand recursion.

Lowest Common Ancestor

Given the value of two nodes in a binary search tree, find the lowest (nearest) common ancestor. You may assume that both values already exist in the tree.

Using the tree shown in Figure 5-7, assume 4 and 14 are the two nodes in question. The lowest common ancestor would be 8 because it's an ancestor to both 4 and 14 and there is no node lower on the tree that is an ancestor to both 4 and 14.

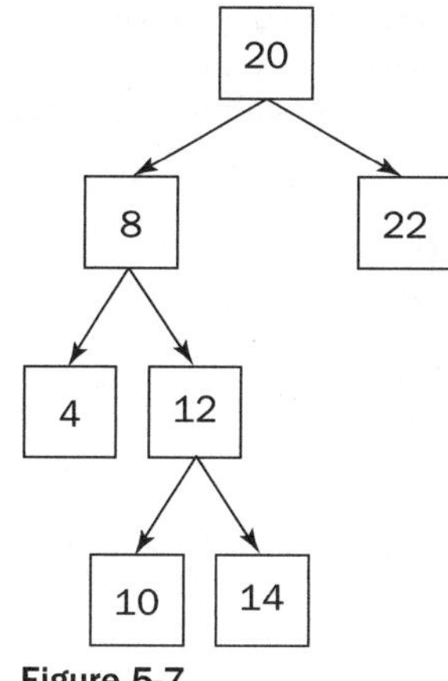

Figure 5-7

Figure 5-7 suggests an intuitive algorithm: Follow the lines up from each of the nodes until they converge. To implement this algorithm, make lists of all the ancestors of both nodes and then search through these two lists to find the first node where they differ. The node right above this divergence will be the lowest common ancestor. This is a good solution, but there is a more efficient one.

The first algorithm doesn't use any of the special properties of a binary search tree. The method works for any type of tree. Try to use some of the special properties of a binary search tree to help you find the lowest common ancestor more efficiently.

Binary search trees have two special properties. First, every node has zero, one, or two children. This fact doesn't seem to help find a new algorithm. Second, the left child's value is less than or equal to the value of the current node, and the right child's value is greater than or equal to the value of the current node. This property looks more promising.

Looking at the example tree, the lowest common ancestor to 4 and 14, the node with value 8, is different from the other ancestors to 4 and 14 in an important way. All the other ancestors are either greater than both 4 and 14 or less than both 4 and 14. Only 8 is between 4 and 14. You can use this insight to design a better algorithm.

The root node is an ancestor to all nodes because there is a path from it to all other nodes. Therefore, you can start at the root node and follow a path through the common ancestors of both nodes. When your target values are both less than the current node, you go left. When they are both greater, you go right. The first node you encounter that is between your target values is the lowest common ancestor.

Based on this description, and referring to the values of the two nodes as value1 and value2, you can derive the following algorithm:

```
Examine the current node
If value1 and value2 are both less than the current node's value
    Examine the left child
If value1 and value2 are both greater than the current node's value
    Examine the right child
Otherwise
    The current node is the lowest common ancestor
```

This solution may seem to suggest using recursion because it is a tree and the algorithm has a recursive structure to it, but recursion is not necessary here. Recursion is most useful when moving through multiple branches of a tree or examining some special pattern of nodes. Here you are only traveling down the tree. It's easy to implement this kind of traversal iteratively:

```
Node findLowestCommonAncestor( Node root, int value1,
                               int value2 ){
    while( root != null ){
        int value = root.getValue();

        if( value > value1 && value > value2 ){
            root = root.getLeft();
        } else if( value < value1 && value < value2 ){
            root = root.getRight();
        } else {
            return root;
        }
    }

    return null; // only if empty tree
}

// Overload it to handle nodes as well
Node findLowestCommonAncestor( Node root, Node child1,
                               Node child2 ){
    if( root == null || child1 == null || child2 == null ){
        return null;
    }

    return findLowestCommonAncestor( root, child1.getValue(),
                                     child2.getValue() );
}
```

What's the running time of this algorithm? You are traveling down a path to the lowest common ancestor. Recall that traveling a path to any one node takes O(log(n)). Therefore, this is an O(log(n)) algorithm. In addition, this is slightly more efficient than a similar recursive solution because you don't have the overhead of repeated function calls.

Summary

Trees and graphs are commonly used data structures for an interview, especially trees. Both data structures consist of nodes that reference other nodes in the structure. A tree is actually a special case of a graph, one that doesn't contain any cycles.

The three major kinds of trees are the binary tree, the binary search tree, and the heap. A binary tree has *left* and *right* children. A binary search tree is a binary tree that orders itself so that all the nodes to the left of a node have values less than or equal to the node's own value and all nodes to the right of a node have values greater than or equal to the node's value. A heap is a tree in which each node's children have values less than or equal to the node's value, which means the heap can be searched in linear time.

Although you should understand the differences between the tree types, most interview problems focus on binary tree operations such as tree traversal.

Arrays and Strings

Arrays and strings are closely related. In the abstract sense, a string is really just an array (possibly read-only) of characters. Most of the string-manipulation problems you'll encounter are therefore based on your understanding of array data types, particularly in languages such as C and C++ in which strings and character arrays are essentially identical. Although other languages — especially the object-oriented ones such as C# and Java — consider strings and character arrays to be separate, there's always a way to convert a string to an array and vice versa. When the two are different, however, it's very important to understand where and why they diverge. In addition, not all array problems will involve strings, so understanding how arrays work in the abstract and how they're implemented by the language you're using is absolutely crucial to answering those array-focused problems.

Arrays

An *array* is a sequence of variables of the same type arranged contiguously in a block of memory. Because arrays play an important role in every major language used in commercial development, we assume you're at least somewhat familiar with their syntax and usage. With that in mind, this discussion focuses on the theory and application of arrays.

Like a linked list, an array provides an essentially linear form of storage, but its properties are significantly different. In a linked list, lookup is always an O(n) operation, but array lookup is O(1) as long as you know the index of the element you want. The provision regarding the index is important — if you know only the value, lookup is still O(n) in the worst case. For example, suppose you have an array of characters. Locating the sixth character is O(1), but locating the character with value 'w' is O(n).

Of course, multidimensional arrays are not exactly linear, but they are implemented as linear arrays of linear arrays (of linear arrays . . . repeated as needed), so even multidimensional arrays are linear in each dimension.

The price for this improved lookup is significantly decreased efficiency in the insertion and deletion of data in the middle of the array. Because an array is essentially a block of contiguous memory, it's not possible to create or eliminate storage between any two elements as it is with a linked list. Instead, you must physically *move* data within the array to make room for an insertion or to close the gap left by a deletion.

Arrays are not dynamic data structures: They have a finite, fixed number of elements. Memory must be allocated for every element in an array, even if only part of the array is used. Arrays are best used when you know how many elements you need to store before the program executes. When the program needs a variable amount of storage, the size of the array imposes an arbitrary limit on the amount of data that can be stored. Making the array large enough so that the program always operates below the limit doesn't solve the problem: Either memory will be wasted or there won't be enough memory to handle the largest data sizes possible.

Some languages do support *dynamic* arrays, which are arrays that can change size to efficiently store as much or as little data as necessary. (Note that in this case we're referring to dynamic arrays as a language feature. Dynamic arrays can be simulated in code by other languages.) This discussion won't go into the details of implementing a dynamic array, but it is important to know that most dynamic array implementations use static arrays internally. A static array cannot be resized, so dynamic arrays are resized by allocating a new array of the appropriate size, copying every element from the old array into the new array, and freeing the old array. This is an expensive operation that must be done as infrequently as possible. (Many strings are implemented as dynamic arrays of characters.)

Each language handles arrays somewhat differently, giving each language a different set of array programming pitfalls. Let's take a look at array usage across several different languages.

C/C++

Despite the differences between C and C++, they are very similar in their treatment of arrays. In most cases, an array name is equivalent to a pointer constant to the first element of the array.[1] This means that you can't initialize the elements of one array with another array using a simple assignment.

> *Pointers and constants can be confusing concepts separately; they are often nearly incomprehensible in combination. When we say pointer constant we mean a pointer declared like* `char *const chrPtr` *that cannot be altered to point at a different place in memory, but that can be used to change the contents of the memory it points to. This is not the same as the more-commonly seen constant pointer, declared like* `const char *chrPtr`*, which can be changed to point at a different memory location but cannot be used to change the contents of a memory location. If you find this confusing, you're certainly not the only one.*

For example,

```
arrayA = arrayB;   /* Compile error: arrayA is not an lvalue */
```

is interpreted as an attempt to make `arrayA` refer to the same area of memory as `arrayB`. If `arrayA` has been declared as an array, this causes a compile error because you can't change the memory location to which `arrayA` refers. To copy `arrayB` into `arrayA`, you have to write a loop that does an element-by-element assignment or use a library function such as `memcpy` that does the copying for you (and usually much more efficiently).

[1] For an excellent discussion of when this analogy breaks down, see *Expert C Programming: Deep C Secrets* by Peter Van Der Linden (Prentice Hall, 1994).

In C and C++, the compiler tracks only the *location* of arrays, not their *size*. The programmer is responsible for tracking array sizes, and there is no bounds checking on array accesses — the language won't complain if you store something in the twentieth element of a ten-element array. As you can imagine, writing outside of the bounds of an array will probably overwrite some other data structure, leading to all manner of curious and difficult-to-find bugs. Development tools are available to help programmers identify out-of-bounds array accesses and other memory-related problems in their C/C++ programs.

Java

Unlike a C array, a Java array is an object in and of itself, separate from the data type it holds. A reference to an array is therefore not interchangeable with a reference to an element of the array. As in C, arrays cannot be copied with a simple assignment: If two array references have the same type, assignment of one to the other is allowed, but it results in both symbols referring to the same array, as shown in the following example:

```
byte[] arrayA = new byte[10];
byte[] arrayB = new byte[10];

arrayA = arrayB; // arrayA now refers to the same array as arrayB
```

Java arrays are static and the language tracks the size of each array, which can be accessed via the implicit `length` data member:

```
if( arrayA.length <= arrayB.length ){
    System.arraycopy( arrayA, 0, arrayB, 0, array.length );
}
```

Each access to an array index is checked against the current size of the array and an exception is thrown if the index is out of bounds. This makes array access a relatively expensive operation when compared to C/C++ arrays, especially with code like this:

```
void parse( char[] arr ){
    for( int i = 0; i < arr.length; ++i ){
        int val;

        if( arr[i] >= '0' && arr[i] <= '9' ){
            val = arr[i] - '0';
        } else if( arr[i] >= 'A' && arr[i] <= 'F' ){
            val = arr[i] - 'A';
        } else if( arr[i] >= 'a' && arr[i] <= 'f' ){
            val = arr[i] - 'a';
        } else {
            // error
        }

        ..... // do something
    }
}
```

Multiple references to the same array element should be simplified by storing the value of the array element into a single variable:

```
void fasterparse( char[] arr ){
    for( int i = 0; i < arr.length; ++i ){
        int  val;
        char ch = arr[i];

        if( ch >= '0' && ch <= '9' ){
            val = ch - '0';
        } else if( ch >= 'A' && ch <= 'F' ){
            val = ch - 'A';
        } else if( ch >= 'a' && ch <= 'f' ){
            val = ch - 'a';
        } else {
            // error
        }

        ..... // do something
    }
}
```

When arrays are allocated, note that the elements in the array are not initialized, even if the array is declared to hold an object type. You must construct the objects yourself and assign them to the elements of the array:

```
Button myButtons[] = new Button[5]; // Buttons not yet constructed
for (int i = 0; i < 5; i++) {
    myButtons[i] = new Button();  // Constructing Buttons
}
// All Buttons constructed
```

C#

C# arrays are similar to Java arrays, but there are some differences. The Java concept of a multidimensional array—an array of arrays such as `int[2][3]` —is called a *jagged* array in C#, and multidimensional arrays are specified using comma-separated arguments, as in `int[2,3]`. Arrays can also be declared to be read-only. All arrays also derive from the `System.array` abstract base class, which defines a number of useful methods for array manipulation.

JavaScript

Arrays in JavaScript are instances of the `Array` object. JavaScript arrays are completely dynamic and resize themselves automatically:

```
Array cities = new Array(); // zero length array
cities[0] = "New York";
cities[1] = "Los Angeles"; // now array is length 2
```

You can change the size of an array simply by modifying its `length` property:

```
cities.length = 1; // drop Los Angeles...
cities[ cities.length ] = "San Francisco"; // new cities[1] value
```

Methods on the `Array` object can be used to split, combine, and sort arrays.

Strings

Strings are sequences of characters. However, what constitutes a *character* depends greatly on the language being used and the settings of the operating system on which the application runs. Gone are the days when a string was just a set of bytes, with each byte representing a character from the ASCII character encoding. Multibyte encodings (either fixed length or variable length) are needed to accurately store text in today's global economy.

With that said, most interview problems will avoid variable-length character encodings to simplify matters. The individual characters will be referred to as *characters* or *bytes* depending mostly on the language being used: Languages such as Java and C# have a built-in Unicode character type, whereas C/C++ does not. In general, most programming examples involving strings will use the natural character type for the language in question.

If you have specific experience with internationalization and localization, don't hesitate to point this out during the interview. You can explain what would have to be done differently to handle a variable-length character encoding, for example, even as you code the solution to only work (as the interviewer requested) with a single-byte character encoding such as ASCII.

No matter how they're encoded, most languages store strings internally as arrays, even if they differ greatly in how they treat arrays and strings. As before, we'll look at each language separately.

C

A C string is nothing more than a `char` array. Just as C doesn't track the size of arrays, it doesn't track the size of strings. Instead, the end of the string is marked with a null character, represented in the language as `'\0'`. (The null character is sometimes referred to as `NULLCHAR`. Using `NULL` is incorrect because `NULL` is specifically reserved for use with pointers.) The character array must have room for the terminator: A 10-character string requires an 11-character array. This scheme makes finding the length of the string an $O(n)$ operation instead of $O(1)$ as you might expect: `strlen()` (the library function that returns the length of a string) must scan through the string until it finds the end.

For the same reason that you can't assign one C array to another, you cannot copy C strings using the = operator. Instead, you generally use the `strcpy()` function.

It is often convenient to read or alter a string by addressing individual characters of the array. If you change the length of a string in this manner, make sure you write a null character after the new last character in the string, and that the character array you are working in is large enough to accommodate the new string and terminator. It's easy to truncate a C string: Just place a null character immediately after the new end of the string.

C++

C-style strings can be used with C++, but the preferred approach is to use the `string` class from the standard libraries whenever possible. The `string` class is a specialization of the `basic_string` template class using a `char` data type. If you want to create strings that store Unicode values (as in Java or C#), you can define a new variant of `basic_string` based on the `wchar_t` (wide character) type.

The string class is very well integrated into the C++ standard libraries. You can use them with streams and iterators. In addition, C++ strings are not null-terminated, so they can store null bytes, unlike C strings. Multiple copies of the same string share the same underlying buffer whenever possible, but because a string is mutable (the string can be changed), new buffers are created as necessary. For compatibility with older code, it is possible to derive a C-style string from a C++ string, and vice versa.

Java

Java strings are objects of the `String` class, a special system class. Although strings can be readily converted to and from character and byte arrays—internally, the class holds the string using a `char` array—they are a distinct type. Java's `char` type holds 16-bit Unicode characters. The individual characters of a string cannot be accessed directly, but only through methods on the `String` class. `String` literals in program source code are automatically converted into `String` instances by the Java compiler. As in C++, the underlying array is shared between instances whenever possible. The length of a string can be retrieved via the `length()` method. Various methods are available to search and return substrings, extract individual characters, trim whitespace characters, and so on.

Java strings are immutable: They cannot be changed once the string has been constructed. Methods that appear to modify a string actually return a new string instance. The `StringBuffer` and `StringBuilder` classes (the former is in all versions of Java and is thread safe, the latter is new starting with Java 5 and is not thread safe) create mutable strings that can be converted to a `String` instance as necessary. The compiler implicitly uses `StringBuffer` instances when two `String` instances are concatenated using the + operator, which is convenient but can lead to inefficient code if you're not careful. For example, the code

```
String s = "";
for( int i = 0; i < 10; ++i ){
    s = s + i + " ";
}
```

is equivalent to

```
String s = "";
for( int i = 0; i < 10; ++i ){
    StringBuffer t = new StringBuffer();
    t.append( s );
    t.append( i );
    t.append( " " );
    s = t.toString();
}
```

which would be much more efficiently coded as:

```
StringBuffer b = new StringBuffer();
for( int i = 0; i < 10; ++i ){
    b.append( i );
    b.append( ' ' );
}
String s = b.toString();
```

Watch for this case whenever you're manipulating strings within a loop.

C#

C# strings are almost identical to Java strings. They are instances of the `String` class (the alternate form `string` is an alias), which is very similar to Java's `String` class. C# strings are also immutable, just like Java strings. Mutable strings are created with the `StringBuilder` class, and similar caveats apply when strings are being concatenated.

JavaScript

Although JavaScript defines a `String` object, many developers are unaware of its existence due to JavaScript's implicit typing. However, the usual string operations are there, as well as more advanced capabilities such as using regular expressions for string matching and replacement.

Array and String Problems

Many string problems involve operations that require converting the string to an array and back for efficient processing of the string.

Find the First Nonrepeated Character

Write an efficient function to find the first nonrepeated character in a string. For instance, the first nonrepeated character in "total" is 'o' and the first nonrepeated character in "teeter" is 'r'. Discuss the efficiency of your algorithm.

At first, this task seems almost trivial. If a character is repeated, it must appear in at least two places in the string. Therefore, you can determine whether a particular character is repeated by comparing it with all other characters in the string. It's a simple matter to perform this search for each character in the string, starting with the first. When you find a character that has no match elsewhere in the string you've found the first nonrepeated character.

What's the time order of this solution? If the string is n characters long, then in the worst case you'll make almost n comparisons for each of the n characters. That gives worst case $O(n^2)$ for this algorithm. You are unlikely to encounter the worst case for single-word strings, but for longer strings, such as a paragraph of text, it's likely that most characters would be repeated, and the most common case might be close to the worst case. The ease with which you arrived at this solution suggests that there are better alternatives—if the answer were truly this trivial, the interviewer wouldn't bother you with the problem. There must be an algorithm with a worst case better than O(n^2).

> *The algorithm described can be improved somewhat by comparing each character with only the characters following it because it has already been compared with the characters preceding it. This would give you a total of* `(n – 1) + (n – 2) + . . . + 1` *comparisons. As discussed in Chapter 3, this is still O(n^2).*

Why was the previous algorithm O(n^2)? One factor of n came from checking each character in the string to determine whether it was nonrepeated. Because the nonrepeated character could be anywhere in the string, it seems unlikely that you'll be able to improve efficiency here. The other factor of n was due to searching the entire string when trying to look up matches for each character. If you improve the efficiency of this search, you'll improve the efficiency of the overall algorithm. The easiest way to improve search efficiency on a set of data is to put it in a data structure that allows more efficient searching. What data structures can be searched more efficiently than O(n)? Binary trees can be searched in O(log(n)). Arrays and hash tables both have constant time element lookup. (Hash tables have worst-case lookup of O(n) but the average case is O(1).) Begin by trying to take advantage of an array or hash table because these data structures offer the greatest potential for improvement.

You'll want to be able to quickly determine whether a character is repeated, so you need to be able to search the data structure by character. This means you have to use the character as the index (in an array) or key (in a hash table). What values would you store in these data structures? A nonrepeated character appears only once in the string, so if you stored the number of times each character appeared, it would help you identify nonrepeating characters. You'll have to scan the entire string before you have the final counts for each character.

> *You can convert a character to an integer in order to use it as an index. If the strings are restricted to ASCII characters, this gives you 128 different possible character values. Unicode characters as used in Java or C#, however, have 65,536 possible values.*

Once you've completed this, you could scan through all the count values in the array or hash table looking for a 1. That would find a nonrepeated character, but it wouldn't necessarily be the first one in the original string.

Therefore, you need to search your count values in the order of the characters in the original string. This isn't difficult—you just look up the count value for each character until you find a 1. When you find a 1, you've located the first nonrepeated character.

Consider whether this new algorithm is actually an improvement. You will always have to go through the entire string to build the count data structure. In the worst case, you might have to look up the count value for each character in the string to find the first nonrepeated character. Because the operations on the array or hash you're using to hold the counts are constant time, the worst case would be two operations for each character in the string, giving $2n$, which is O(n) —a major improvement over the previous attempt.

Both hash tables and arrays provide constant-time lookup; you need to decide which one you will use. On the one hand, hash tables have a higher lookup overhead than arrays. On the other hand, an array would initially contain random values that you would have to take time to set to zero, whereas a hash table initially has no values. Perhaps the greatest difference is in memory requirements. An array would need an element for every possible value of a character. This would amount to a relatively reasonable 128 elements if you were processing ASCII strings, but if you had to process Unicode strings you would need more than 65,000 elements, assuming a 16-bit Unicode encoding. In contrast, a hash table would require storage for only the characters that actually exist in the input string. Therefore, arrays are a better choice for long strings with a limited set of possible character values; hash tables are more efficient for shorter strings or when there are many possible character values.

You could implement the solution either way. Assume the code may need to process Unicode strings (a safe bet these days) and choose the hash table implementation. You might choose to write the function in Java or C#, which have built-in support for both hash tables and Unicode. In outline form, the function you'll be writing looks like this:

```
First, build the character count hash table:
    For each character
        If no value is stored for the character, store 1
        Otherwise, increment the value
Second, scan the string:
    For each character
        Return character if count in hash table is 1
    If no characters have count 1, return null
```

Now implement the function. Because you don't know what class your function would be part of, implement it as a public static function (this is equivalent to a normal C function). Remember that the Java `Hashtable` stores references to `Object`, which means you can store the reference type `Integer`, but not the fundamental type `int`:

```
public static Character firstNonRepeated( String str ){
    Hashtable charHash = new Hashtable();
    int i, length;
    Character c;
    Integer intgr;

    length = str.length();

    // Scan str, building hash table
    for (i = 0; i < length; i++) {
        c = new Character(str.charAt(i));
        intgr = (Integer) charHash.get(c);
        if (intgr == null) {
            charHash.put(c, new Integer(1));
        } else {
            // Increment count corresponding to c
            charHash.put(c, new Integer(intgr.intValue() + 1));
        }
    }

    // Search hashtable in order of str
    for (i = 0; i < length; i++) {
        c = new Character(str.charAt(i));
        if (((Integer)charHash.get(c)).intValue() == 1)
            return c;
    }
    return null;
}
```

The preceding code is actually quite inefficient from a memory standpoint, however. It allocates a lot of objects unnecessarily. The emphasis is not actually on how many times a character is repeated. You just want to know whether it occurs *zero* times, *one* time, or *more than one* time. Instead of storing integers in the hash table, why not just reserve two `Object` values for use as your "one time" and "more than one time" flags (with the null object meaning "zero times," of course) and store those in the hash table. Here's the simplified version:

```
public static Character firstNonRepeated( String str ){
    Hashtable charHash = new Hashtable();
    int i, length;
    Character c;
    Object seenOnce = new Object();
    Object seenTwice = new Object();

    length = str.length();

    // Scan str, building hash table
    for( i = 0; i < length; i++ ){
        c = new Character(str.charAt(i));
        Object o = charHash.get(c);
        if( o == null ){
            charHash.put( c, seenOnce );
        } else if( o == seenOnce ){
            // Increment count corresponding to c
            charHash.put( c, seenTwice );
        }
    }

    // Search hashtable in order of str
    for( i = 0; i < length; i++ ){
        c = new Character(str.charAt(i));
        if( charHash.get(c) == seenOnce ){
            return c;
        }
    }
    return null;
}
```

A (significantly) further speedup could be achieved by implementing a faster `char` to `Character` mapping, possibly using an array to cache the mappings, or at least the most frequent mappings (such as for ASCII characters). Or use a hash table implementation that could directly store character `char` values.

Remove Specified Characters

Write an efficient function in C# that deletes characters from a string. Use the prototype

```
string removeChars( string str, string remove );
```

where any character existing in `remove` must be deleted from `str`. For example, given a `str` of "Battle of the Vowels: Hawaii vs. Grozny" and a `remove` of "aeiou", the function should transform `str` to "Bttl f th Vwls: Hw vs. Grzny". Justify any design decisions you make and discuss the efficiency of your solution.

Because this problem involves string manipulation and the string class is immutable, you'll need to either convert the string to a character array or use a `StringBuilder` for your manipulations. Using an array will save you a lot of overhead, so that's what you should use.

This problem breaks down into two separate tasks. For each character in `str`, you must determine whether it should be deleted. Then, if appropriate, you must delete the character. The second task, deletion, is discussed first.

Your initial task is to delete an element from an array. An array is a contiguous block of memory, so you can't simply remove an element from the middle as you might with a linked list. Instead, you'll have to rearrange the data in the array so it remains a contiguous sequence of characters after the deletion. For example, if you want to delete "c" from the string "abcd" you could either shift "a" and "b" forward one position (toward the end) or shift "d" back one position (toward the beginning). Either approach leaves you with the characters "abd" in contiguous elements of the array.

In addition to shifting the data, you need to decrease the size of the string by one character. If you shift characters before the deletion forward, you need to eliminate the first element; if you shift the characters after the deletion backward you need to eliminate the last element. Because you're already keeping track of the string's length (strings are not null-terminated as they are in C), shifting characters backward and decrementing the string length is the cleanest choice.

How would the proposed algorithm fare in the worst-case scenario in which you need to delete all the characters in `str`? For each deletion, you would shift all the remaining characters back one position. If `str` were n characters long, you would move the last character $n - 1$ times, the next to last $n - 2$ times, and so on, giving worst-case $O(n^2)$ for the deletion. Moving the same characters many times seems extremely inefficient. How might you avoid this?

> *If you start at the end of the string and work back toward the beginning, it's somewhat more efficient but still $O(n^2)$ in the worst case.*

What if you allocated a temporary string buffer and built your modified string there instead of in place? Then you could simply copy the characters you need to keep into the temporary string, skipping the characters you want to delete. When you finish building the modified string, you can copy it from the temporary buffer back into `str`. This way, you move each character at most twice, giving $O(n)$ deletion. However, you've incurred the memory overhead of a temporary buffer the same size as the original string, and the time overhead of copying the modified string back over the original string. Is there any way you could avoid these penalties while retaining your $O(n)$ algorithm?

To implement the $O(n)$ algorithm just described, you need to track a source position for the read location in the original string and a destination position for the write position in the temporary buffer. These positions both start at zero. The source position is incremented every time you read, and the destination position is incremented every time you write. In other words, when you copy a character you increment both positions, but when you delete a character you increment only the source position. This means the source position will always be the same as or ahead of the destination position. Once you read a character from the original string (that is, the source position has advanced past it), you no longer need that character — in fact, you're just going to copy the modified string over it. Because the destination position in the original string is always a character you don't need anymore, you can write directly into the original string, eliminating the temporary buffer entirely. This is still an $O(n)$ algorithm, but without the memory and time overhead of the earlier version.

Now that you know how to delete characters, consider the task of deciding whether to delete a particular character. The easiest way to do this is to compare the character to each character in `remove` and delete it if it matches any of them. How efficient is this? If `str` is n characters long and `remove` is m characters long, then in the worst case you make m comparisons for each of n characters, so the algorithm is $O(nm)$. You can't avoid checking each of the n characters in `str`, but perhaps you can make the lookup that determines whether a given character is in `remove` better than $O(m)$.

If you've already read the solution to the section "Find the First Nonrepeated Character," this should sound very familiar. Just as you did in that problem, you can use `remove` to build an array or hash table that has constant time lookup, thus giving an $O(n)$ solution. The trade-offs between hashes and arrays have been discussed. In this case, an array is most appropriate when `str` and `remove` are long and characters have relatively few possible values (for example, ASCII strings). A hash table may be a better choice when `str` and `remove` are short or characters have many possible values (for example, Unicode strings). This time, the assumption is that you're processing long ASCII strings and using an array instead of a hash table.

> *Why build an array? Isn't* `remove` *already an array? Yes, it is, but it is an array of characters indexed by an arbitrary (that is, meaningless for this problem) position, requiring you to search through each element. The array that is referred to here would be an array of Boolean values indexed by all the possible values for a* `char`*. This enables you to determine whether a character is in* `remove` *by checking a single element.*

Your function will have three parts:

1. Set all the elements in your lookup array to `false`.
2. Iterate through each character in `remove`, setting the corresponding value in the lookup array to `true`.
3. Iterate through `str` with a source and destination index, copying each character only if its corresponding value in the lookup array is `false`.

Now that you've combined both subtasks into a single algorithm, analyze the overall efficiency for `str` of length n and `remove` of length m. Because the size of a character is fixed for a given platform, zeroing the array is constant time. You perform a constant time assignment for each character in `remove`, so building the lookup array is $O(m)$. Finally, you do at most one constant time lookup and one constant time copy for each character in `str`, giving $O(n)$ for this stage. Summing these parts yields $O(n + m)$, so the algorithm has linear running time.

Having justified and analyzed your solution, you're ready to code it:

```
string removeChars( string str, string remove ){
    char[] s = str.toCharArray();
    char[] r = remove.toCharArray();
    bool[] flags = new bool[128]; // assumes ASCII!
    int    len = s.Length;
    int    src, dst;

    // Set flags for characters to be removed
    for( src = 0; src < len; ++src ){
        flags[r[src]] = true;
    }
```

```
        src = 0;
        dst = 0;

        // Now loop through all the characters,
        // copying only if they aren't flagged
        while( src < len ){
            if( !flags[ (int)s[src] ] ){
                s[dst++] = s[src];
            }
            ++src;
        }

        return new string( s, 0, dst );
    }
```

Reverse Words

Write a function that reverses the order of the words in a string. For example, your function should transform the string "Do or do not, there is no try." to "try. no is there not, do or Do". Assume that all words are space delimited and treat punctuation the same as letters.

Just for variety, solve this problem in C, not Java or C#, and assume that you're only dealing with ASCII characters that can be safely stored in byte arrays.

You probably already have a pretty good idea how you're going to start this problem. Because you need to operate on words, you have to be able to recognize where words start and end. You can do this with a simple token scanner that iterates through each character of the string. Based on the definition given in the problem statement, your scanner will differentiate between *nonword characters*—namely, the space character—and *word characters*, which for this problem are all characters except space. A word begins, not surprisingly, with a word character and ends at the next nonword character or the end of the string.

The most obvious approach is to use your scanner to identify words, write these words into a temporary buffer, and then copy the buffer back over the original string. To reverse the order of the words, you will have to either scan the string backward to identify the words in reverse order or write the words into the buffer in reverse order (starting at the end of the buffer). It doesn't matter which method you choose; the following discussion identifies the words in reverse order.

As always, consider the mechanics of how this works before you begin coding. First, you need to allocate a temporary buffer of the appropriate size. Next, you'll enter the scanning loop, starting with the last character of the string. When you find a nonword character, you can write it directly to the buffer. When you find a word character, however, you can't write it immediately to the temporary buffer. Because you're scanning the string in reverse, the first word character you encounter is the last character of the word, so if you were to copy the characters in the order you find them, you'd write the characters within each word backward. Instead, you need to keep scanning until you find the first character of the word and then copy each character of the word in the correct, nonreversed order. When you're copying the characters of a word, you need to identify the end of the word so that you know when to stop. You could do this by checking whether each character is a word character, but because you already know the position of the last character in the word, a better solution is to continue copying until you reach that position.

> *You may think you could avoid this complication by scanning the string forward and writing the words in reverse. However, you then have to solve a similar, related problem of calculating the start position of each word when writing to the temporary buffer.*

An example may help to clarify this. Suppose you are given the string "piglet quantum." The first word character you encounter is 'm'. If you copy the characters as you found them, you end up with the string "mutnauq telgip", which is not nearly as good a name for a techno group as the string you were supposed to produce, "quantum piglet". To get "quantum piglet" from "piglet quantum" you need to scan until you get to 'q' and then copy the letters in the word in the forward direction until you get back to 'm' at position 13. Next, copy the space character immediately because it's a nonword character. Then, just as for "quantum", you would recognize the character 't' as a word character, store position 5 as the end of the word, scan backward to 'p', and finally write the characters of "piglet" until you got to position 5.

Finally, after you scan and copy the whole string, write a null character to terminate the string in the temporary buffer and call `strcpy` to copy the buffer back over the original string. Then you can deallocate the temporary buffer and return from the function. This process is illustrated graphically in Figure 6-1.

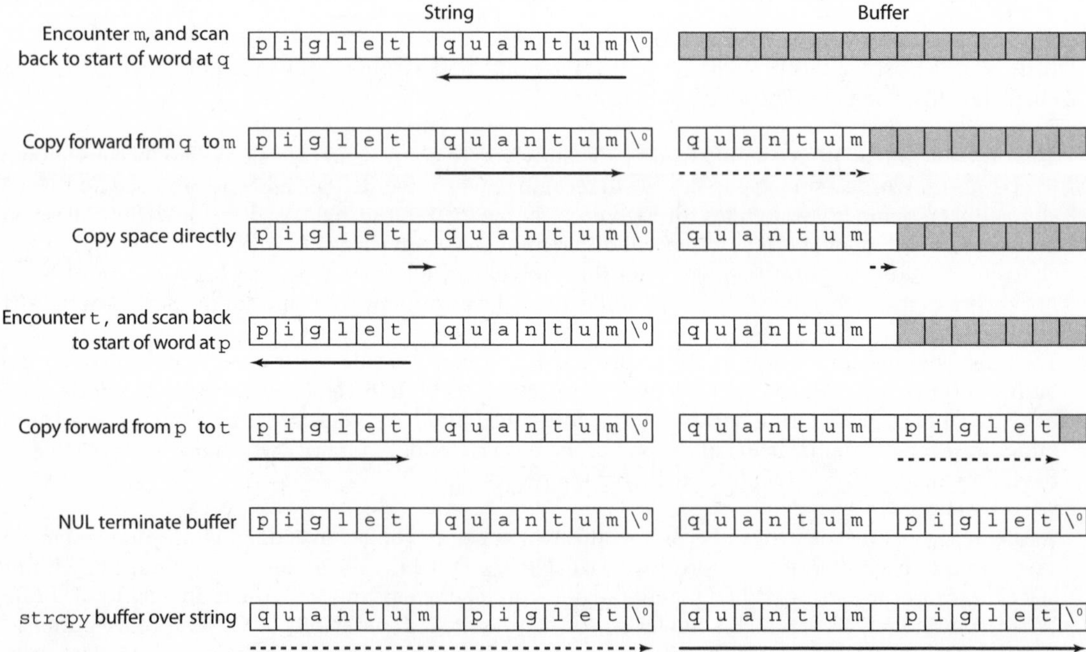

Figure 6-1

It's obviously important that your scanner stop when it gets to the first character of the string. Although this sounds simple, it can be easy to forget to check that the read position is still in the string, especially when the read position is changed at more than one place in your code. In this function, you move the read position in the main token scanning loop to get to the next token and in the word scanning loop to get to the next character of the word. Make sure neither loop runs past the beginning of the string.

Programmed in C, the algorithm described so far looks like the following:

```
bool reverseWords( char str[] ){
    char *buffer;
    int tokenReadPos, wordReadPos, wordEnd, writePos = 0;

    /* Position of the last character is length - 1 */
    tokenReadPos = strlen(str) - 1;

    buffer = (char *) malloc(tokenReadPos + 2);
    if( !buffer )
        return false; /* reverseWords failed */

    while( tokenReadPos >= 0 ){

        if( str[tokenReadPos] == ' ' ){ /* Non-word characters */

            /* Write character */
            buffer[writePos++] = str[tokenReadPos--];

        } else {  /* Word characters */

            /* Store position of end of word */
            wordEnd = tokenReadPos;

            /* Scan to next non-word character */
            while( tokenReadPos >= 0 && str[tokenReadPos] != ' ' )
                tokenReadPos--;

            /* tokenReadPos went past the start of the word */
            wordReadPos = tokenReadPos + 1;

            /* Copy the characters of the word */
            while( wordReadPos <= wordEnd ){
                buffer[writePos++] = str[wordReadPos++];
            }
        }
    }
    /* null terminate buffer and copy over str */
    buffer[writePos] = '\0';
    strcpy(str, buffer);

    free(buffer);

    return true; /* ReverseWords successful */
}
```

The preceding token scanner-based implementation is the general-case solution for this type of problem. It is reasonably efficient, and its functionality could easily be extended. It is important that you are able to implement this type of solution, but the solution is not perfect. All the scanning backward, storing positions, and copying forward is somewhat lacking in algorithmic elegance. The need for a temporary buffer is also less than desirable.

Often, interview problems have obvious general solutions and less-obvious special-case solutions. The special-case solution may be less extensible than a general solution, but more efficient or elegant. Reversing the words of a string is such a problem. You have seen the general solution, but a special-case solution also exists. In an interview, you might have been steered away from the general solution before you got to coding it. The general solution is followed through to code because token scanning and string scanning are important techniques to illustrate.

One way to improve an algorithm is to focus on a particular, concrete deficiency and try to remedy that. Because elegance, or lack thereof, is hard to quantify, you might try to eliminate the need for a temporary buffer from your algorithm. You can probably see that this is going to require a significantly different algorithm. You can't simply alter the preceding approach to write to the same string it reads from—by the time you get halfway through you will have overwritten the rest of the data you need to read.

Rather than focus on what you can't do without a buffer, you should turn your attention to what you can do. It is possible to reverse an entire string in place by exchanging characters. Try an example to see whether this might be helpful: "in search of algorithmic elegance" would become "ecnagele cimhtirogla fo hcraes ni." Look at that! The words are in exactly the order you need them, but the characters in the words are backward. All you have to do is reverse each word in the reversed string. You can do that by locating the beginning and end of each word using a scanner similar to the one used in the preceding implementation and calling a reverse function on each word substring.

Now you just have to design an in-place reverse string function. The only trick is to remember that there's no one-statement method of exchanging two values in C—you have to use a temporary variable and three assignments. Your reverse string function should take a string, a start index, and an end index as arguments. Begin by exchanging the character at the start index with the character at the end index, and then increment the start index and decrement the end index. Continue like this until the start and end index meet in the middle (in a string with odd length) or end is less than start (in a string with even length) —put more succinctly, continue while end is greater than start.

In C, these functions would look like the following:

```
void reverseWords( char str[] ){
    int start = 0, end = 0, length;

    length = strlen(str);

    /* Reverse entire string */
    reverseString(str, start, length - 1);

    while( end < length ){
        if( str[end] != ' ' ){ /* Skip non-word characters */

            /* Save position of beginning of word */
            start = end;

            /* Scan to next non-word character */
            while( end < length && str[end] != ' ' )
                end++;
```

```
                /* Back up to end of word */
                end--;

                /* Reverse word */
                reverseString( str, start, end );
            }
            end++; /* Advance to next token */
        }
    }

    void reverseString( char str[], int start, int end ){
        char temp;
        while( end > start ){
            /* Exchange characters */
            temp = str[start];
            str[start] = str[end];
            str[end] = temp;

            /* Move indices towards middle */
            start++; end--;
        }
    }
```

This solution does not need a temporary buffer and is considerably more elegant than the previous solution. It's also more efficient, mostly because it doesn't suffer from dynamic memory overhead and doesn't need to copy a result back from a temporary buffer.

Integer/String Conversions

> **Write two conversion routines. The first routine converts a string to a signed integer. You may assume that the string only contains digits and the minus character ('-'), that it is a properly formatted integer number, and that the number is within the range of an `int` type. The second routine converts a signed integer stored as an `int` back to a string.**

Every language has library routines to do these conversions. For example, in C# the `Convert.ToInt32()` and `Convert.ToString()` methods are available. Java uses the `Integer.parseInt()` and `Integer.toString()` methods. You should mention to the interviewer that under normal circumstances, you know better than to duplicate functionality provided by standard libraries. This doesn't get you off the hook—you still have to implement the functions called for by the problem.

From String to Integer

You can start with the string-to-integer routine, which is passed a valid string representation of an integer. Think about what that gives you to work with. Suppose you were given '137'. You would have a three-character string with the character encoding for '1' at position 0, '3' at position 1, and '7' at position 2. Recall from grade school that the 1 represents 100 because it is in the hundreds place, the 3 represents 30 because it is in the tens place, and the 7 is just 7 because it is in the ones place. Summing these values gives the complete number: 100 + 30 + 7 = 137.

This gives you a framework for dissecting the string representation and building it back into a single integer value. You need to determine the numeric (integer) value of the digit represented by each character, multiply that value by the appropriate place value, and then sum these products.

Consider the character-to-numeric-value conversion first. What do you know about the values of digit characters? In all common character encodings the values are sequential: '0' has a value one less than '1', which in turn is followed by '2', '3', and so on (of course, if you didn't know this, you'd have to ask the interviewer). Therefore, the value of a digit character is equal to the digit plus the value of 0 (note that 'the value of 0' is the nonzero code number representing the character '0', not the number zero). This means you subtract the value of '0' from a digit character to find the numeric value of the digit. You don't even have to know what the value of '0' is, just say `-'0'`, which the compiler will interpret as "subtract the value of '0'."

Next you need to know what place value each digit must be multiplied by. Working through the digits left to right seems problematic because you don't know what the place value of the first digit is until you know how long the number is. For example, the first character of "367" is identical to that of "31", although it represents 300 in the first case and 30 in the second case. The most obvious solution is to scan the digits from right to left because the rightmost position is always the ones place, the next to rightmost is always the tens, and so on. This enables you to start at the right end of the string with a place value of 1 and work backward through the string, multiplying the place value by 10 each time you move to a new place. This method, however, requires two multiplications per iteration, one for multiplying the digit by the place value and another for increasing the place value. That seems a little inefficient.

Perhaps the alternative of working through the characters left to right was too hastily dismissed. Is there a way you could get around the problem of not knowing the place value for a digit until you've scanned the whole string? Returning to the example of "367", when you encounter the first character, '3', you register a value of 3. If the next character were the end of the string, the number's value would be 3. However, you encounter '6' as the next character of the string. Now the '3' represents 30 and the 6 represents '6'. On the next iteration, you read the last character, '7,' so the '3' represents 300, the '6' represents 60 and the '7' represents 7. In summary, the value of the number you've scanned so far increases by a factor of 10 every time you encounter a new character. It really doesn't matter that you don't initially know whether the '3' represents 3, 30, or 30,000—every time you find a new digit you just multiply the value you've already read by 10 and add the value of the new digit. You're no longer tracking a place value, so this algorithm saves you a multiplication on each iteration. The optimization described in this algorithm is frequently useful in computing checksums and is considered clever enough to merit a name: *Horner's Rule.*

Up to this point, the discussion has only touched on positive numbers. How can you expand your strategy to include negative numbers? A negative number will have a '-' character in the first position. You'll want to skip over the '-' character so you don't interpret it as a digit. After you've scanned all the digits and built the number, you'll need to change the number's sign so that it's negative. You can change the sign by multiplying by –1. You have to check for the '-' character before you scan the digits so you know whether to skip the first character, but you can't multiply by negative 1 until after you've scanned all the digits. One way around this problem is to set a flag if you find the '-' character and then multiply by –1 only if the flag is set.

In summary, the algorithm is as follows:

```
Start number at 0
If the first character is '-'
    Set the negative flag
    Start scanning with the next character
For each character in the string
    Multiply number by 10
    Add (digit character - '0') to number
Return number
```

Coding this in C# results in the following:

```
int strToInt( string str ){
    int i = 0, num = 0;
    bool isNeg = false;
    int len = str.Length();

    if( str[0] == '-' ){
        isNeg = true;
        i = 1;
    }

    while( i < len ){
        num *= 10;
        num += ( str[i++] - '0' );
    }

    if( isNeg )
        num *= -1;

    return num;
}
```

Before you declare this function finished, check it for cases that may be problematic. At minimum, you should check –1, 0, and 1, so you've checked a positive value, a negative value, and a value that's neither positive nor negative. You should also check a multidigit value like 324 to ensure that the loop has no problems. The function appears to work properly for these cases, so you can move on to `intToStr`, its opposite.

From Integer to String

In `intToStr`, you will be performing the inverse of the conversion you did in `strToInt`. Given this, much of what you discovered in writing `strToInt` should be of use to you here. For example, just as you converted digits to integer values by subtracting '0' from each digit, you can convert integer values back to digits by adding '0' to each digit.

Before you can convert values to characters, you need to know what those values are. Consider how you might do this. Suppose you have the number 732. Looking at this number's decimal representation on paper, it seems a simple matter to identify the digit values 7, 3, and 2. However, you must remember that the computer isn't using a decimal representation, but rather the binary representation 1011011100.

Because you can't select decimal digits directly from a binary number, you'll have to calculate the value of each digit. It seems logical to try to find the digit values either left to right or right to left.

Try left to right first. Integer dividing 732 by the place value (100) gives the first digit, 7. However, now if you integer divide by the next place value (10), you get 73, not 3. It looks as if you need to subtract the hundreds value you found before moving on. Starting over with this new process gives you the following:

```
732 ÷ 100 = 7 (first digit); 732 - 7 _ 100 = 32
32 ÷ 10 = 3 (second digit); 32 - 3 _ 10 = 2
2 ÷ 1 = 2 (third digit)
```

To implement this algorithm, you're going to have to find the place value of the first digit and divide the place value by 10 for each new digit. This algorithm seems workable but complicated. What about working right to left?

Starting again with 732, what arithmetic operation can you perform to yield 2, the rightmost digit? 732 modulo 10 will give you 2. Now how can you get the next digit? 732 modulo 100 gives you 32. You could integer divide this by 10 to get the second digit, 3, but now you have to track two separate place values.

Modulo gives the remainder of an integer division. In C/C++ and C-like languages such as Java and C#, the modulo operator is %.

What if you did the integer divide before the modulo? Then you'd have 732 integer divide by 10 is 73; 73 modulo 10 is 3. Repeating this for the third digit you have 73 / 10 = 7; 7 % 10 = 7. This seems like an easier solution—you don't even have to track place values, you just divide and modulo until there's nothing left.

The major downside of this approach is that you find the digits in reverse order. Because you don't know how many there will be until you've found them all, you don't know where in the string to begin writing. You could run through the calculations twice—once to find the number of digits so you know where to start writing them and again to actually write the digits—but this seems wasteful. Perhaps a better solution is to write the digits out backward as you discover them and then reverse them into the proper order when you're done. Because the largest possible value of an integer yields a relatively short string, you could write the digits into a temporary buffer and then reverse them into the final string.

Again, negative numbers have been ignored so far. Unfortunately, the modulo of a negative number is not handled consistently across different languages. The easiest way around this problem is to avoid the problem entirely. In `strToInt`, you treated the number as if it were positive and then made an adjustment at the end if it were, in fact, negative. How might you employ this type of strategy here? You could start by multiplying the number by –1 if it were negative. Then it would be positive, so treating it as a positive number wouldn't be a problem. The only wrinkle would be that you'd need to write a '-' if the number had originally been negative, but that isn't difficult—just set a flag indicating that the number is negative when you multiply by –1.

You've solved all the important subproblems in `intToStr`—now assemble these solutions into an outline you can use to write your code.

```
If number less than zero:
     Multiply number by -1
     Set negative flag
```

```
While number not equal to 0
     Add '0' to number % 10 and write this to temp buffer
     Integer divide number by 10
If negative flag is set
     Write '-' into next position in temp buffer
Write characters in temp buffer into output string in reverse order:
```

Rendering this in Java might give the following:

```
public static final int MAX_DIGITS = 10;

String intToStr( int num ){
    int i = 0;
    boolean isNeg = false;
    /* Buffer big enough for largest int and - sign */
    char[] temp = new char[ MAX_DIGITS + 1 ];

    /* Check to see if the number is negative */
    if( num < 0 ){
        num *= -1;
        isNeg = true;
    }

    /* Fill buffer with digit characters in reverse order */
    while( num != 0 ){
        temp[i++] = (char)((num % 10) + '0');
        num /= 10;
    }

    StringBuffer b = new StringBuffer();

    if( isNeg )
        b.append( '-' );

    while( i > 0 ){
        b.append( temp[--i] );
    }

    return b.toString();
}
```

Again, check the same potentially problematic cases you tried for `strToInt` (multidigit, –1, 0, and 1). Multidigit numbers, –1, and 1 cause no problems, but if `num` is 0 you never go through the body of the `while` loop. This causes the function to write an empty string instead of "0." How can you fix this bug? You need to go through the body of the `while` loop at least once, so that you write a '0' even if `num` starts at 0. You can ensure that the body of the loop is executed at least once by changing it from a `while` loop to a `do...while loop`. This fix yields the following code, which can handle converting 0 as well as positive and negative values to strings:

```
public static final int MAX_DIGITS = 10;

String intToStr( int num ){
    int i = 0;
    boolean isNeg = false;
```

```
        /* Buffer big enough for largest int and - sign */
        char[] temp = new char[ MAX_DIGITS + 1 ];

        /* Check to see if the number is negative */
        if( num < 0 ){
            num *= -1;
            isNeg = true;
        }

        /* Fill buffer with digit characters in reverse order */
        do {
            temp[i++] = (char)((num % 10) + '0');
            num /= 10;
        } while( num != 0 );

        StringBuffer b = new StringBuffer();

        if( isNeg )
            b.append( '-' );

        while( i > 0 ){
            b.append( temp[--i] );
        }

        return b.toString();
    }
```

Summary

Programmers use strings and arrays all the time, so it's not surprising to see problems about them showing up in a programming interview. A string can even be thought of as an array of characters — and if not actually implemented that way, there's usually an easy way to convert it to an array and back.

Arrays are not treated identically in all languages. All languages support static arrays, but few offer native support for dynamic arrays. C++ and C don't do any bounds checking of array access, whereas Java and C# do.

String manipulation is so fundamental that it's normally handled via built-in library routines or system classes. Languages like C# and Java consider strings to be immutable, making changes to a string non-trivial and requiring the use of special mutable string classes. If you're not careful, string manipulation can greatly degrade the performance of your algorithms.

You should know how to convert a string to an array of characters and back for each language you're using, because your answers to many interview problems will require such conversions.

Recursion

Recursion is a deceptively simple concept: Any routine that calls itself is recursive. Despite this apparent simplicity, understanding and applying recursion can be surprisingly complex. One of the major barriers to understanding recursion is that general descriptions tend to become highly theoretical, abstract, and mathematical. Although there is certainly value in that approach, this chapter will instead follow a more pragmatic course, focusing on example, application, and comparison of recursive and iterative (nonrecursive) algorithms.

Understanding Recursion

Recursion is most useful for tasks that can be defined in terms of similar subtasks. For example, sort, search, and traversal problems often have simple recursive solutions. A recursive routine performs a task in part by calling itself to perform the subtasks. At some point, the routine encounters a subtask that it can perform without calling itself. This case, in which the routine does not recurse, is called the *base case*; the former, in which the routine calls itself to perform a subtask, is referred to as the *recursive case*.

Recursive algorithms have two types of cases: recursive cases and base cases.

These concepts can be illustrated with a simple and commonly used example: the factorial operator. *n!* (pronounced "n factorial") is essentially the product of all integers between *n* and 1. For example, 4! = 4 - 3 - 2 - 1 = 24. *n!* can be more formally defined as follows:

```
n! = n (n - 1)!
0! = 1! = 1
```

This definition leads easily to a recursive implementation of factorial. The task is determining the value of *n!*, and the subtask is determining the value of *(n – 1)!* In the recursive case, when *n* is greater than 1, the routine calls itself to determine the value of *(n – 1)!* and multiplies that by *n*. In the base case, when *n* is 0 or 1, the routine simply returns 1. Rendered in any C-like language, this looks like the following:

```
int factorial( int n ){
    if (n > 1) {  /* Recursive case */
        return factorial(n-1) * n;
    } else {        /* Base case */
        return 1;
    }
}
```

Figure 7-1 illustrates the operation of this routine when computing 4!. Notice that *n* decreases by 1 each time the routine recurses. This ensures that the base case will eventually be reached. If a routine is written incorrectly such that it does not always reach a base case, it will recurse infinitely. In practice, there is usually no such thing as infinite recursion: Eventually a stack overflow occurs and the program crashes—a similarly catastrophic event. (There is a form of recursion, called *tail recursion,* that can be optimized by the compiler to use the same stack frame for each recursive call. An appropriately optimized tail recursive algorithm could recurse infinitely because it wouldn't overflow the stack.)

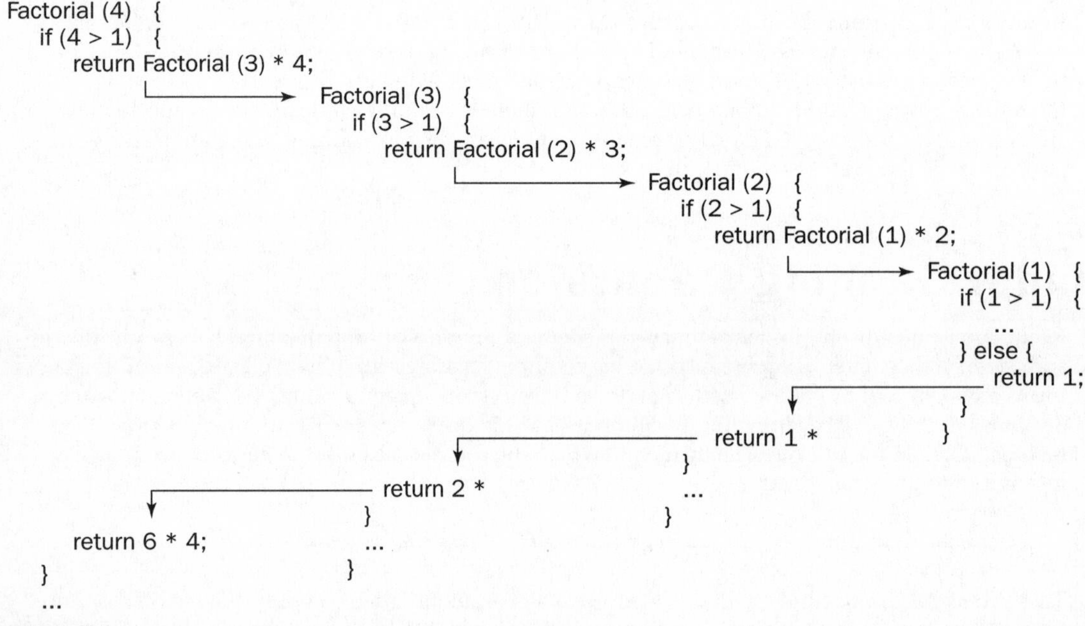

Figure 7-1

Every recursive case must eventually lead to a base case.

This implementation of factorial represents an extremely simple example of a recursive routine. In many cases, your recursive routines may need additional data structures or an argument that tracks the recursion level. Often the best solution in such cases is to move the data structure or argument initialization code into a separate routine. This wrapper routine, which performs initialization and then calls the purely recursive routine, provides a clean, simple interface to the rest of the program.

For example, if you need a factorial routine that returns all of its intermediate results (factorials less than *n*), as well as the final result (*n!*), you most naturally return these results as an integer array, which means the routine needs to allocate an array. You also need to know where in the array each result should be written. These tasks are most easily accomplished using a wrapper routine, as follows:

```
int[] allFactorials( int n ){ /* Wrapper routine */
    int[] results = new int[ n == 0 ? 1 : n ];
    doAllFactorials( n, results, 0 );
    return results;
}

int doAllFactorials( int n, int[] results, int level ){
    if( n > 1 ){  /* Recursive case */
        results[level] = n * doAllFactorials( n - 1, results, level + 1 );
        return results[level];
    } else {        /* Base case */
        results[level] = 1;
        return 1;
    }
}
```

You can see that using a wrapper routine enables you to hide the array allocation and recursion level tracking to keep the recursive routine very clean. In this case, it's possible to determine the appropriate array index from `n`, avoiding the need for the `level` argument, but in many cases there is no alternative to tracking the recursion level as shown here.

It may be useful to write a separate wrapper routine to do initialization for a complex recursive routine.

Although recursion is a very powerful technique, it is not always the best approach, and rarely is it the most efficient approach. This is due to the relatively large overhead for routine calls on most platforms. For a simple recursive routine like factorial, many computer architectures spend more time on call overhead than the actual calculation. Iterative routines, which use looping constructs instead of recursive routine calls, do not suffer from this overhead and are frequently more efficient.

Iterative solutions are usually more efficient than recursive solutions.

Any problem that can be solved recursively can also be solved iteratively. Iterative algorithms are often quite easy to write, even for tasks that might appear to be fundamentally recursive. For example, an iterative implementation of factorial is relatively simple. It may be helpful to expand the definition of factorial, such that you describe *n!* as the product of every integer between *n* and 1, inclusive. You can use a `for` loop to iterate through these values and calculate the product:

```
int factorial( int i ){
    int n, val = 1;
    for( n = i; n > 1; n-- )  /* n = 0 or 1 falls through */
        val *= n;
    return val;
}
```

This implementation is significantly more efficient than our previous recursive implementation because no routine calls are involved. Although it represents a different way of thinking about the problem, it's not really any more difficult to write than the recursive implementation.

For some problems, there are no obvious iterative alternatives like the one just shown. It's always possible, though, to implement a recursive algorithm without using recursive calls. Recursive calls are generally used to preserve the current values of local variables and restore them when the subtask performed by the recursive call is completed. Because local variables are allocated on the program's stack, each recursive instance of the routine has a separate set of the local variables, so recursive calls implicitly store variable values on the program's stack. You can therefore eliminate the need for recursive calls by allocating your own stack and manually storing and retrieving local variable values from this stack.

Implementing this type of stack-based interactive routine tends to be significantly more complicated than implementing an equivalent routine using recursive calls. In languages like Java or C#, a stack-based iterative implementation of a recursive algorithm won't be more efficient than the recursive version. Given the large increase in complexity, you should implement recursive algorithms with recursive calls unless instructed otherwise. An example of a recursive algorithm implemented without recursive calls is given in the solution to the "Preorder Traversal, No Recursion" problem in Chapter 5.

> *A recursive algorithm can be implemented without recursive calls by using a stack, but it's usually more trouble than it's worth.*

In an interview, a working solution is of primary importance; an efficient solution is secondary. Unless you've been told otherwise, go with whatever type of working solution comes to you first. If it's a recursive solution, you might want to mention the inefficiencies inherent in recursive solutions to your interviewer, so it's clear that you know about them. In the rare instance that you see a recursive solution and an iterative solution of roughly equal complexity, you should probably mention them both to the interviewer, indicating that you're going to work out the iterative solution because it's likely to be more efficient.

Recursion Problems

Recursive algorithms offer elegant solutions to problems that would be quite awkward to code nonrecursively. Interviewers like these kinds of problems because the answers are often short without being too simple.

Binary Search

Implement a function to perform a binary search on a sorted array of integers to find the index of a given integer. Use this method declaration:

```
int binarySearch( int[] array, int lower, int upper, int target );
```

Comment on the efficiency of this search and compare it with other search methods.

In a binary search, you compare the central element in your sorted search space (an array, in this case) with the item you're looking for. There are three possibilities. If it's less than what you're searching for, you eliminate the first half of the search space. If it's more than the search value, you eliminate the second half of the search space. In the third case, the central element is equal to the search item and you stop the search. Otherwise, you repeat the process on the remaining portion of the search space. If it's not already familiar to you from computer science courses, this algorithm may remind you of the optimum strategy in the children's number-guessing game in which one child guesses numbers in a given range and a second responds "higher" or "lower" to each incorrect guess.

Because a binary search can be described in terms of binary searches on successively smaller portions of the search space, it lends itself to a recursive implementation. Your method will need to be passed the array it is searching, the limits within which it should search, and the element for which it is searching. You can subtract the lower limit from the upper limit to find the size of the search space, divide this size by two, and add it to the lower limit to find the index of the central element. Next compare this element to the search element. If they're equal, return the index. Otherwise, if the search element is smaller, then the new upper limit becomes the central index – 1; if the search element is larger, the new lower limit is the central index + 1. Recurse until you match the element you're searching for.

Before you code, consider what error conditions you'll need to handle. One way to think about this is to consider what assumptions you're making about the data you are being given and then consider how these assumptions might be violated. One assumption, explicitly stated in the problem, is that only a sorted array can be searched, so you'll want to detect unsorted lists. You can do this by checking whether the value at the upper limit is less than the value at the lower limit, although this won't catch all unsorted lists. If the limits are wrong, you should return an error code. (Another way to handle this case would be to call a sort routine and then restart the search, but that's more than you need to do in an interview.)

Another assumption implicit in a search may be a little less obvious: The element you're searching for is assumed to exist in the array. If you don't terminate the recursion until you find the element, you'll recurse infinitely when the element is missing from the array. You can avoid this by returning an error code if the upper and lower limits are equal and the element at that location is not the element you're searching for. Finally, you assume that the lower limit is less than or equal to the upper limit. For simplicity, you can just return an error code in this case, although in a real program you'd probably want to either define this as an illegal call and use an assert to check it (for more efficient programs) or silently reverse the limits when they are out of order (for easier programming).

Now you can translate these algorithms and error checks into C# code:

```
const int NOT_IN_ARRAY = -1;
const int ARRAY_UNORDERED = -2;
const int LIMITS_REVERSED = -3;

int binarySearch( int[] array, int lower, int upper, int target ){
    int center, range;

    range = upper - lower;
    if (range < 0) {
        return LIMITS_REVERSED;
    } else if( range == 0 && array[lower] != target ){
        return NOT_IN_ARRAY;
```

```
        }

        if( array[lower] > array[upper] )
            return ARRAY_UNORDERED;

        center = ((range)/2) + lower;

        if( target == array[center] ){
            return center;
        } else if( target < array[center] ){
            return binarySearch( array, lower, center - 1, target );
        } else {
            return binarySearch( array, center + 1, upper, target );
        }
    }
```

Note that the example returns an error code instead of throwing an exception. You could use this as a chance to discuss the pros and cons of exception throwing with the interviewer.

Although the preceding routine completes the given task, it is not as efficient as it could be. As discussed at the beginning of this chapter, recursive implementations are generally less efficient than equivalent iterative implementations.

If you analyze the recursion in the previous solution, you can see that each recursive call serves only to change the search limits. There's no reason why you can't change the limits on each iteration of a loop and avoid the overhead of recursion. The method that follows is a more-efficient, iterative analog of the recursive binary search:

```
    int iterBinarySearch( int[] array, int lower, int upper, int target ){
        int center, range;

        if( lower > upper )
            return LIMITS_REVERSED;

        while( true ){
            range = upper - lower;
            if( range == 0 && array[lower] != target )
                return NOT_IN_ARRAY;

            if( array[lower] > array[upper] )
                return ARRAY_UNORDERED;

            center = ((range)/2) + lower;

            if( target == array[center] ){
                return center;
            } else if( target < array[center] ){
                upper = center - 1;
            } else {
                lower = center + 1;
            }
        }
    }
```

A binary search is O(log(n)) because half of the search is eliminated (in a sense, searched) on each iteration. This is more efficient than a simple search through all the elements, which would be O(n). However, in order to perform a binary search the array must be sorted, an operation that is usually O(n log(n)), unless of course the array is always kept in sorted order.

Permutations of a String

Implement a routine that prints all possible orderings of the characters in a string. In other words, print all permutations that use all the characters from the original string. For example, given the string "hat", your function should print the strings "tha", "aht", "tah", "ath", "hta", and "hat". Treat each character in the input string as a distinct character, even if it is repeated. Given the string "aaa", your routine should print "aaa" six times. You may print the permutations in any order you choose.

Manually permuting a string is a relatively intuitive process, but describing an algorithm for the process can be difficult. In a sense, the problem here is like being asked to describe how you tie your shoes: You know the answer, but you probably still have to go through the process a few times to figure out what steps you're taking.

Try applying that method to this problem: Manually permute a short string and try to reverse-engineer an algorithm out of the process. Take the string "abcd" as an example. Because you're trying to construct an algorithm from an intuitive process, you want to go through the permutations in a systematic order. Exactly which systematic order you use isn't terribly important — different orders are likely to lead to different algorithms, but as long as you're systematic about the process you should be able to construct an algorithm. You want to choose a simple order that will make it easy to identify any permutations that you might accidentally skip.

You might consider listing all the permutations in alphabetical order. This means the first group of permutations will all start with "a". Within this group, you first have the permutations with a second letter of "b", then "c", and finally "d". Continue in a like fashion for the other first letters.

abcd	bacd	cabd	dabc
abdc	badc	cadb	dacb
acbd	bcad	cbad	dbac
acdb	bcda	cbda	dbca
adbc	bdac	cdab	dcab
adcb	bdca	cdba	dcba

Before you continue, make sure you didn't miss any permutations. Four possible letters can be placed in the first position. For each of these four possibilities, there are three remaining possible letters for the second position. Thus, there are 4×3 = 12 different possibilities for the first two letters of the permutations. Once you've selected the first two letters, two different letters remain available for the third position, and the last remaining letter is put in the fourth position. If you multiply 4×3×2×1 you have a total of 24 different permutations; there are 24 permutations in the previous list, so nothing has been missed.

This calculation can be expressed more succinctly as 4!—you may recall that *n!* is the number of possible arrangements of *n* objects.

Now examine the list of permutations for patterns. The rightmost letters vary faster than the leftmost letters. For each letter that you choose for the first (leftmost) position, you write out all the permutations beginning with that letter before you change the first letter. Likewise, once you've picked a letter for the second position, you write out all permutations beginning with this two-letter sequence before changing the letters in either the first or second position. In other words, you can define the permutation process as picking a letter for a given position and performing the permutation process starting at the next position to the right before coming back to change the letter you just picked. This sounds like the basis for a recursive definition of permutation. Try to rephrase it in explicitly recursive terms: To find all permutations starting at position *n*, successively place all allowable letters in position *n*, and for each new letter in position *n* find all permutations starting at position $n + 1$ (the recursive case). When *n* is greater than the number of characters in the input string, a permutation has been completed; print it and return to changing letters at positions less than *n* (the base case).

You almost have an algorithm; you just need to define "all allowable letters" a little more rigorously. Because each letter from the input string can appear only once in each permutation, "all allowable letters" can't be defined as every letter in the input string. Think about how you did the permutations manually. For the group of permutations beginning with "b", you never put a "b" anywhere but the first position because when you selected letters for later positions, "b" had already been used. For the group beginning "bc" you used only "a" and "d" in the third and fourth positions because both "b" and "c" had already been used. Therefore, "all allowable letters" means all letters in the input string that haven't already been chosen for a position to the left of the current position (a position less than *n*). Algorithmically, you could check each candidate letter for position *n* against all the letters in positions less than *n* to determine whether it had been used. You can eliminate these inefficient scans by maintaining an array of Boolean values corresponding to the positions of the letters in the input string and using this array to mark letters as used or unused, as appropriate.

In outline form, this algorithm looks like the following:

```
If you're past the last position
    Print the string
    Return
Otherwise
    For each letter in the input string
    If it's marked as used, skip to the next letter
    Else place the letter in the current position
        Mark the letter as used
        Permute remaining letters starting at current position + 1
        Mark the letter as unused
```

Separating the base case from the recursive case as performed here is considered good style and may make the code easier to understand, but it does not provide optimum performance. You can significantly optimize the code by invoking the base case directly without a recursive call if the next recursive call invokes the base case. In this algorithm, that involves checking whether the letter just placed was the last letter—if so, you print the permutation and make no recursive call; otherwise, a recursive call is made. This eliminates n! function calls, reducing the function call overhead by approximately a factor of n (where n is the length of the input string). Short-circuiting the base case in this manner is called arms-length recursion *and is considered poor style, especially in academic circles. Whichever way you choose to code the solution, it is worthwhile to mention the advantages of the alternate approach to your interviewer.*

Here's a Java version of this algorithm:

```
void permute( String str ){
    int          length = str.length();
    boolean[]    used = new boolean[ length ];
    StringBuffer out = new StringBuffer();
    char[]       in = str.toCharArray();

    doPermute( in, out, used, length, 0 );
}

void doPermute( char[] in, StringBuffer out,
                boolean[] used, int length, int level ){
    if( level == length ){
        System.out.println( out.toString() );
        return;
    }

    for( int i = 0; i < length; ++i ){
        if( used[i] ) continue;

        out.append( in[i] );
        used[i] = true;
        doPermute( in, out, used, length, level + 1 );
        used[i] = false;
        out.setLength( out.length() - 1 );
    }
}
```

Structurally, this function uses a wrapper method called `permute` to allocate two arrays, one for the flags and one to hold the input characters, and a `StringBuffer` for building the output string. Then it calls the recursive portion, `doPermute`, to actually do the permutation. The characters are appended to the `StringBuffer` as appropriate. When the recursive call returns, the last character is dropped simply by reducing the buffer's length.

Combinations of a String

Implement a function that prints all possible combinations of the characters in a string. These combinations range in length from one to the length of the string. Two combinations that differ only in ordering of their characters are the same combination. In other words, "12" and "31" are different combinations from the input string "123", but "21" is the same as "12".

This is a companion problem to finding the permutations of the characters in a string. If you haven't yet worked through that problem, you may want to do so before you tackle this one.

Following the model of the solution to the permutation problem, try working out an example by hand and see where that gets you. Because you are trying to divine an algorithm from the example, you again need to be systematic in your approach. You might try listing combinations in order of length. The input string "wxyz" is used in the example. Because the ordering of letters within each combination is arbitrary, they are kept in the same order as they are in the input string to minimize confusion.

w	wx	wxy	wxyz
x	wy	wxz	
y	wz	wyz	
z	xy	xyz	
	xz		
	yz		

Some interesting patterns seem to be emerging, but there's nothing clear yet, certainly nothing that seems to suggest an algorithm. Listing output in terms of the order of the input string (alphabetical order, for this input string) turned out to be helpful in the permutation problem. Try rearranging the combinations you generated and see if that's useful here.

w	x	y	z
wx	xy	yz	
wxy	xyz		
wxyz	xz		
wxz			
wy			
wyz			
wz			

This looks a little more productive. There is a column for each letter in the input string. The first combination in each column is a single letter from the input string. The remainder of each column's combinations consist of that letter prepended to each of the combinations in the columns to the right. Take, for example, the "x" column. This column has the single letter combination "x". The columns to the right of it have the combinations "y", "yz", and "z", so if you prepend "x" to each of these combinations you find the remaining combinations in the "x" column: "xy", "xyz", and "xz". You could use this rule to generate all of the combinations, starting with just "z" in the rightmost column and working your way to the left, each time writing a single letter from the input string at the top of the column and then completing the column with that letter prepended to each of the combinations in columns to the right. This is a recursive method for generating the combinations. It is space inefficient because it requires storage of all previously generated combinations, but it indicates that this problem can be solved recursively. See if you can gain some insight on a more-efficient recursive algorithm by examining the combinations you've written a little more closely.

Look at which letters appear in which positions. All four letters appear in the first position, but "w" never appears in the second position. Only "y" and "z" appear in the third position, and "z" is in the fourth position in the only combination that has a fourth position ("wxyz"). Therefore, a potential algorithm might involve iterating through all allowable letters at each position: w–z in the first position, x–z in the second position, and so on. Check this idea against the example to see if it works: It seems to successfully generate all the combinations in the first column. However, when you select "x" for the first position, this candidate algorithm would start with "x" in the second position, generating an illegal combination of "xx". Apparently the algorithm needs some refinement.

To generate the correct combination "xy", you really need to begin with "y", not "x", in the second position. When you select "y" for the first position (third column), you need to start with "z" because "yy" is illegal and "yx" and "yw" have already been generated as "xy" and "wy". This suggests that in each output position you need to begin iterating with the letter in the input string following the letter selected for the preceding position in the output string. Call this letter your input start letter.

It may be helpful to summarize this a little more formally. You need to track the output position as well as the input start position. Begin with the first position as the output position, and the first character of the input as the input start position. For a given position, sequentially select all letters from the input start position to the last letter in the input string. For each letter you select, print the combination and then generate all other combinations beginning with this sequence by recursively calling the generating function with the input start position set to the next letter after the one you've just selected and the output position set to the next position. You should check this idea against the example to make sure it works. It does — no more problems in the second column. Before you code, it may be helpful to outline the algorithm just to make sure you have it.

For comparison, the performance side of the arms-length recursion style/performance trade-off discussed in the permutation problem was chosen. The performance and style differences between the two possible approaches are not as dramatic for the combination algorithm as they were for the permutation algorithm.

```
For each letter from input start position to end of input string
    Select the letter into the current position in output string
    Print letters in output string
    If the current letter isn't the last in the input string
Generate remaining combinations starting at next position with iteration starting
at next letter beyond the letter just selected
```

After all that hard work, the algorithm looks pretty simple! You're ready to code it. Here's a C# version:

```
void combine( string str ){
    int           length = str.Length;
    char[]        instr = str.ToCharArray();
    StringBuilder outstr = new StringBuilder();

    doCombine( instr, outstr, length, 0, 0 );
}

void doCombine( char[] instr, StringBuilder outstr, int length,
                int level, int start ){
    for( int i = start; i < length; i++ ){
        outstr.Append( instr[i] );
        Console.WriteLine( outstr );

        if( i < length - 1 ){
            doCombine( instr, outstr, length, level + 1, i + 1 );
        }

        outstr.Length = outstr.Length - 1;
    }
}
```

This solution is sufficient in most interviews. Nevertheless, you can make a rather minor optimization to `doCombine` that eliminates the `if` statement. Given that this is a recursive function, the performance increase is probably negligible compared to the function call overhead, but you might want to see if you can figure it out just for practice.

You can eliminate the `if` statement by removing the final iteration from the loop and moving the code it would have executed during that final iteration outside the loop. The general case of this optimization is referred to as *loop partitioning*, and `if` statements that can be removed by loop partitioning are called *loop index dependent conditionals*. Again, this optimization doesn't make much difference here, but it can be important inside nested loops.

Telephone Words

People often give others their telephone number as a word representing the seven-digit number. For example, if my telephone number were 866-2665, I could tell people my number is "TOOCOOL," instead of the hard-to-remember seven-digit number. Note that many other possibilities (most of which are nonsensical) can represent 866-2665. You can see how letters correspond to numbers on a telephone keypad in Figure 7-2.

Figure 7-2

Write a routine that takes a seven-digit telephone number and prints out all of the possible "words" or combinations of letters that can represent the given number. Because the 0 and 1 keys have no letters on them, you should change only the digits 2–9 to letters. You'll be passed an array of seven integers, with each element being one digit in the number. You may assume that only valid phone numbers will be passed to your routine. You can use the helper routine

```
char getCharKey( int telephoneKey, int place )
```

which takes a telephone key (0–9) and a place of either 1, 2, 3 and returns the character corresponding to the letter in that position on the specified key. For example, `GetCharKey(3, 2)` **will return 'E' because the telephone key 3 has the letters "DEF" on it and 'E' is the second letter.**

It's worthwhile to define some terms for this problem. A telephone number consists of digits. Three letters correspond to each digit (except for 0 and 1, but when 0 and 1 are used in the context of creating a word, you can call them letters). The lowest letter, middle letter, and highest letter will be called the digit's low value, middle value, and high value, respectively. You will be creating words, or strings of letters, to represent the given number.

First, impress the interviewer with your math skills by determining how many words can correspond to a seven-digit number. This requires combinatorial mathematics, but if you don't remember this type of math, don't panic. First, try a one-digit phone number. Clearly, this would have three words. Now, try a two-digit phone number — say, 56. There are three possibilities for the first letter, and for each of these there are three possibilities for the second letter. This yields a total of nine words that can correspond to this number. It appears that each additional digit increases the number of words by a factor of 3. Thus, for 7 digits, you have 3^7 words, and for a phone number of length n, you have 3^n words. Because 0 and 1 have no corresponding letters, a phone number with 0s or 1s in it would have fewer words, but 3^7 is the upper bound on the number of words for a seven-digit number.

Now you need to figure out an algorithm for printing these words. Try writing out some words representing one of the author's old college phone numbers, 497-1927, as an example. The most natural manner in which to list the words is alphabetical order. This way, you always know which word comes next and you are less likely to miss words. You know that there is on the order of 3^7 words that can represent this number, so you won't have time to write them all out. Try writing just the beginning and the end of the alphabetical sequence. You will probably want to start with the word that uses the low letter for each digit of the phone number. This guarantees that your first word is the first word in alphabetical order. Thus, the first word for 497-1927 becomes 'G' for 4 because 4 has "GHI" on it, 'W' for 9, which has "WXY" on it, 'P' for 7, which has "PRS" on it, and so on, resulting in "GWP1WAP".

As you continue to write down words, you ultimately create a list that looks like the following:

```
GWP1WAP
GWP1WAR
GWP1WAS
GWP1WBP
GWP1WBR
...
IYS1YCR
IYS1YCS
```

It was easy to create this list because the algorithm for generating the words is relatively intuitive. Formalizing this algorithm is more challenging. A good place to start is by examining the process of going from one word to the next word in alphabetical order.

Because you know the first word in alphabetical order, determining how to get to the next word at any point gives you an algorithm for writing all the words. One important part of the process of going from one word to the next seems to be that the last letter always changes. It continually cycles through a pattern of P-R-S. Whenever the last letter goes from S back to P, it causes the next-to-last letter to change.

Try investigating this a little more to see if you can come up with specific rules. Again, it's probably best to try an example. You may have to write down more words than in the example list to see a pattern (a three-digit phone number should be sufficient, or the previous list will work if it's expanded a bit). It looks as if the following is always true: Whenever a letter changes, its right neighbor goes through all of its values before the original letter changes again. Conversely, whenever a letter resets to its low value, its left neighbor increases to the next value.

From these observations, there are probably two reasonable paths to follow as you search for the solution to this problem. You can start with the first letter and have a letter affect its right neighbor, or you can start with the last letter and have a letter affect its left neighbor. Both of these approaches seem reasonable, but you'll have to choose one. For now, try the former and see where that gets you.

You should examine exactly what you're trying to do at this point. You're working with the observation that whenever a letter changes, it causes its right neighbor to cycle through all of its values before it changes again. You're now using this observation to determine how to get from one word to the next word in alphabetical order. It may help to formalize this observation: Changing the letter in position i causes the letter in position $i + 1$ to cycle through its values. When you can write an algorithm in terms of how elements i and $i + 1$ interact with each other, it often indicates recursion, so try to figure out a recursive algorithm.

You have already discovered most of the algorithm. You know how each letter affects the next; you just need to figure out how to start the process and determine the base case. Looking again at the list to try to figure out the start condition, you'll see that the first letter cycles only once. Therefore, if you start by cycling the first letter, this causes multiple cycles of the second letter, which causes multiple cycles of the third letter—exactly as desired. After you change the last letter, you can't cycle anything else, so this is a good base case to end the recursion. When the base case occurs, you should also print out the word because you've just generated the next word in alphabetical order. The one special case you have to be aware of occurs when there is a 0 or 1 in the given telephone number. You don't want to print out any word three times, so you should check for this case and cycle immediately if you encounter it.

In list form, the steps look like this:

```
If the current digit is past the last digit
    Print the word because you're at the end
Else
    For each of the three digits that can represent the current digit, going from
low to high
        Have the letter represent the current digit
        Move to next digit and recurse
        If the current digit is a 0 or a 1, return
```

The code is as follows:

```
static final int PHONE_NUMBER_LENGTH = 7;

void printTelephoneWords( int[] phoneNum ){
    char[] result = new char[ PHONE_NUMBER_LENGTH ];

    doPrintTelephoneWords( phoneNum, 0, result );
```

```
}

void doPrintTelephoneWords( int[] phoneNum, int curDigit,
                            char[] result ){
    if( curDigit == PHONE_NUMBER_LENGTH ){
        System.out.println( new String( result ) );
        return;
    }

    for( int i = 1; i <= 3; i++ ){
        result[ curDigit ] = getCharKey( phoneNum[curDigit], i );
        doPrintTelephoneWords( phoneNum, curDigit + 1, result );
        if( phoneNum[curDigit] == 0 ||
            phoneNum[curDigit] == 1) return;
    }
}
```

What is the running time of this algorithm? It can be no less than O(3^n) because there are 3^n solutions, so any correct solution must be at least O(3^n). Getting each new word requires only constant time operations so the running time is indeed O(3^n).

Reimplement `PrintTelephoneWords` without using recursion.

The recursive algorithm doesn't seem to be very helpful in this situation. Recursion was inherent in the way that you wrote out the steps of the algorithm. You could always try emulating recursion using a stack-based data structure, but there may be a better way involving a different algorithm. In the recursive solution, you solved the problem from left to right. You also made an observation that suggested the existence of another algorithm going from right to left: Whenever a letter changes from its high value to its low value, its left neighbor is incremented. Explore this observation and see if you can find a nonrecursive solution to the problem.

Again, you're trying to figure out how to determine the next word in alphabetical order. Because you're working from right to left, you should look for something that always happens on the right side of a word as it changes to the next word in alphabetical order. Looking back at the original observations, you noticed that the last letter always changes. This seems to indicate that a good way to start is to increment the last letter. If the last letter is at its high value and you increment it, you reset the last letter to its low value and increment the second-to-last letter. Suppose, however, that the second-to-last number is already at its high value. Try looking at the list to figure out what you need to do. From the list, it appears that you reset the second-to-last number to its low value and increment the third-to-last number. You continue carrying your increment like this until you don't have to reset a letter to its low value.

This sounds like the algorithm you want, but you still have to work out how to start it and how to know when you're finished. You can start by manually creating the first string as you did when writing out the list. Now you need to determine how to end. Look at the last string and figure out what happens if you try to increment it. Every letter resets to its low value. You could check whether every letter is at its low value, but this seems inefficient. The first letter resets only once, when you've printed out all of the words. You can use this to signal that you're done printing out all of the words. Again, you have to consider the cases where there is a 0 or a 1. Because 0 and 1 effectively can't be incremented (they always stay as 0 and 1), you should always treat a 0 or a 1 as if it were at its highest letter value and increment its left neighbor. In outline form, the steps are as follows:

```
Create the first word character by character
Loop infinitely:
     Print out the word
     Increment the last letter and carry the change
     If the first letter has reset, you're done
```

Here is the solution based on this sort of algorithm:

Note that you can cut down on the calls to `getCharKey` *by storing each letter's three values in variables, rather than making repeated calls to see whether a value is low, middle, or high. This makes the code a little more difficult, and this sort of optimization is probably unnecessary in the context of this solution.*

```
static final int PHONE_NUMBER_LENGTH = 7;

void printTelephoneWords( int phoneNum[] ){
    char[] result = new char[ PHONE_NUMBER_LENGTH ];
    int i;

    /* Initialize the result (in our example,
     * put GWP1WAR in result).
     */
    for( i = 0; i < PHONE_NUMBER_LENGTH; i++ )
        result[i] = getCharKey( phoneNum[i], 1 );

    /* Main loop begins */
    while( true ){
        for( i = 0; i < PHONE_NUMBER_LENGTH; ++i ){
            System.out.print( result[i] );
        }
        System.out.print( '\n' );

        /* Start at the end and try to increment from right
         * to left.
         */
        for( i = PHONE_NUMBER_LENGTH - 1; i >= -1; i-- ){
            /* You're done because you
             * tried to carry the leftmost digit.
             */
            if( i == -1 ) return;

            /* Otherwise, we're not done and must continue. */

            /* You want to start with this condition so that you can
             * deal with the special cases, 0 and 1 right away.
             */
            if( getCharKey( phoneNum[i], 3 ) == result[i] ||
                phoneNum[i] == 0 || phoneNum[i] == 1 ){
                result[i] = getCharKey( phoneNum[i], 1 );
                /* No break, so loop continues to next digit */
```

```
                } else if ( getCharKey( phoneNum[i], 1 ) == result[i] ){
                    result[i] = getCharKey( phoneNum[i], 2 );
                    break;
                } else if ( getCharKey( phoneNum[i], 2 ) == result[i] ){
                    result[i] = getCharKey( phoneNum[i], 3 );
                    break;
                }
            }
        }
    }
```

What's the running time on this algorithm?

Again, there must be at least 3^n solutions, so the algorithm can be no better than $O(3^n)$ if it is correct. There is slight constant overhead in finding each word, but you can ignore it. Therefore, this is also an $O(3^n)$ solution.

Summary

Recursion occurs whenever a routine calls itself, directly or indirectly, as part of its processing. One or more base cases are needed to end the recursion; otherwise, the algorithm loops indefinitely — a common problem to watch out for.

A recursive algorithm can always be recoded to use iteration in place of recursion by using a stack to maintain the algorithm's state, which is essentially what the program is doing anyway. Sometimes, however, an iterative alternative to a recursive algorithm can be found, and such solutions are generally more efficient than their recursive counterparts.

Concurrency

Not that long ago, it wasn't unusual for programs to have a single thread of execution, even if they were running on a multithreading system. Even today, code you write for an application or Web server tends to be single-threaded, even if the server itself is multithreaded. Why? Because multithreaded programming (often referred to as *concurrency*) is hard to do correctly, even when the programming language directly supports it. The incorrect use of threads can easily halt your program's execution or corrupt its data.

However, if you're writing applications with a graphical user interface or that perform lengthy I/O operations, chances are good that you'll need to do some of the work using a background thread or two. Even JavaScript programmers doing AJAX-style programming encounter threading issues — even though neither the language nor the standard libraries explicitly support multithreading — because the Web server responses are processed asynchronously, and hence the JavaScript that runs to process the response possibly accesses data used by other parts of the application. That's why good programmers take the time to learn how to write multithreaded programs correctly.

Basic Thread Concepts

This chapter starts by reviewing what threads are and how you can control them.

Threads

A *thread* is the fundamental unit of execution within an application: A running application consists of at least one thread. Each thread has its own stack and runs independently from the application's other threads. Threads share the resources used by the application as it runs, such as file handles or memory, which is why problems can occur. Data corruption is a common side effect of having two threads simultaneously write data to the same block of memory, for example.

Threads can be implemented in different ways. On most systems, threads are created and managed by the operating system. Sometimes, however, the threads are actually implemented by a software layer above the operating system, such as the runtime system for an interpreted programming language. Conceptually, however, they behave the same, and the remainder of this chapter assumes that the operating system manages the threads. (Such threads are often called *native* or *kernel-level* threads.)

Because the number of threads that can be executed at any given instant is limited by the number of processors in the computer, the operating system will rapidly switch from thread to thread, giving each thread a small window of time in which to run. This is known as *preemptive threading,* because the operating system can suspend a thread's execution at any point in order to let another thread run. (A cooperative model, on the other hand, requires a thread to explicitly suspend its own execution in order to let other threads run.) Swapping one thread out and another in is referred to as a *context switch.*

System Threads versus User Threads

It's useful to distinguish between system threads and user threads. A system thread is created and managed by the system. The first (main) thread of an application is a system thread, and the application often exits when the first thread terminates. User threads are explicitly created by the application to do tasks that cannot or should not be done by the main thread.

Applications that display user interfaces must be particularly careful with how they use threads. The main thread in such an application is usually called the *event thread,* because it waits for and delivers events (such as mouse clicks and key presses) to the application for processing. Generally speaking, causing the event thread to block for any length of time is considered bad programming practice, because it leads to (at best) an unresponsive application or (at worst) a frozen computer. Applications avoid these issues by creating threads to handle time-consuming operations, especially those involving network access.

Monitors and Semaphores

In order to avoid data corruption and other problems, applications must control how threads interact with shared resources, referred to as *thread synchronization*. The two fundamental thread synchronization constructs are *monitors* and *semaphores*. Which you use depends on what your system or language supports.

A monitor is a set of routines that are protected by a mutual exclusion lock. A thread cannot execute any of the routines in the monitor until it acquires the lock, which means that only one thread at a time can execute within the monitor; all other threads must wait for the currently executing thread to give up control of the lock. A thread can suspend itself in the monitor and wait for an event to occur, in which case another thread is given the chance to enter the monitor. At some point the suspended thread is notified that the event has occurred, allowing it to awake and reacquire the lock at the earliest possible opportunity.

A semaphore is a simpler construct, just a lock that protects a shared resource. Before using a shared resource, the application must acquire the lock. Any other thread that tries to use the resource is blocked until the owning thread releases the lock, at which point one of the waiting threads (if any) acquires the lock and is unblocked. This is the most basic kind of semaphore, a mutual exclusion, or *mutex,* semaphore. There are other semaphore types, such as counting semaphores (which let a maximum of *n* threads access a resource at any given time) and *event* semaphores (which notify one or all waiting threads that an event has occurred), but they all work in much the same way.

Monitors and semaphores are equivalent, but *monitors* are simpler to use because they handle all details of lock acquisition and release. When using semaphores, an application must be very careful to release any locks a thread has acquired when it terminates; otherwise, no other thread that needs the shared resource can proceed. In addition, every routine that accesses the shared resource must explicitly acquire a lock before using the resource, something that is easily forgotten when coding. Monitors always and automatically acquire the necessary locks.

Most systems provide a way for the thread to timeout if it can't acquire a resource within a certain amount of time, allowing the thread to report an error and/or try again later.

There is a cost to using monitors and semaphores, of course, because extra time is required to acquire the necessary locks whenever a shared resource is accessed.

Deadlocks

As soon as two or more threads contend for a shared resource, the possibility of deadlock occurs, which happens when two threads each have a lock on a resource needed by the other thread. Because neither thread can continue running, the threads are said to be deadlocked. Typically, the only way to resolve a deadlock is to forcefully terminate one of the threads, which is not a great solution. The best solution is deadlock avoidance — using careful programming to ensure that deadlock can never occur.

A Threading Example

Consider the following example of a banking system to illustrate basic threading concepts and why thread synchronization is necessary. The system consists of a program running on a single central computer that controls multiple automated teller machines (ATMs) in different locations. Each ATM has its own thread so that the machines can be used simultaneously and easily share the bank's account data.

Now imagine that the banking system has an `Account` class with a method to deposit and withdraw money from a user's account. The following code is written as a Java class but the code is almost identical to what you'd write in C#:

```
public class Account {
    int    userNumber;
    String userLastName;
    String userFirstName;
    double userBalance;

    public boolean deposit( double amount ){
        double newBalance;

        if( amount < 0.0 ){
            return false; /* Can't add negative amt */
        } else {
            newBalance = userBalance + amount;
            userBalance = newBalance;
            return true;
        }
    }

    public boolean withdraw( double amount ){
```

```
            double newBalance;

            if( amount < userBalance ){
                return false; /* Insufficient funds */
            } else {
                newBalance = userBalance - amount;
                userBalance = newBalance;
                return true;
            }
        }
    }
```

Suppose a husband and wife, Ron and Sue, walk up to different ATMs to withdraw $100 each from their joint account. The thread for the first ATM deducts $100 from the couple's account, but the thread is switched out after executing this line:

```
newBalance = userBalance - amount;
```

Processor control then switches to the thread for Sue's ATM, which is also deducting $100. When that thread deducts $100, the account balance is still $500 because the variable, `userBalance`, has not yet been updated. Sue's thread executes until completing this function and updates the value of `userBalance` to $400. Then, control switches back to Ron's transaction. Ron's thread has the value $400 in `newBalance`. Therefore, it simply assigns this value to `userBalance` and returns. Thus, Ron and Sue have deducted $200 total from their account, but their balance still indicates $400, or a net $100 withdrawal. This is a great feature for Ron and Sue, but a big problem for the bank.

Fixing this problem is trivial in Java. Just use the `synchronized` keyword to create a monitor:

```
public class Account {
    int    userNumber;
    String userLastName;
    String userFirstName;
    double userBalance;

    public synchronized boolean deposit( double amount ){
        double newBalance;

        if( amount < 0.0 ){
            return false; /* Can't add negative amt */
        } else {
            newBalance = userBalance + amount;
            userBalance = newBalance;
            return true;
        }
    }

    public synchronized boolean withdraw( double amount ){
        double newBalance;

        if( amount < userBalance ){
            return false; /* Insufficient funds */
        } else {
            newBalance = userBalance - amount;
```

```
                userBalance = newBalance;
                return true;
            }
        }
    }
```

The first thread that enters either `deposit` or `withdraw` blocks all other threads from entering either method. This protects the `userBalance` class data from being changed simultaneously by different threads. The preceding code can be made marginally more efficient by using a monitor around any code that uses or alters the value of `userBalance`:

```
public class Account {
    int    userNumber;
    String userLastName;
    String userFirstName;
    double userBalance;

    public boolean deposit( double amount ){
        double newBalance;

        if( amount < 0.0 ){
            return false; /* Can't add negative amt */
        } else {
            synchronized( this ){
                newBalance = userBalance + amount;
                userBalance = newBalance;
            }
            return true;
        }
    }

    public boolean withdraw( double amount ){
        double newBalance;

        synchronized( this ){
            if( amount < userBalance ){
                return false; /* Insufficient funds */
            } else {
                newBalance = userBalance - amount;
                userBalance = newBalance;
                return true;
            }
        }
    }
}
```

In fact, in Java a synchronized method such as:

```
synchronized void someMethod(){
    .... // the code to protect
}
```

is exactly equivalent to:

```
void someMethod(){
    synchronized( this ){
        .... // the code to protect
    }
}
```

The `lock` statement in C# can be used in a similar manner, but only within a method:

```
void someMethod(){
    lock( this ){
        .... // the code to protect
    }
}
```

In either case, the parameter passed to `synchronize` or `lock` is the object to use as the lock.

Note that the C# `lock` isn't as flexible as the Java `synchronized` because the latter allows threads to suspend themselves while waiting for another thread to signal them that an event has occurred. In C# this must be done using event semaphores.

Concurrency Problems

An interviewer can quickly learn how well you understand multithreaded programming by asking you to solve one or two classic problems involving multiple threads of execution.

Busy Waiting

Explain the term "busy waiting" and how it can be avoided.

This is a simple problem, but one with important performance implications for any multithreaded application.

Consider a thread that spawns another thread to complete a task. Assume that the first thread needs to wait for the second thread to finish its work, and that the second thread terminates as soon as its work is done. The simplest approach is to have the first thread wait for the second thread to die:

```
Thread task = new TheTask();
task.start();

while( task.isAlive() ){
    ; // do nothing
}
```

This is called *busy waiting* because the waiting thread is still active, but it's not actually accomplishing anything. It's "busy" in the sense that the thread is still executed by the processor, even though the thread is doing nothing but waiting for the second thread to finish. This actually "steals" processor cycles away from the second thread (and any other active threads in the system), cycles that could be better spent doing real work.

Busy waiting is avoided using a monitor or a semaphore, depending on what's available to the programmer. The waiting thread simply sleeps (suspends itself temporarily) until the other thread notifies it that it's done. In Java, any shared object can be used as a notification mechanism:

```
Object theLock = new Object();
synchronized( theLock ){
    Thread task = new TheTask( theLock );
    task.start();

    try {
        theLock().wait();
    }
    catch( InterruptedException e ){
        .... // do something if interrupted
    }
}

.....

class TheTask extends Thread {
    private Object theLock;

    public TheTask( Object theLock ){
        this.theLock = theLock;
    }

    public void run(){
        synchronized( theLock ){
            .... // do the task

            theLock.notify();
        }
    }
}
```

In fact, the preceding code can be simplified somewhat by using the class instance itself for the signaling:

```
Thread task = new TheTask();
synchronized( task ){
    task.start();

    try {
        task.wait();
    }
    catch( InterruptedException e ){
        .... // do something if interrupted
    }
}

.....

class TheTask extends Thread {
    public void run(){
```

```
            synchronized( this ){
                .... // do the task

                this.notify();
            }
        }
    }
```

For extra bonus points, ask the interviewer if the first thread is an event thread. Blocking an event thread is almost never acceptable, so waiting indefinitely for a lock to be released won't cut it in a real-world application. That's why most graphical user interface toolkits provide a way for applications to queue pseudo-events for processing by the event thread, which is what the second thread would do when it finished its task.

Producer/Consumer

Write a Producer thread and a Consumer thread that share a fixed-size buffer and an index to access the buffer. The Producer should place numbers into the buffer, while the Consumer should remove the numbers. The order in which the numbers are added or removed is not important.

This is one of the canonical concurrency problems. The first step is to answer the problem without using any concurrency control, and then comment on what the problems are. The algorithm isn't very difficult when concurrency isn't an issue. The data buffer looks like this:

```
public class IntBuffer {
    private int   index;
    private int[] buffer = new int[8];

    public void add( int num ){
        while( true ){
            if( index < buffer.length ){
                buffer[index++] = num;
                return;
            }
        }
    }

    public int remove(){
        while( true ){
            if( index > 0 ){
                return buffer[--index];
            }
        }
    }
}
```

The producer and consumer are almost trivial:

```
public class Producer extends Thread {
    private IntBuffer buffer;

    public Producer( IntBuffer buffer ){
        this.buffer = buffer;
    }

    public void run(){
        Random r = new Random();
        while( true ){
            int num = r.nextInt();
            buffer.add( num );
            System.out.println( "Produced " + num );
        }
    }
}

public class Consumer extends Thread {
    private IntBuffer buffer;

    public Consumer( IntBuffer buffer ){
        this.buffer = buffer;
    }

    public void run(){
        while( true ){
            int num = buffer.remove();
            System.out.println( "Consumed " + num );
        }
    }
}
```

Then, somewhere in the code you start the threads:

```
IntBuffer b = new IntBuffer();
Producer p = new Producer( b );
Consumer c = new Consumer( b );
p.start();
c.start();
```

There are two problems with this approach, however. First, it uses busy waiting, which wastes a lot of CPU time. Second, there is no access control for the shared resource, the buffer: If a context switch occurs as the index is being updated, the next thread may read from or write to the wrong element of the buffer.

You may think at first that making the `add` and `remove` methods synchronized will fix the problem:

```
public class IntBuffer {
    private int   index;
    private int[] buffer = new int[8];

    public synchronized void add( int num ){
```

```
        while( true ){
            if( index < buffer.length ){
                buffer[index++] = num;
                return;
            }
        }
    }

    public synchronized int remove(){
        while( true ){
            if( index > 0 ){
                return buffer[--index];
            }
        }
    }
}
```

This won't fix anything, however. Instead, the first thread to call `add` or `remove` will prevent the other thread from even entering the other method. Nothing will happen: One of the threads will busy-wait indefinitely and the other will be permanently suspended. The code inside the methods needs to be changed so that the producer suspends itself when the buffer is full and waits for a slot to open up, while the consumer suspends itself if the buffer is empty and waits for a new value to arrive:

```
public class IntBuffer {
    private int   index;
    private int[] buffer = new int[8];

    public synchronized void add( int num ){
        while( index == buffer.length - 1 ){
            try {
                wait();
            }
            catch( InterruptedException e ){
            }
        }

        buffer[index++] = num;
        notifyAll();
    }

    public synchronized int remove(){
        while( index == 0 ){
            try {
                wait();
            }
            catch( InterruptedException e ){
            }
        }

        int ret = buffer[--index];
        notifyAll();
        return ret;
    }
}
```

This code actually allows multiple producers and consumers to use the same buffer simultaneously, so it's even more general-purpose than the two-thread-only solution you'd be expected to come up with.

The Dining Philosophers

Five introspective and introverted philosophers are sitting at a circular table. In front of each philosopher is a plate of food. A fork (or a chopstick) lies between each philosopher, one by the philosopher's left hand and one by the right hand. A philosopher cannot eat until he or she has both forks in hand. Forks are picked up one at a time. If a fork is unavailable, the philosopher simply waits for the fork to be freed. When a philosopher has two forks, he or she eats a few bites and then returns both forks to the table. If a philosopher cannot obtain both forks for a long time, he or she will starve. Is there an algorithm that will ensure that no philosophers starve?

This is another concurrency classic, and although it may seem quite contrived — in the real world no one would starve because each philosopher would simply ask the adjacent philosophers for their forks — it accurately reflects real-world concurrency issues involving multiple shared resources. The point of the problem is to see whether you understand the concept of deadlock and know how it avoid it.

Start by trying a few simple tests to determine when deadlock happens and what you can do to avoid it. It won't take you long to figure out that deadlock occurs quite readily. Consider the following implementation in which each philosopher picks up the forks in the same order, left followed by right:

```
public class DiningPhilosophers {

    // Each "fork" is just an Object we synchronize on
    private Object[]      forks;

    private Philosopher[] philosophers;

    // Prepare the forks and philosophers

    private DiningPhilosophers( int num ){

        forks = new Object[ num ];
        philosophers = new Philosopher[ num ];

        for( int i = 0; i < num; ++i ){
            forks[i] = new Object();
            philosophers[i] = new Philosopher( i, i, ( i + 1 ) % num );
        }
    }

    // Start the eating process

    public void startEating() throws InterruptedException {
        for( int i = 0; i < philosophers.length; ++i ){
```

```
            philosophers[i].start();
        }

        // Suspend the main thread until the first philosopher
        // stops eating, which will never happen -- this keeps
        // the simulation running indefinitely

        philosophers[0].join();
    }

    // Entry point for simulation

    public static void main( String[] args ){
        try {
            DiningPhilosophers d = new DiningPhilosophers( 5 );
            d.startEating();
        }
        catch( InterruptedException e ){
        }
    }

    // Each philosopher runs in its own thread.

    private class Philosopher extends Thread {

        private int id;
        private int fork1;
        private int fork2;

        Philosopher( int id, int fork1, int fork2 ){
            this.id = id;
            this.fork1 = fork1;
            this.fork2 = fork2;
        }

        public void run() {

            status( "Ready to eat using forks " + fork1 +
                    " and " + fork2 );

            pause(); // pause to let others get ready

            while( true ){
                status( "Picking up fork " + fork1 );

                synchronized( forks[ fork1 ] ){

                    status( "Picking up fork " + fork2 );

                    synchronized( forks[ fork2 ] ){
                        status( "Eating" );
                    }
                }
            }
```

```
        }

        private void pause(){
            try {
                sleep( 200 );
            }
            catch( InterruptedException e ){
                // do nothing
            }
        }

        private void status( String msg ){
            System.out.println( "Philosopher " + id +
                                ": " + msg );
        }
    }
}
```

This application deadlocks when all philosophers have simultaneously picked up their left fork: Because no right fork is available to any philosopher, no philosopher can eat.

One solution is to add a timeout to the waiting: If a philosopher is not able to eat within a predetermined amount of time after acquiring the first fork, then the philosopher drops the fork and tries again. The flaw with this solution is that it's possible for one or more philosophers to starve because they *never* acquire both forks. This is referred to as *livelock*.

The best solution requires a very simple change to the application. Instead of having all the philosophers pick up the left fork first, have *one* of the philosophers pick up the right fork first:

```
    // Prepare the forks and philosophers

    private DiningPhilosophers( int num ){

        forks = new Object[ num ];
        philosophers = new Philosopher[ num ];

        for( int i = 0; i < num; ++i ){
            forks[i] = new Object();

            int fork1 = i;
            int fork2 = ( i + 1 ) % num;

            if( i == 0 ){
                philosophers[0] = new Philosopher( 0, fork2, fork1 );
            } else {
                philosophers[i] = new Philosopher( i, fork1, fork2 );
            }
        }
    }
```

This one change to the fork pickup order is enough to break the deadlock and ensure that forks are always available to enable hungry philosophers to eat.

Summary

Using multiple threads of execution within an application makes programming the application much more complicated. There's the chance of corruption whenever one thread reads data that another thread is modifying, for example. Or threads may block with no chance of resuming their operation.

Concurrency issues are normally handled using monitors or semaphores. These facilities enable applications to control access to shared resources and to signal other threads when data is ready to be processed. Misuse of these constructs can lead to problems such as deadlock, however, so careful programming is needed to ensure that multithreaded programs work correctly and as expected.

Object-Oriented Programming

These days, most programming is done using an object-oriented (OO) language such as Java, C#, or C++. Even JavaScript, though not an OO language, supports some features of OO programming through prototype objects and the clever use of function definitions. As such, it's important to have a good grasp of fundamental OO principles, so this entire chapter is devoted to the topic.

Fundamentals

Although not widely used until the turn of the century, object-oriented programming's roots date back several decades to languages such as Simula and Smalltalk. OO programming has been the subject of much academic research and debate, especially since the widespread adoption of OO programming languages by practicing developers.

Classes and Objects

There are many different ways and no clear consensus on how to describe and define object orientation as a programming technique, but all of them revolve around the notions of *classes* and *objects*. A *class* is an abstract definition of something that has *attributes* (sometimes called *properties* or *states*) and *actions* (*capabilities* or *methods*). An *object* is a specific instance of a class that has its own state separate from any other object instance. Here's a class definition for `Point`, which is a pair of integers that represents the *x* and *y* values of a point in a Cartesian coordinate system:

```
public class Point {
    private int x;
    private int y;

    public Point( int x, int y ){
        this.x = x;
        this.y = y;
```

```
    }

    public Point( Point other ){
        x = other.getX();
        y = other.getY();
    }

    public int getX(){ return x; }

    public int getY(){ return y; }

    public Point relativeTo( int dx, int dy ){
        return new Point( x + dx, y + dy );
    }

    public String toString(){
        StringBuffer b = new StringBuffer();
        b.append( '(' );
        b.append( x );
        b.append( ',' );
        b.append( y );
        b.append( ')' );

        return b.toString();
    }
}
```

To represent a specific point, simply create an instance of the `Point` class with the appropriate values:

```
Point p1 = new Point( 5, 10 );
Point p2 = p1.relativeTo( -5, 5 );

System.out.println( p2.toString() ); // prints (0,15)
```

This simple example shows one of the principles of OO programming, that of *encapsulation* — the hiding of implementation details.

Inheritance and Polymorphism

Two other important principles are those of inheritance and polymorphism, which are closely related. *Inheritance* enables a class to provide behavior for a more-specialized version of the class. When class B *inherits* from class A (Java uses the term *extends*), class A is B's *parent* or *base* class and class B is A's *subclass*. All the behaviors defined by class A are also part of class B, though possibly in a modified form. In fact, an instance of class B can be used wherever an instance of class A is required.

Polymorphism is the ability to provide multiple implementations of an action and to select the correct implementation based on the surrounding context. For example, a class might define two versions of a method with different parameters. Or the same method might be defined both in a parent class and a subclass, the latter *overriding* the former for instances of the subclass. Method selection may occur when the code is compiled or when the application is run.

The classic example of inheritance and polymorphism is a shapes library representing the different shapes in a vector-based drawing application. At the top of the hierarchy is the `Shape` class, which defines the things that all shapes have in common:

```
public abstract class Shape {
    protected Point center;

    protected Shape( Point center ){
        this.center = center;
    }

    public Point getCenter(){
        return center; // because Point is immutable
    }

    public abstract Rectangle getBounds();

    public abstract void draw( Graphics g );
}
```

We can then specialize the shapes into `Rectangle` and `Ellipse` subclasses:

```
public class Rectangle extends Shape {
    private int h;
    private int w;

    public Rectangle( Point center, int w, int h ){
        super( center );
        this.w = w;
        this.h = h;
    }

    public Rectangle getBounds(){
        return this;
    }

    public int getHeight(){ return h; }

    public int getWidth(){ return w; }

    public void draw( Graphics g ){
        .... // code to paint rectangle
    }
}

public class Ellipse extends Shape {
    private int a;
    private int b;

    public Ellipse( Point center, int a, int b ){
        super( center );
        this.a = a;
        this.b = b;
```

```
        }

        public Rectangle getBounds(){
            return new Rectangle( center, a * 2, b * 2 );
        }

        public int getSemiMajorAxis(){ return a; }

        public int getSemiMinorAxis(){ return b; }

        public void draw( Graphics g ){
            .... // code to paint ellipse
        }
    }
```

The `Rectangle` and `Ellipse` classes could be further specialized into `Square` and `Circle` subclasses, but we won't bother doing so here.

Even though many shapes may be defined in the library, the part of the application that draws them on the screen doesn't need to do much work at all:

```
    void paintShapes( Graphics g, List<Shape> shapes ){
        for( Shape s : shapes ){
            s.draw( g );
        }
    }
```

Note that the preceding code could be rewritten to work on older Java systems as follows:

```
    void paintShapes( Graphics g, List shapes ){
        Iterator it = shapes.iterator();
        while( it.hasNext() ){
            Shape s = (Shape) it.next();
            s.draw( g );
        }
    }
```

Adding a new shape to the library is just a matter of subclassing one of the existing classes and implementing the things that are different.

Construction and Destruction

Objects are instances of classes. Creating an object is called *constructing* the object. Part of the process involves invoking a *constructor* method in the class. The constructor initializes the state of the object, which usually involves calling (either explicitly or implicitly) the constructors of its parent classes so that they can initialize their part of the object's state.

Destroying objects is not as straightforward as constructing them. In C++ a method called the *destructor* is invoked to clean up an object's state. Destructors are invoked automatically when an object goes out of scope or when the delete operation is used to destroy a dynamically created object — keeping track of object instances is important to avoid leaking memory. In languages such as C# and Java, however, the garbage collector is responsible for finding and destroying unused objects, in which case the time and place (it usually happens on a separate, system-defined thread) of the destruction is out of the application's control. An optional *finalizer* method is invoked by the system prior to the object's destruction to give it the opportunity to clean itself up before its "final" destruction. (Note, however, that in C# and Java it's possible for objects to "resurrect" themselves from destruction in their finalizers.)

Object-Oriented Programming Problems

Problems you are presented relating to object-oriented programming are likely to focus on the concepts of object orientation, particularly on issues relevant to the languages the company is using in its coding.

Interfaces and Abstract Classes

Explain the difference between an interface and an abstract class in object-oriented programming.

The specific answer to this depends, of course, on which language you're developing with, but start the answer by giving some general definitions:

- An *interface* declares a set of related methods, outside of any class.
- An *abstract class* is an incomplete class definition that declares but does not define all of its methods.

Conceptually, then, an interface defines an *application programming interface (API)* that is independent of any class hierarchy. In fact, interfaces can be used in non-OO programming models, such as component-based models like COM and CORBA. However, you're focusing on the use of interfaces in an object-oriented context, where they are useful in their own right. Interfaces are the ultimate encapsulators, because they hide all the details of the classes that implement their methods from the user of the interface. They're particularly important — almost necessary, in fact — in languages that only support single inheritance (classes can only inherit from one base class). A class that exposes its members via an interface is said to *implement* the interface.

Unlike an interface, an abstract class is a proper class: It can have data members and can be a subclass of other classes. Unlike a concrete (nonabstract) class, however, some of its behaviors are deliberately left to be defined by its own subclasses. Abstract classes cannot be instantiated because of this — only instances of concrete subclasses can be created.

An interface is almost identical to an abstract class with no data members and no method definitions. In C++ this is exactly how you'd define an interface: by declaring a class with no data members and only pure virtual functions — something like this, for example:

```
class StatusCallback {
  public:
    virtual void updateStatus( int oState, int nState ) = 0;
}
```

A class could then "implement" the interface by deriving from it:

```
class MyClass : SomeOtherClass, StatusCallback {
  public:
    void updateStatus( int oState, int nState ){
        if( nState > oState ){
            ..... // do stuff
        }
    }

    .... // remainder of class
}
```

In Java, an interface is defined using the `interface` keyword:

```
public interface StatusCallback {
    void updateStatus( int oState, int nState );
}
```

The interface is then implemented by a class:

```
public class MyClass implements StatusCallback {
    public void updateStatus( int oState, int nState ){
        .... // do stuff
    }

    .... // remainder of class
}
```

A common pattern you'll see with languages that support both interfaces and abstract classes is the provision of a *default implementation* of an interface via an abstract class. For example, the following interface:

```
public interface XMLReader {
    public XMLObject fromString( String str );
    public XMLObject fromReader( Reader in );
}
```

might have this default implementation:

```
public abstract class XMLReaderImpl {
    public XMLObject fromString( String str ){
        fromString( new StringReader( str ) );
    }

    public abstract XMLObject fromReader( Reader in );
}
```

A programmer who wanted to implement `XMLReader` would then have the option of creating a class that subclasses `XMLReaderImpl` (likely as a nested class) and only implement one method instead of two.

Virtual Methods

Describe what virtual methods are and why they are useful.

A virtual method is a method whose implementation is determined at run time based on the actual type (class) of the invoking object. Nonstatic Java methods are always virtual, so Java programmers may have trouble answering this one; but in C# and C++, methods are only virtual when declared with the `virtual` keyword—nonvirtual methods are the default.

Virtual methods are used for polymorphism. Consider the following three C++ classes:

```
class A {
  public:
    void print() { cout << "A"; }
}

class B : A {
  public:
    void print() { cout << "B"; }
}

class C : B {
  public:
    void print() { cout << "C"; }
}
```

Because `print` is declared as nonvirtual, the method that is invoked depends on the type used at *compile time*:

```
A *a = new A();
B *b = new B();
C *c = new C();

a->print(); // "A"
b->print(); // "B"
c->print(); // "C"
((B *)c)->print(); // "B"
((A *)c)->print(); // "A"
((A *)b)->print(); // "A"
```

Now redeclare `print` as virtual:

```
class A {
  public:
    virtual void print() { cout << "A"; }
}

class B : A {
  public:
    virtual void print() { cout << "B"; }
```

```
}

class C : B {
  public:
    virtual void print() { cout << "C"; }
}
```

Now the *run-time* type of the object determines the method invoked:

```
A *a = new A();
B *b = new B();
C *c = new C();

a->print(); // "A"
b->print(); // "B"
c->print(); // "C"
((B *)c)->print(); // "C"
((A *)c)->print(); // "C"
((A *)b)->print(); // "B"
```

A C++ version of the `Shape` class defined at the beginning of the chapter would need to declare the `draw` method as virtual in order for the `paintShapes` method — which would only have references to `Shape` instances — to work.

Once you explain what virtual methods are and why they're useful, talk about their advantages and disadvantages. The primary advantage was just described: the run-time method selection. Virtual methods are also used to declare abstract methods. The disadvantages are that it takes longer to invoke a virtual method (at a minimum, one lookup needs to be done in a table to find the right method — you can't jump directly to the method as you can with nonvirtuals) and that extra memory is required to store the information needed for the lookup.

Multiple Inheritance

Why do C# and Java disallow the multiple inheritance of classes?

In C++ it's legal for a class to inherit (directly or indirectly) from more than one class, which is referred to as *multiple inheritance*. C# and Java, however, limit classes to *single inheritance* — each class inherits from a single parent class.

Multiple inheritance is a useful way to create classes that combine aspects of two disparate class hierarchies, something that often happens when using different class frameworks within a single application. If two frameworks define their own base classes for exceptions, for example, you can use multiple inheritance to create exception classes that can be used with either framework.

The problem with multiple inheritance is that it can lead to ambiguity. The classic example is when a class inherits from two other classes, each of which inherits from the same class:

```
class A {
  protected:
    bool flag;
};

class B : public A {};

class C : public A {};

class D : public B, public C {
  public:
    void setFlag( bool nflag ){
        flag = nflag; // ambiguous
    }
};
```

In this example, the `flag` data member is defined by class `A`. But class `D` descends from class `B` and class `C`, which both derive from `A`, so in essence *two copies* of `flag` are available because there are two instances of `A` in `D`'s class hierarchy. Which one do you want to set? The compiler will complain that the reference to `flag` in `D` is ambiguous. One fix is to explicitly disambiguate the reference:

```
B::flag = nflag;
```

Another fix is to declare `B` and `C` as *virtual base classes*, which means that only one copy of `A` will exist in the hierarchy, eliminating any ambiguity.

There are other complexities with multiple inheritance, such as the order in which the base classes are initialized when a derived object is constructed, or the way members can be inadvertently hidden from derived classes. Because of these complexities, some languages restrict themselves to the much simpler single inheritance model. On the other hand, single inheritance is also very restrictive, because only classes with a common ancestor can share behaviors. Interfaces mitigate this restriction somewhat by allowing classes in different hierarchies to *expose* common interfaces even if they're not implemented by sharing code.

Summary

Object-oriented programming languages are in widespread use today, so a firm understanding of basic OO principles is necessary for most jobs. This means understanding the difference between classes and objects as well as concepts such as polymorphism and inheritance.

Be sure you understand how each programming language you use handles the different aspects of OO programming.

Databases

With the rise of Web-based applications, more and more programmers find themselves using databases for data storage and manipulation, so don't be surprised if you are asked questions about your experience with databases. Although different kinds of databases are available, the *relational database* is by far the most common type, so that's what this chapter covers.

Database Fundamentals

There are tools available to help you create and manage databases, many of which hide the complexities of the underlying data structures. Ruby on Rails, for example, abstracts all database access and makes most direct access unnecessary, as do component technologies such as Enterprise JavaBeans and many object-oriented frameworks. Still, you need an understanding of how relational databases work to make good design decisions.

Relational Databases

Relational databases originated in the 1960s from the work of E. F. Codd, a computer scientist who designed a database system based on the concepts of relational algebra. However, you don't need to understand relational algebra or other mathematical concepts to use a relational database.

Data in a relational database is stored in *tables*, which consist of *rows* and *columns*. (A set of tables is referred to as a *schema*.) Each table has at least one column, but there may be no rows. Each column has a type associated with it, which limits the type of data that can be stored in the column, as well as additional constraints. Although the columns are ordered, the rows aren't. Any ordering that is required is done when the data is fetched (via a *query*) from the database.

Most tables have *keys*, although it's not a requirement (but it is good design). A key is a column or set of columns that uniquely identifies a particular row in the table. One of the keys is designated to be the *primary key*. For example, in a table of employees, you would use the employee identification number — guaranteed to be unique for each employee — as the primary key.

A table can be linked to another table using a *foreign key*. A foreign key is usually a primary key value taken from the other table. Foreign keys ensure that data isn't deleted prematurely: You can't delete a row from a table if the foreign key of another table references the row. This is known as *referential integrity*, and it ensures that related tables are always in a consistent state with respect to each other.

There are different ways to manipulate databases, but the most common way is through the use of a *structured query language*.

Structured Query Language (SQL)

SQL is the *lingua franca* of relational database manipulation. It provides mechanisms for most kinds of database manipulations. Understandably, SQL is a big topic, and numerous books are devoted just to SQL and relational databases. Nevertheless, the basic tasks of storing and retrieving data are fairly simple with SQL. Let's look at some of the highlights of SQL.

Most interview database problems involve writing queries for a database with a given schema, so you won't usually need to design a schema yourself. This introduction works with the following schema:

```
Player (
  name   CHAR(20),
  number INT(4)
)

Stats (
  number      INT(4),
  totalPoints INT(4),
  year        CHAR(20)
)
```

Some sample data for `Player` is shown in Table 10-1, and a sample `Stats` table is shown in Table 10-2.

Table 10-1. Player Sample Data

name	number
Larry Smith	23
David Gonzalez	12
George Rogers	7
Mike Lee	14
Rajiv Williams	55

Table 10-2. Stats Sample Data

number	totalPoints	year
7	59	Freshman
55	90	Senior
23	15	Senior
86	221	Junior
36	84	Sophomore

The first thing to notice about the schema is that neither table has a primary key defined, although the `number` column in both tables is a natural key because the player number uniquely identifies each player. In fact, the `number` column in the `Stats` table is really a foreign key—a reference to the number column in the `Player` table. You might suggest to the interviewer that the schema could be improved with the following changes:

```
Player (
  name   CHAR(20),
  number INT(4) PRIMARY KEY
)

Stats (
  number      INT(4) PRIMARY KEY,
  totalPoints INT(4),
  year        CHAR(20),
  FOREIGN KEY number REFERENCES Player
)
```

With these changes, the database takes an active role in ensuring the correctness of the data. For example, you can't add a row to the `Stats` table that references a player not listed in the `Player` table: The foreign key relationship between `Stats.number` and `Player.number` forbids this. At this point you could have a very detailed discussion with the interviewer about the advantages and disadvantages of primary keys and foreign keys in database design.

One fundamental SQL statement is `INSERT`, which is used to add values to a table. For example, to insert a player named Bill Henry with the number 50 into the `Player` table, you would use the following statement:

```
INSERT INTO Player VALUES('Bill Henry', 50)
```

`SELECT` is the SQL statement most commonly seen in interviews. A `SELECT` statement retrieves data from a table. For example, the statement

```
SELECT * FROM Player
```

will return all of the values in the table `Player`:

```
+----------------+--------+
| name           | number |
+----------------+--------+
| Larry Smith    |     23 |
| David Gonzalez |     12 |
| George Rogers  |      7 |
| Mike Lee       |     14 |
| Rajiv Williams |     55 |
| Bill Henry     |     50 |
+----------------+--------+
```

You can specify which columns you want to return like this:

```
SELECT name FROM Player
```

The preceding code returns the following:

```
+----------------+
| name           |
+----------------+
| Larry Smith    |
| David Gonzalez |
| George Rogers  |
| Mike Lee       |
| Rajiv Williams |
| Bill Henry     |
+----------------+
```

You may want to be more restrictive about which values you return. For example, if you want to return only the names of the players with numbers less than 10 or greater than 40, you would use the following statement:

```
SELECT name FROM Player WHERE number < 10 OR number > 40
```

That would return the following:

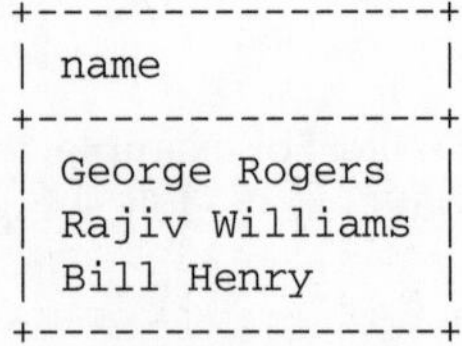

```
+----------------+
| name           |
+----------------+
| George Rogers  |
| Rajiv Williams |
| Bill Henry     |
+----------------+
```

Often, you will want to use data from two tables. For example, you may want to print out the names of all players along with the number of points that each player has scored. To do this, you will have to *join* the two tables on the `number` field. The `number` field is called a *common key* because it represents the same unique value in both tables. The query is as follows:

```
SELECT name, totalPoints FROM Player, Stats WHERE Player.number = Stats.number
```

It returns this:

```
+----------------+-------------+
| name           | totalPoints |
+----------------+-------------+
| George Rogers  |          59 |
| Rajiv Williams |          90 |
+----------------+-------------+
```

The *aggregates*, `MAX`, `MIN`, `SUM`, and `AVG`, are another commonly used SQL feature. These aggregates enable you to retrieve the maximum, minimum, sum, and average, respectively, for a particular column. For example, you may want print out the average number of points each player has scored. To do this, you would use the following query:

```
SELECT AVG(totalPoints) FROM Stats
```

It yields this:

```
+------------------+
| AVG(totalPoints) |
+------------------+
|          93.8000 |
+------------------+
```

Other times, you may want to use the aggregates over a subset of the data. For example, you may want to print out the year along with the average number of points that each year's players have scored. You will need to use the `GROUP BY` clause to do this, as in the following query:

```
SELECT year, AVG(totalPoints) FROM Stats GROUP BY year
```

It gives this result:

```
+-----------+------------------+
| year      | AVG(totalPoints) |
+-----------+------------------+
| Freshman  |          59.0000 |
| Junior    |         221.0000 |
| Senior    |          52.5000 |
| Sophomore |          84.0000 |
+-----------+------------------+
```

Most interview problems focus on using these sorts of insert and select statements. You're less likely to encounter SQL problems related to other features, such as `UPDATE` statements, `DELETE` statements, permissions, security, or optimization. One thing you should definitely understand is *transactions*.

Database Transactions

The integrity of the data stored in a database is paramount: If the data is ever corrupted, every application that depends on the database may fail or be in error. While referential integrity helps keep the data consistent, the best way to ensure data integrity is to use a database *transaction*.

A transaction groups a set of related database manipulations together into a single unit. If any operation within the transaction fails, the entire transaction fails and any changes made by the transaction are abandoned (*rolled back*). Conversely, if all the operations succeed, then all the changes are *committed* together as a group.

Chapter 8 included a simple example involving the addition and removal of money from a bank account. If you expand the example to involve the *transfer* of money between two accounts, you'll see why transactions are so important. A transfer is really two operations: removing money from the first account and then adding it to the second account. If an error occurs immediately after the money is removed from the first account, you want the system to detect the problem and redeposit the withdrawn money into the original account. These are the kinds of problems that transactions solve.

The four properties of a transaction are as follows:

- **Atomicity** — The database system guarantees that either all operations with the transaction succeed or else they all fail.
- **Consistency** — The transaction must ensure that the database is in a correct, consistent state at the start and the end of the transaction. No referential integrity constraints can be broken, for example.
- **Isolation** — All changes to the database within a transaction are isolated from all other queries and transactions until the transaction is committed.
- **Durability** — Once committed, changes made in a transaction are permanent. The database system must have some way to recover from crashes and other problems so that the current state of the database is never lost.

These four properties are generally referred to as *ACID*. As you might imagine, there is a significant penalty performance to be paid if all four properties are to be guaranteed on each transaction. The isolation requirement can be particularly onerous on a system with many simultaneous transactions, so most systems allow the isolation requirements to be relaxed in different ways in order to provide improved performance.

Note that ACID compliance is *not* a relational database requirement, but most modern databases support it.

Database Problems

If you indicate on your résumé that you have some database experience, an interviewer will probably ask you a few questions to determine the depth of your knowledge in this area.

Simple SQL

Given a database with the table

```
Olympics(
    city CHAR(16),
    year INT(4)
)
```

write a SQL statement to insert Montreal and 1976 into the database.

This is an extremely easy problem that an interviewer might use to determine whether you have ever used SQL before or whether you were padding your résumé when you mentioned it. If you know SQL, you're all set. It's a straightforward SQL `INSERT` statement; no tricks at all. If you don't really know SQL, you're in trouble. The correct answer is

```
INSERT INTO Olympics VALUES( 'Montreal', 1976 )
```

Company and Employee Database

You are given a database with the following tables:

```
Company (
    companyName CHAR(30),
    id          INT(4) PRIMARY KEY
)

EmployeesHired (
    id            INT(4) PRIMARY KEY,
    numHired      INT(4),
    fiscalQuarter INT(4),

    FOREIGN KEY id REFERENCES Company
)
```

You may make the assumption that the only possible fiscal quarters are 1 through 4. Sample data for this schema is presented in Table 10-3.

Table 10-3. Company and Employee Sample Data

companyName	id
Hillary Plumbing	6
John Lawn Company	9
Dave Cookie Company	19
Jane Electricity	3

Id	numHired	fiscalQuarter
3	3	3
3	2	4
19	4	1
6	2	1

Write a SQL statement that returns the names of all the companies that hired employees in fiscal quarter 4.

This problem involves retrieving data from two tables. You will have to join the two tables to get all of the needed information. `id` is the only key common to both tables so you want to join on the value `id`. Once you have joined the two tables, you can select the company name where the fiscal quarter is 4. This SQL statement looks like this:

```
SELECT companyName FROM Company, EmployeesHired
WHERE Company.id = EmpolyeesHired.id AND fiscalQuarter = 4
```

There is a small problem with this SQL statement. Consider what might happen if a company did not hire anyone in Q4. There could still be a tuple (a row of data) such as `EmployeesHired(6, 0, 4)`. The company with `id` 6 would be returned by the preceding query even though it didn't hire anyone during fiscal quarter 4. To fix this bug, you need to ensure that `numHired` is greater than 0. The revised SQL statement looks like this:

```
SELECT companyName FROM Company, EmployeesHired
WHERE Company.id = EmpolyeesHired.id AND fiscalQuarter = 4 AND numHired > 0
```

Now, using the same schema, write a SQL statement that returns the names of all companies that did not hire anyone in fiscal quarters 1 through 4.

The best way to start this problem is by looking at the previous answer. You know how to get the names of all of the companies that hired an employee in quarter 4. If you remove the `WHERE` condition that `fiscalQuarter = 4`, you will have a query that returns the names of all companies that hired employees during all fiscal quarters. If you use this query as a *subquery* and select all of the companies that are not in the result, you will get all of the companies that did not hire anyone in fiscal quarters 1 through 4. As a slight optimization, you can select just the `id` from the `EmployeesHired` table and print out the companies that do not have an `id` returned. The query looks like this:

```
SELECT companyName FROM Company WHERE id NOT IN
(SELECT id from EmployeesHired WHERE numHired > 0)
```

Finally, return the names of all companies and the total number of employees that each company hired during fiscal quarters 1 through 4.

You're asked to retrieve the totals of some sets of values, which indicates that you will have to use the `SUM` aggregate. In this problem, you don't want the sum of the entire column, you want only a sum of the values that have the same `id`. To accomplish this task, you will need to use the `GROUP BY` feature. This feature enables you to apply `SUM` over grouped values of data. Other than the `GROUP BY` feature, this query is very similar to the first query except you omit the `fiscalQuarter = 4` in the `WHERE` clause. The query looks like this:

```
SELECT companyName, SUM(numHired)
FROM Company, EmployeesHired
WHERE Company.id = EmployeesHired.id
GROUP BY companyName
```

Max, No Aggregates

Given the following SQL database schema

```
Test (
    num INT(4)
)
```

write a SQL statement that returns the maximum value from `num` **without using an aggregate (**`MAX`**,** `MIN`**, etc.).**

In this problem, your hands are tied behind your back — you have to find a maximum without using the feature designed for finding the maximum. A good way to start is by drawing a table with some sample data as shown in Table 10-4.

Table 10-4. Sample Values for num

num
5
23
-6
7

In this sample data, you want to print out the value 23. 23 has the property that all other numbers are less than it. Though true, this way of looking at things doesn't offer much help with constructing the SQL statement. A similar but more useful way to say the same thing is that 23 is the *only* number that does not have a number that is greater than it. If you could return every value that does not have a number greater than it, you would return only 23, and you would have solved the problem. Try designing a SQL statement to print out every number that does not have a number greater than it.

First, you will want to figure out which numbers do have numbers greater than themselves. This is a more manageable query. Begin by joining the table with itself to create all possible pairs for which each value in one column is greater than the corresponding value in the other column, as in the following query:

```
SELECT Lesser.num, Greater.num
FROM Test AS Greater, Test AS Lesser
WHERE Lesser.num < Greater.num
```

Using the sample data, this yields the results shown in Table 10-5.

Table 10-5. Temporary Table Formed after Join

Lesser	Greater
-6	23
5	23
7	23
-6	7
5	7
-6	5

As desired, every value is in the lesser column except the maximum value of 23. Thus, if you use the previous query as a subquery and select every value not in it, you will get the maximum value. This query would look like the following:

```
SELECT num FROM Test WHERE num NOT IN
(SELECT Lesser.num FROM Test AS Greater, Test AS Lesser
WHERE Lesser.num < Greater.num)
```

There is one minor bug in this query. If the maximum value is repeated in the `Test` table, it will be returned twice. To prevent this, use the `DISTINCT` keyword. This changes the query to the following:

```
SELECT DISTINCT num FROM Test WHERE num NOT IN
(SELECT Lesser.num FROM Test AS Greater, Test AS Lesser
WHERE Lesser.num < Greater.num)
```

Three-Valued Logic

Given the following table

```
Address (
    street CHAR(30) NOT NULL,
    apartment CHAR(10),

    city CHAR(40) NOT NULL,
)
```

write a SQL statement that returns nonapartment addresses only.

This problem seems very simple. The solution that comes to mind is most probably this query, which the interviewer might even supply unprompted:

```
SELECT * FROM Address WHERE apartment = null
```

This won't return any addresses, however, and the reason has to do with SQL's use of *ternary*, or *three-valued*, logic. Ternary logic is not familiar to many programmers, but it's an important concept to grasp in order to write effective queries.

Logical operations in SQL have *three* possible values, not two. Those three values are `TRUE`, `FALSE` and `UNKNOWN`. As you might expect, `UNKNOWN` means that a value is unknown or unrepresentable. The familiar `AND`, `OR`, and `NOT` operations, for example, return different values in the presence of an `UNKNOWN` value, as shown in Tables 10-6, 10-7, and 10-8.

Table 10-6. Ternary AND Operations

AND	TRUE	FALSE	UNKNOWN
TRUE	TRUE	FALSE	UNKNOWN
FALSE	FALSE	FALSE	FALSE
UNKNOWN	UNKNOWN	FALSE	UNKNOWN

Table 10-7. Ternary OR Operations

OR	TRUE	FALSE	UNKNOWN
TRUE	TRUE	TRUE	TRUE
FALSE	TRUE	FALSE	UNKNOWN
UNKNOWN	TRUE	UNKNOWN	UNKNOWN

Table 10-8. Ternary NOT Operations

NOT	
TRUE	FALSE
FALSE	TRUE
UNKNOWN	UNKNOWN

The trick is in the use of the equality operator ('=') to test for a `NULL` column value. In most databases, a comparison to `NULL` returns `UNKNOWN`—even when comparing `NULL` to `NULL`. The proper way to check for a `NULL` or non-`NULL` column is to use the `IS NULL` or `IS NOT NULL` syntax. Thus, the original query should be restated as follows:

```
SELECT * FROM Address WHERE apartment IS NULL
```

Not accounting for `UNKNOWN` values in `WHERE` clause conditions is a common error.

Summary

Databases are used by many of today's applications, especially Web-based applications. Most database systems are based on the concepts of relational database theory, so you can expect any problems you encounter to be about accessing and manipulating relational data. To do this you'll need to understand basic SQL commands such as `SELECT` and `INSERT`.

Transactions are used to group multiple changes to a database together into a single unit such that either all the changes succeed and are made permanent (the transaction is committed) or all fail and are undone (the transaction is rolled back). The ACID acronym describes the four fundamental properties of a transaction: atomicity, consistency, isolation, and durability. Most relational databases support ACID transactions, although the isolation levels are often variable in order to allow for better performance.

Other Programming Topics

A couple of interview topics are less common than those we've looked at so far. These topics do appear frequently enough in interviews, though, to merit discussion. The first topic is graphics, and the second is bit manipulation. The latter topic in particular often occurs early in an interview as a warm-up to the more-challenging problems.

Graphics

A computer screen consists of pixels arranged in a Cartesian coordinate system. This is commonly called a *raster pixel display*. Computer graphics algorithms change the colors of sets of pixels. Often, the algorithm for generating a raster pixel image is based on a geometric equation. Because a computer screen has a finite number of pixels, translating from a geometric equation to a pixel display can be quite complex. Geometric equations usually have real-number (floating-point) solutions, but pixels are found only at fixed, regularly spaced locations. Therefore, every point that is calculated must be adjusted to pixel coordinates. This requires some kind of rounding, but rounding to the nearest pixel coordinate is not always the correct approach. It is often necessary to round numbers in unusual ways or add error-correcting terms. When rounding is done carelessly, it often leads to gaps in what should be continuous lines. Take care to check your graphics algorithms for distortion or gaps due to poor rounding or error correction.

Consider something as simple as drawing a line segment, for example. Suppose you were trying to implement a function that takes two endpoints and draws a line between them. After doing a little algebra, you could easily get an equation in the form of $y = mx + b$. Then, you could calculate y for a range of x values and draw the points making up the line. This function seems trivial.

The devil, though, is in the details of this problem. First, you must account for vertical lines. In this case, m is infinity, so the simple procedure can't draw the line. Similarly, imagine that the line is not vertical, but close to vertical. For example, suppose that the horizontal distance spanned by the line were 2 pixels, but the vertical distance were 20 pixels. In this case, only two pixels would be drawn — not much of a line. To correct for this problem, you would have to rework your equation to $x = (y - b) / m$. Now, if the line is closer to vertical, then you vary y and use this equation; if it is closer to horizontal, then you use the original procedure.

Even this won't solve all your problems. Suppose you need to draw a line with a slope of 1 — for example, $y = x$. In this case, using either procedure, you would draw the pixels (0, 0), (1, 1), (2, 2) . . . . This is mathematically correct, but the line looks too thin on the screen because the pixels are much more spread out than in other lines. A diagonal line of length 100 has fewer pixels in it than a horizontal line of length 80. An ideal line-drawing algorithm would have some mechanism to guarantee that all lines have nearly equal pixel density.

Another problem involves rounding. If you calculate a point at (.99, .99) and use a type cast to convert this to integers, then the floating-point values will be truncated and the pixel will be drawn at (0, 0). You need to explicitly round the values so that the point is drawn at (1, 1).

If graphics problems seem like never-ending series of special cases, then you understand the issues involved. Note that even if you were to work out all the problems with the line-drawing algorithm described, it still wouldn't be very good. Although this algorithm effectively illustrates the problems encountered in graphics programming, its reliance on floating-point calculations makes it very slow. High-performance algorithms that use only integer math are far more complicated than what is discussed here.

Computer graphics involves drawing with pixels. Always check for rounding errors, gaps, and special cases.

Bit Manipulation

Many computer languages have facilities to allow programmers access to the individual bits of a variable. Bit operators may appear more frequently in interviews than in day-to-day programming, so they merit a review. It's very common to be presented with a "bit twiddling" problem early in the interview, as the problems tend to be short and may have multiple possible answers that enable the interviewer to probe the depth of your knowledge.

Binary Two's Complement Notation

To work with bit operators, you have to start thinking on the levels of bits. Numbers are usually internally represented in a computer in *binary two's complement notation*. If you're already familiar with binary numbers, you almost understand binary two's complement notation, because binary two's complement notation is almost the same as plain binary notation. In fact, it's identical for positive numbers.

The only difference appears with negative numbers. (An integer usually consists of 32 or 64 bits, but to keep things simple the example uses 8-bit integers.) In binary two's complement notation, a positive integer such as 13 is `00001101`, exactly the same as in regular binary notation. Negative numbers are a little trickier. Two's complement notation makes a number negative by applying the rule "flip each bit and add 1" to the number's positive binary representation. For example, to get the number –1, you start with 1, which is `00000001` in binary. Flipping each bit results in `11111110`. Adding 1 gives you `11111111`, which is the two's complement notation for –1. If you're not familiar with this, it may seem weird, but it makes addition and subtraction very simple. For example, you can add `00000001` (1) and `11111111` (-1) simply by adding the binary digits from right to left, carrying values as necessary, to end up with (`00000000`) 0.

The first bit in binary two's complement notation is a sign bit. If the first bit is 0, the number is non-negative; otherwise, it's negative. This has important implications when shifting bits within a number.

Bitwise Operators

Most languages, especially the C-like ones, include a series of *bitwise operators*, operators that affect the individual bits of an integer value. C and C++ bitwise operators share the same syntax and behaviors. The bitwise operators in C#, Java, and JavaScript are the same as the C/C++ except for the shift operators.

The simplest bit operator is the unary operator (~) called *NOT*. This operator flips or reverses all the bits that it operates on. Thus, every 1 becomes a 0, and every 0 becomes a 1. For example, if ~ is applied to `00001101`, then the result is `11110010`.

Three other bitwise operators are | (*OR*), & (*AND*), and ^ (*XOR*). They are all binary operators applied in a bitwise fashion. This means that the ith bit of one number is combined with the ith bit of the other number to produce the ith bit of the resulting value. The rules for these operators are as follows:

&: If both bits are 1, the result is a 1. Otherwise, the result is 0. For example:

```
  01100110
& 11110100
  01100100
```

|: If either bit is a 1, the result is 1. If both bits are 0, the result is 0. For example:

```
  01100110
| 11110100
  11110110
```

^: If the bits are the same, the result is 0. If the bits are different, the result is 1. For example:

```
  01100110
^ 11110100
  10010010
```

Don't confuse the *bitwise* & and | operators with the *logical* && and || operators. The bitwise operators take two integers and return an integer result; the logical operators take two Booleans and return a Boolean result.

The remaining bit operators are the shift operators, operators that shift the bits within a value to the left or the right. C, C++, and C# have left (<<) and right (>>) shift operators. Java and JavaScript have one left shift (<<) operator but two right shift (>> and >>>) operators.

The value to the right of the operator indicates how many positions to shift the bits. For example, 8 << 2 means shift the bits of the value "8" two positions to the left. Bits that "fall off" either end of a value (the overflow bits) are lost.

The << operator is common to all five languages. It shifts the bits to the left, filling the exposed bits on the right with 0. For example, `01100110 << 5` results in `11000000`. Note that the value can change sign depending on the state of the new first bit.

The >> operator is also common to all five languages, but its behavior varies depending on what happens to the exposed bits on the left. When positive numbers are used, the result is always a positive number because 0's are shifted into the empty spaces. However, negative numbers are treated differently. In C and C++, the value of a shifted negative number may be positive or negative, depending on the implementation. Therefore, `10100110 >> 5` may result in either `00000101` or `11111101`. In C#, all the exposed bits except for the first bit are set to 0, but the first bit stays at 1 to keep the number negative. For example, `10100110 >> 5` results in `10000101`. Java and JavaScript perform *sign extension* when shifting right, filling the empty spaces with 1's for negative numbers, so `10100110 >> 5` becomes `11111101`.

The >>> operator is unique to Java and JavaScript. It does a *logical* shift right, filling the empty spaces with 0 no matter what the value, so `10100110 >>> 5` becomes `00000101`.

Optimizing with Shifts

The shift operators enable you to multiply and divide by powers of 2 very quickly. For non-negative numbers, shifting to the right one bit is equivalent to dividing by 2, and shifting to the left one bit is equivalent to multiplying by 2. For negative numbers, it obviously depends on the language being used.

The equivalence of shifting and multiplying or dividing by a power of the base also occurs in the more familiar base 10 number system. Consider the number 17. In base 10, 17 << 1 results in the value 170, which is exactly the same as multiplying 17 by 10. Similarly, 17 >> 1 produces 1, which is the same as integer dividing 17 by 10.

Graphics and Bit Operations Problems

The following problems test your knowledge of basic graphics and bit operations.

Eighth of a Circle

Write a function that draws the upper eighth of a circle centered at (0, 0) with a given radius, where the upper eighth is defined as the portion starting at 12 and going to 1:30 on a clock face. Use the following prototype:

```
void drawEighthOfCircle( int radius );
```

The coordinate system and an example of what you are to draw are shown in Figure 11-1. You will use a function with the following prototype to draw pixels:

```
void setPixel( int xCoord, int yCoord );
```

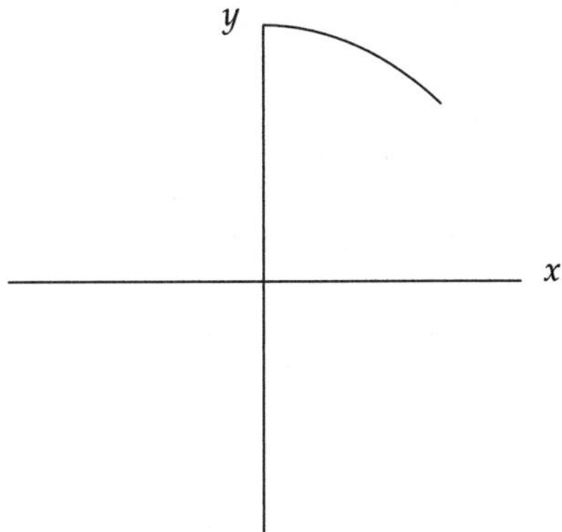

Figure 11-1

This problem is not as contrived as it seems. If you were trying to implement a full-circle drawing routine, you would want to do as little calculation as possible to maintain optimum performance. Given the pixels for one-eighth of a circle, you can easily determine the pixels for the remainder of the circle from symmetry.

If a point (x, y) is on a circle, so are the points (–x, y), (x, –y), (–x, –y), (y, x), (–y, x), (y, –x), and (–y, –x).

This problem is an example of a *scan conversion*, converting a geometric drawing to a pixel-based raster image. You will need an equation for a circle before you can calculate anything. The common mathematical function that produces a circle is as follows:

$$x^2 + y^2 = r^2$$

The definition is nice because it contains x's, y's, and r's, just like your problem and your coordinate system. You have to figure out how to determine pairs of coordinates (x, y) on the circle using the equation, $x^2 + y^2 = r^2$. The easiest way to find a pair of coordinates is to set a value for one and then calculate the other. It's more difficult to set y and calculate x because after the scan conversion there will be several x values for certain y values. Therefore, you should set x and calculate y. Doing some algebra, you can calculate y with the following equation:

$$y = \pm\sqrt{r^2 - x^2}$$

In this problem you are dealing with only positive values of y, so you can ignore the negative root. This produces the following:

$$y = \sqrt{r^2 - x^2}$$

For example, given an x coordinate of 3 and a radius of 5, $y = \sqrt{5^2 - 3^2} = 4$. You now know how to calculate y, given x. Next, you need to determine the range of x values. x clearly starts at 0, but where does it end? Look again at the figure and try to figure out how you visually know that you are at the end of the one-eighth of the circle. In visual terms, this happens when you are farther out then you are up. In mathematical terms, this means that the x value becomes greater than the y value. Thus, you can use the x range from 0 until $x > y$. If you put these pieces together, you have an algorithm for drawing a circle. In outline form, it appears as follows:

```
Start with x = 0 and y = r.
While (y > x)

    Determine the y coordinate using the equation: y = +√(r² − x²)
    Set the pixel (x, y)
    Increment x
```

This algorithm looks correct, but there is a subtle bug in it. The problem arises from treating the y coordinate as an integer, when often y will be a decimal value. For example, if y had the value 9.99, `setPixel` would truncate it to 9, rather than round to the y pixel of 10 as you probably want. One way to solve this problem is to round all values to the nearest whole integer by adding 0.5 to the y value before calling `setPixel`.

This change results in a much better-looking circle. The code for this algorithm is as follows:

```
void drawEighthOfCircle(int radius ){
    int x, y;
    x = 0;
    y = radius;
    while( y <= x ){
        y = Math.sqrt((radius * radius) - (x * x)) + 0.5;
        setPixel( x, y );
        x++;
    }
}
```

What's the efficiency of this algorithm? Its running time is O(n), where n is the number of pixels that you need to set. This is the best possible running time because any algorithm would have to call `setPixel` at least n times to draw the circle correctly. The function also uses the `sqrt` function and multiplies during each iteration of the while loop. The `sqrt` function and the multiplications are likely to be slow operations. Therefore, this function probably isn't practical for most graphical applications where speed is critical. There are faster circle-drawing algorithms that don't make repeated calls to slow functions like `sqrt` or have repeated multiplications, but you wouldn't be expected to implement them during an interview.

Rectangle Overlap

You are given two rectangles, each defined by an upper left (UL) corner and a lower right (LR) corner. Both rectangles' edges will always be parallel to the *x* or *y* axis, as shown in Figure 11-2. Write a function that determines whether the two rectangles overlap. The function should return 1 if the rectangles overlap and 0 if they do not. For convenience, you may use the following classes:

```
class Point {
    public int x;
    public int y;

    public Point( int x, int y ){
        this.x = x;
        this.y = y;
    }
}

class Rect {
    public Point ul;
    public Point lr;

    public Rect( Point ul, Point lr ){
        this.ul = ul;
        this.lr = lr;

    }
}
```

The method should take two `Rect` objects and return true if they overlap, false if they don't.

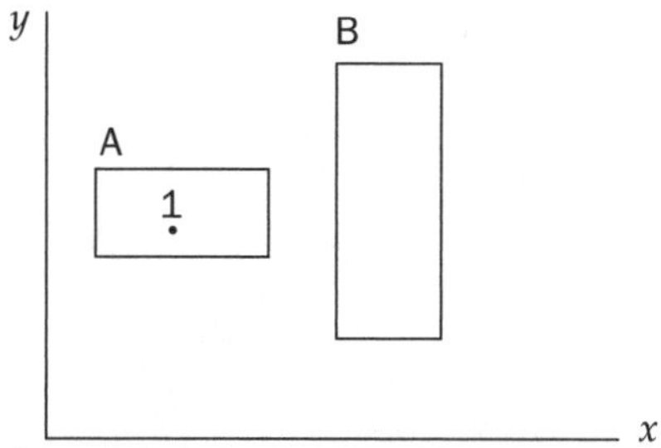

Figure 11-2

Before you jump into the problem, it's important to work out a few properties about rectangles and their vertices. First, given the upper left (UL) point and lower right (LR) corners, it is not difficult to get the upper right (UR) and lower left (LL) corners. The coordinates of the upper right corner are the upper left's *y* and the lower right's *x*. The lower left corner is at the upper left's *x* and the lower right's *y*.

It is also useful to be able to determine whether a point falls inside a rectangle. A point is inside a rectangle if the point's x is greater than the rectangle's UL corner's x and less than the rectangle's LR corner's x, and the point's y is greater than the rectangle's LR corners's y and less than the rectangle's UL corner's y. You can see this in Figure 11-2, where point 1 is inside rectangle A. Now we can move on to the problem.

This problem seems pretty straightforward. Start by considering the ways in which two rectangles can overlap. Try to divide the different ways into various cases. A good place to begin is by examining where the corners of a rectangle end up when it overlaps another. Perhaps you could enumerate the ways in which two rectangles can overlap by counting the number of corners of one rectangle that are inside the other rectangle. The cases that you must consider are when one of the rectangles will have 0, 1, 2, 3, or 4 corners inside the other. Take these cases one at a time. Begin by considering a case in which no corners of either rectangle are inside the other. This is illustrated in Figure 11-3.

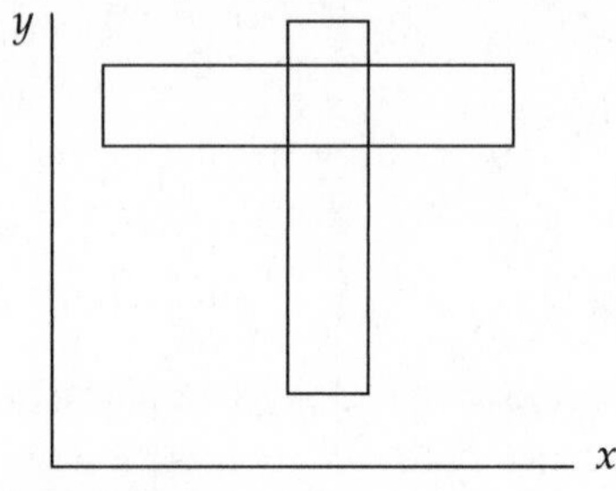

Figure 11-3

Consider what conditions have to be true for two rectangles to overlap without having any corners inside each other. First, the wider rectangle must be shorter than the narrower rectangle. Next, the two rectangles must be positioned so the overlap occurs. This means that the narrower rectangle's x coordinates must be between the wider rectangle's x coordinates and the shorter rectangle's y coordinates must be between the taller rectangle's y coordinates. If all of these conditions are true, you have two rectangles that overlap without having any corners inside of each other.

Now consider the second case, in which rectangles may overlap with one corner inside the other. This is illustrated in Figure 11-4. This case is relatively easy. You can simply check whether any of the four corners of one rectangle are inside the other rectangle.

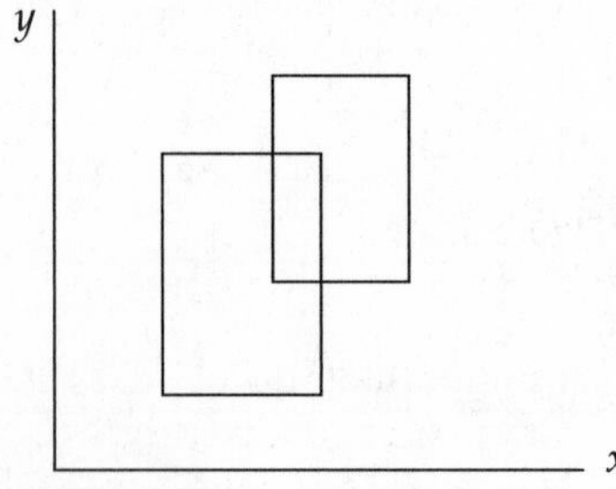

Figure 11-4

In the third case, the rectangles may overlap if two points of one rectangle are inside the other. This occurs when one rectangle is half in and half out of the other rectangle, as illustrated in Figure 11-5. Here, one rectangle has no corners inside the other, and one rectangle has two corners inside the other. If you check the corners of the rectangle with no corners inside the other, you will not find overlap. If you check the rectangle with two corners overlapping, you must check at least three corners to determine overlap. However, you can't determine ahead of time which rectangle will have no corners inside the other. Therefore, you must check three corners of each rectangle to test for overlap properly.

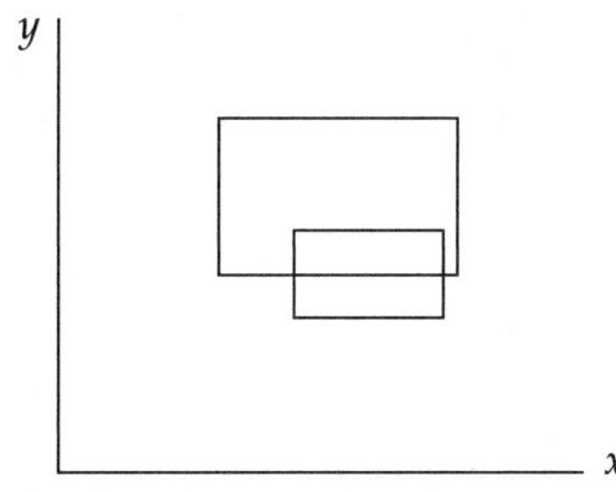

Figure 11-5

The three-point case is very simple: It's just not possible. No matter how you draw the rectangles, you can't arrange them so that one rectangle has exactly three corners inside the other.

The four-corner case is possible. This happens if one rectangle completely subsumes the other, as shown in Figure 11-6. If you check one corner of both rectangles, you can correctly determine overlap in this case.

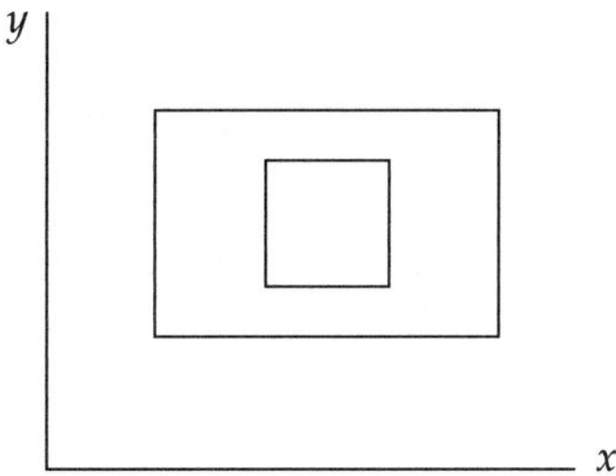

Figure 11-6

Now, put your tests for determining overlap in the zero-corner, one-corner, two-corner, and four-corner cases together to encompass all of these cases. These tests check the widths, heights, and positions of both rectangles, the four corners of one rectangle, the three corners of each rectangle, and the one corner of each rectangle, respectively. You could test each of these cases individually, but that's very repetitive. Instead, try to develop a single test that encompasses all of these cases. Start by checking the widths, heights, and positions of both rectangles to cover the zero-corner case. Next, check the four corners of one rectangle to cover the one-corner case. Then, to include the two-corner case, you'll also have to check three corners of the other rectangle. Luckily, the four-corner case is already covered if you check four corners of one rectangle and three of the other because you're clearly checking one corner of each. The composite test to determine rectangle overlap is to check the following:

- The heights, widths and positions of both rectangles
- Whether any of four corners of one rectangle are inside the other
- Whether any of three corners from the second rectangle are inside the first

This solution to test for overlap is correct, but it seems inefficient. It checks the heights, widths, and positions of both rectangles as well as seven of eight possible corners—and each corner check requires four comparisons. This results in 34 comparisons to calculate the answer.

Perhaps there is a better solution. Another way to think about the problem is to consider when the rectangles don't overlap, as opposed to when they do overlap. If you know when the rectangles don't overlap, you know when they do overlap. The conditions for not overlapping are much more straightforward. Call the two rectangles A and B. A and B do not overlap when A is above B, or A is below B, or A is to the left of B, or A is to the right of B. It is possible for more than one of these conditions to be true at the same time. For example, A could be above and to the right of B. If any one of these conditions is true, the two rectangles do not overlap. The specifics of these conditions can be summarized as follows.

The two rectangles do not overlap when

- A's UL's x value is greater than B's LR's x value or
- A's UL's y value is less than B's LR's y value or
- A's LR's x value is less than B's UL's x value or
- A's LR's y value is greater than B's UL's y value.

This solution is much simpler, requiring only four comparisons and one negation. You can implement the function as follows:

```
boolean overlap( Rect a, Rect b ){
    return !( a.ul.x > b.lr.x ||
              a.ul.y < b.lr.y ||
              a.lr.x < b.ul.x ||
              a.lr.y > b.ul.y );
}
```

This function works, but you can do even better. It's possible to get rid of the logical *NOT*. A bit of logic theory called DeMorgan's Law may be helpful here. This law states the following:

$\neg(\text{A OR B}) = \neg\text{A AND }\neg\text{B}$
$\neg(\text{A AND B}) = \neg\text{A OR }\neg\text{B}$

The symbol ¬ means NOT in the logic world.

In addition, you should recognize that

$\neg(A > B)$ is equivalent to $(B \leq A)$

Working through these rules, you'll get the following function:

```
boolean overlap( Rect a, Rect b){
    return( a.ul.x <= b.lr.x &&
            a.ul.y >= b.lr.y &&
            a.lr.x >= b.ul.x &&
            a.lr.y <= b.ul.y );
}
```

To ensure that you didn't make a mistake, it's a good idea to verify that these conditions make sense. The preceding function determines that two rectangles overlap if

- A's left edge is to the left of B's right edge and
- A's upper edge is above B's bottom edge and
- A's right edge is to the right of B's left edge and
- A's bottom edge is below B's upper edge.

These conditions mean that rectangle B cannot be outside of rectangle A, so there must be some overlap. This makes sense.

Big-endian or Little-endian

Write a function that determines whether a computer is big-endian or little-endian.

This problem tests your knowledge of computer architectures as much as it tests your ability to program. The interviewer wants to know whether you are familiar with the term *endian*. If you are familiar with it, you should define it or at least try to point out the differences between big-endian and little-endian, even if you forget which is which. If you are not familiar with the term, you'll have to ask the interviewer to explain it.

Endianness refers to the order in which a computer stores the bytes of a multibyte value. (Or, technically, the units of a multiunit value — for example, the computer may use a 16-bit unit size instead of an 8-bit unit size. We restrict ourselves to 8-bit units for simplicity, however.) Almost all modern computers use multibyte sequences to represent certain primitive data types.

For example, an integer is usually 4 bytes. The bytes within an integer can be arranged in any order, but they are almost always either least-significant byte (LSB) to most-significant byte (MSB) or MSB to LSB. Significance refers to the place value a byte represents within a multibyte value. If a byte represents the lowest place values in a (two-byte) word the byte is the LSB. For example, in the number 5A6C, 6C is the LSB. Conversely, if a byte represents the highest place values in the word, it is the MSB. In the 5A6C example, 5A is the MSB.

In a big-endian machine the MSB has the lowest address; in a little-endian machine the LSB has the lowest address. For example, a big-endian machine stores the 2-byte hexadecimal value A45C by placing A4 in the first byte and 5C in the second. In contrast, a little-endian machine stores 5C in the first byte and A4 in the second.

Endianness is important to know when reading or writing data structures, especially across networks, so that different applications can communicate with each other. Sometimes the endianness is hidden from the developer: Java uses a fixed endianness to store data, regardless of the underlying platform's endianness, so data exchanges between two Java applications won't normally be affected by endianness. But other languages, C in particular, don't specify an endianness for data storage, leaving the implementation free to choose the endianness that works best for the platform. C is used to solve this problem.

To answer the problem, you have to choose some multibyte data type to work with. It's not important which one you choose, just that the type is more than one byte. A 32-bit integer is a good choice. You need to determine how you can test this integer to figure out which byte is LSB and which is MSB. If you set the value of the integer to 1, you can distinguish between the MSB and the LSB because in an integer with the value 1, the LSB has the value 1 and the MSB has the value 0.

Unfortunately, it's not immediately clear how to access the bytes of an integer. You might try using the bit operators because they allow access to individual bits in a variable. However, they are not particularly useful because the bit operators act as if the bits are arranged in order from least-significant bit to most-significant bit. For example, if you use the shift left operator to shift the integer 8 bits, the operator works on the integer as if it were 32 consecutive bits regardless of the true internal byte order. This property prevents you from using the bit operators to determine byte order.

How might you be able to examine the individual bytes of an integer? A character is a single-byte data type. It could be useful to view an integer as four consecutive characters. To do this, you create a pointer to the integer. Then, you can cast the integer pointer to a character pointer. This enables you to access the integer like an array of 1-byte data types. Using the character pointer, you can examine the bytes and determine the format.

Specifically, to determine the computer's endianness, get a pointer to an integer with the value of 1. Then, cast the pointer to a `char *`. This changes the size of the data to which the pointer points. When you dereference this pointer you access a 1-byte character instead of a 4-byte integer. Thus, you can test the first byte and see if it is 1. If the byte's value is 1, then the machine is little-endian because the LSB is at the lowest memory address. If the byte's value is 0, then the machine is big-endian because the MSB is at the lowest memory address. In outline form, here is the procedure:

```
Set an integer to 1
Cast a pointer to the integer as a char *
If the dereferenced pointer is 1, the machine is little-endian
If the dereferenced pointer is 0, the machine is big-endian
```

The code for this test is as follows:

```
/* Returns true if the machine is little-endian, false if the
 * machine is big-endian
 */
bool endianness(){
    int   testNum;
    char *ptr;

    testNum = 1;
    ptr = (char *) &testNum;
    return (*ptr); /* Returns the byte at the lowest address */
}
```

This solution is sufficient for an interview. However, as the goal of an interview is not just to solve problems, but also to impress your interviewer, you may want to consider a slightly more elegant way to solve this problem. It involves using a feature of C/C++ called `union` types. A union is like a `struct`, except that all of the members are allocated starting at the same location in memory. This enables you to access the same data with different variable types. The syntax is almost identical to a `struct`. Using a `union`, the code is as follows:

```
/* Returns true if the machine is little-endian, false if the
 * machine is big-endian
 */
bool endianness(){
    union {
        int theInteger;
        char singleByte;
    } endianTest;

    endianTest.theInteger = 1;
    return endianTest.singleByte;
}
```

Number of Ones

> **Write a function that determines the number of 1 bits in the computer's internal representation of a given integer.**

This problem may at first sound like a base conversion problem in which you have to design an algorithm to convert a base 10 number to a two's complement binary number. That approach is circuitous because the computer already internally stores its numbers in two's complement binary. Instead of doing a base conversion, try counting the 1's directly.

You can count the number of 1's by checking the value of each bit. Ideally, you'd like to use an operator that would tell you the value of a specified bit. That way, you could iterate over all of the bits and count how many of them were 1's. Unfortunately, this ideal operator doesn't exist.

You can begin by trying to create a procedure that determines the value of each bit using the existing bit operators. Focus on figuring out a way to get the value of the lowest bit. One way to do this is to AND the given integer with the value 1. Let's use 8-bit integers to keep our examples manageable, in which case 1 is stored as 00000001. The result would be either 00000000 if the given integer's lowest bit had the value 0, or 00000001 if the given integer's lowest bit had the value 1. In general, you can get the value of any bit if you create the correct *mask*. In this case, the mask is an integer with all the bits set to 0 except the bit you're checking, which is set to 1. When you AND a mask with the value you're checking, the result is either a 0, indicating that the bit you are checking has the value 0, or a non-zero result, indicating that the bit you are checking has the value 1.

You could create a mask for each of the bits and count the number of 1 bits. For example, the first mask would be 00000001, followed by masks of 00000010, 00000100, 00001000, and so on. This would work, but your interviewer probably doesn't want to watch you write out that many masks. Consider the differences between each mask. Each mask is the same as the previous mask, but the 1 bit is moved one place to the left. Instead of predefining your masks, you can construct them using the shift left operator. Simply start with a mask of 00000001 and repeatedly shift the integer one bit to the left to generate all the necessary masks. This is a good technique, and if you work it out to its conclusion, it yields an acceptable answer. However, there's a prettier and slightly faster solution that uses only one mask.

Think about what you can do with a single mask. You are trying to examine each bit of the integer, so you need to mask a different bit on each iteration. So far, you've been accomplishing this by shifting the mask and keeping the integer in place, but if you shifted the integer, you could examine all of its bits using the same mask. The most natural mask to use is 00000001, which yields the least-significant bit. If you keep shifting the integer right, each bit will eventually become the rightmost bit. Try working through 00000101 as an example. The rightmost bit is 1 so you would add 1 to your count and shift the integer right, yielding 00000010. This time the rightmost bit is 0. Shifting right again produces 00000001. The least significant bit in this integer is 1, so you would increment your count to 2. When you shift right a third time, the integer becomes 00000000. When the integer's value reaches zero there are no 1 bits remaining, so you can stop counting. As in this example, you may not have to iterate through all the bits to count all the 1's, so in many cases this algorithm is more efficient than the multiple mask algorithm. In outline, the single mask algorithm is as follows:

```
Start with count = 0
While the integer is not 0
    If the integer AND 1 equals 1, increment count
    Shift the integer one bit to the right
Return count
```

Finally, check for any error cases in this code; you'll want to look for problems with positive numbers, negative numbers, and zero. If the integer has the value of 0, the algorithm immediately and correctly returns that there are zero 1's in the binary representation. Now consider the case where you are passed a negative number. The number will be shifted to the right, but the new bit added on the left will depend on how the shift operator treats negative values. Let's avoid the problem entirely and use Java's >>> operator for our example. In the other C-like languages, you can also avoid the problem by reading the value as an unsigned integer. (That solution doesn't work with Java because there are no unsigned integer types in Java.) Using either the >>> or an unsigned integer means that the shift operator will not sign extend, and the new bits that are added during the right shifting will be 0's. The number will eventually become all 0's. Finally, consider the case where you are given a positive integer. This is the sample case that you worked with, and the algorithm works correctly here.

The code for this algorithm is as follows:

```
int numOnesInBinary( int number )
{
     int numOnes = 0;
     while( number != 0 ){
          if( ( number & 1 ) == 1 )
               numOnes++;
          number = number >>> 1;
     }
     return numOnes;
}
```

What's the running time of this function? The function will iterate through the `while` loop until all the 1's have been counted. In the best case, the given integer is 0, and the function never executes the while loop. In the worst case, this is O(n), where n is the size, in bits, of an integer.

Unless you're incredibly good at bitwise operations, this is the best solution you're likely to come up with in an interview. There are better solutions, though. Consider what happens at the bit level when you subtract 1 from a number. Subtracting 1 produces a value that has all the same bits as the original integer except that all the low bits up to and including the lowest 1 are flipped. For example, subtracting 1 from the value 01110000 results in the value 01101111.

If you apply the AND operation to the integer and the result of the subtraction, the result is a new number that is the same as the original integer except that the rightmost 1 is now a 0. For example, 01110000 AND (01110000 – 1) = 01110000 AND 01101111 = 01100000.

You can count the number of times that you can perform this process before the integer's value reaches 0. This is the number of 1's in the computer's representation of the number. In outline form this algorithm is as follows:

```
Start with count = 0
While the integer is not zero
    AND the integer with the integer - 1
    Increment count
Return count
```

Here is the code:

```
int numOnesInBinary( int number ){
     int numOnes = 0;
     while( number != 0 ){
          number = number & (number - 1);
          numOnes++;
     }
     return numOnes;
}
```

This solution has a running time of O(m), where m is the number of 1's in the solution. There may be even better solutions. Keep in mind that this solution was presented for interest, and the first solution is all that would be expected in an interview.

Summary

Problems involving bit manipulation and computer graphics are fairly common in interviews, especially bit-manipulation problems. As such, it's best to be prepared to handle some simple problems on these topics. The graphics problems likely won't be very advanced, unless of course you're applying for a graphics-oriented position. Concentrate more on the bit-manipulation problems, which are often one of the first problems presented during an interview.

Counting, Measuring, and Ordering Puzzles

In addition to technical and programming problems, you will often encounter brainteasers in your interviews. Brainteasers are mathematics and logic puzzles that have no direct relation to computer programming. Some interviewers feel these problems are silly because they have no direct bearing on the job at hand and won't ask any of them. Many interviewers, though, think brainteasers are useful in assessing problem-solving ability — perhaps the most important job skill for a programmer. Interviewers may also be influenced by the knowledge that industry leaders such as Google use brainteasers in their interviews. Whatever the motivation, in some interviews as many as a third of the problems you are presented may be brainteasers.

In the authors' opinion, performance on brainteasers says a lot about your experience with working mathematical puzzles and very little about whether you will be a valuable employee. The discussion and examples in this and the next chapter aim to give you this experience so you can be successful with brainteasers. Brainteasers share many common themes, so gaining both familiarity with these commonalities and some experience with brainteasers in general can be a great help in solving these puzzles when they are presented during an interview.

Tackling Brainteasers

One of the most important themes to keep in mind is that the solutions to brainteasers are almost never straightforward or obvious. Unlike the programming or technical parts of the interview, where you will sometimes be given simple problems just to see whether you know something, brainteasers always require thought and effort. This means that any solution that seems immediately obvious is probably incorrect or not the best solution. For example, suppose you're asked, "From the time you get on a ski lift to the time you get off, what proportion of the chairs do you pass?" Most people's immediate gut-level response is that you pass half of the chairs. This response is obvious and makes some sense. At any given time, half of the chairs are on each side of the lift, and you pass chairs only on the other side. It's also wrong — because both sides of the lift are moving, you pass all the other chairs.

This answer assumes you get on and off at the extreme ends of the lift. On most real ski lifts, you pass almost all the other chairs.

This property of brainteasers works most strongly to your advantage when you are faced with a problem that has only two possible answers (for example, any *yes or no* question). Whichever answer seems at first to be correct is probably wrong. Of course, it's probably not a good idea to say, "The answer must be yes because if it were no this would be a very simple problem and you wouldn't have bothered to ask it." You can, however, use this knowledge to guide your thinking.

Remember that the obvious answer is almost never the right answer.

Although the correct solutions to brainteasers are usually complex, they rarely require time-consuming computations or mathematics beyond trigonometry. Just as writing pages of code is a warning sign that you're headed in the wrong direction, using calculus or spending a long time number-crunching is a strong indicator that you're not headed toward the best solution to one of these puzzles.

Solve the Right Problem

Many of these problems are difficult because they suggest an incorrect assumption that leads you to the wrong answer. Based on this knowledge, you might conclude that the best approach is to avoid making any assumptions. Unfortunately, that's not really practical — even understanding a problem is very difficult without making a whole series of assumptions. For example, suppose you are given the problem of finding an arrangement that maximizes the number of oranges you can fit in the bottom of a square box. You would probably automatically assume that the oranges are small spherical fruit, that they are all about the same size, that "in the bottom" means in contact with the bottom surface of the box, and that the oranges must remain intact (you can't puree them and pour them in). These assumptions may seem ridiculous — they are all rather obvious and they are all correct. The point is that assumptions are inherent in all communication or thought; you can't begin to work on a problem without assumptions.

Carrying this example further, you might assume you could model this problem in 2D using circles in a square, and that the solution would involve some sort of orderly, repeating pattern. Based on these assumptions and the knowledge that a honeycomb-like hexagonal array provides the tightest pack of circles covering a plane, you might conclude that the best solution is to place the oranges in a regular hexagonal array. Depending on the relative sizes of the oranges and the box, this conclusion would be incorrect.

Although you can't eliminate assumptions, it can be useful to try to identify and analyze them. As you identify your assumptions, categorize them as almost certainly correct, probably correct, or possibly incorrect. Starting with the assumption you feel is least likely to be correct, try reworking the problem without each assumption. Keep in mind that these puzzles are rarely trick questions, so your definitional assumptions are usually correct.

For instance, in the preceding example, it would be reasonable to classify the assumptions that oranges are spherical fruit and that they must remain intact and in contact with the bottom of the box as almost certainly correct. How would you categorize the assumption that you can reduce this puzzle to a 2D problem of circles in a square? If you think about it, you can see that the oranges make contact with each other in a single plane, and that in this plane you're essentially dealing with circles inside a square. This isn't exactly a proof, but it's solid enough to decide that this assumption is probably correct. On the other hand, you'll find you have more trouble supporting the assumption that the oranges should be in an orderly repeating pattern. It seems reasonable, and it is true for an infinite plane, but it's not clear that the similarities between a plane and the box bottom are sufficient for this assumption to be true. In general, beware of any assumption that you "feel" is true but can't quite explain — this is often the incorrect assumption. You would therefore conclude that the assumption that the oranges must form an ordered array is possibly incorrect. In fact, this assumption *is* incorrect. In many cases the best packing involves putting most of the oranges in an ordered array and the remaining few in unordered positions. Analyzing your assumptions is a particularly good strategy when you think you've found the only logically possible solution but you're told it's incorrect. It's often the case that your logic was good but based on a flawed assumption.

If the solution that seems logical is wrong, you made a false assumption. Categorize your assumptions, and try to identify those that are false.

Don't Be Intimidated

Some problems are intimidating because they are so complex or difficult that you can't see a path to the solution. You may not even know where to start. Don't let this lock you up. You don't have to devise a plan for getting all the way to the solution before you start — things will come to you as you work:

- ❑ **Break a problem into parts** — If you can identify a subproblem, try solving that, even if you're not sure it's critical to solving the main problem.
- ❑ **Try a simplified problem** — Try solving a simplified version of the problem; you may gain insights that will be useful in solving the full problem.
- ❑ **Try specific examples** — If the problem involves some sort of process, try working through a few specific examples. You may notice a pattern you can generalize to other cases. Above all, keep talking, keep thinking, and keep working.

The pieces of the puzzle are much more likely to fall into place when your mind is in motion than when you are sitting at the starting line praying for a revelation. Even if you don't make much progress, it looks much better to the interviewer when you actively attack a problem than when you sit back stumped, looking clueless and overwhelmed.

Remember that you came to the interview to demonstrate that you will be a valuable employee. Analyzing the problems and patiently trying a variety of approaches shows this almost as well as solving problems does.

Don't be intimidated by complexity. Try a subproblem, a simplified version, or some examples. Be patient, keep working, and keep talking.

Beware of Simple Problems

Other problems are tricky for the opposite reason: They are so simple or restricted that it seems that there's no way to solve the problem within the given constraints. In these circumstances, brainstorming can be useful. Try to enumerate all the possible actions that are legal within the constraints of the problem, even those that seem counterproductive. If the problem involves physical objects, consider every object, the properties of every object, what you might do to or with each object, and how the objects might interact.

When you're stuck on a problem like this, there may be something allowed by the problem that you're missing. If you make a list of everything allowed by the constraints of the problem, it will include the key to the solution that hasn't occurred to you. It's often easier to enumerate all the possibilities than it is to specifically come up with the one thing you haven't thought of.

When you do this enumeration, don't do it silently; think aloud or write it down. This shows the interviewer what you're doing and helps you be more methodical and thorough.

When you're stuck on a simple, restricted problem, brainstorm all the possibilities to identify the one you're missing.

Estimation Problems

There's one more type of problem worth discussing. This is the estimation problem, where you're asked to use a rational process to estimate the size of some statistic you don't know. These problems are relatively rare in interviews for pure development positions, but they may be more common in interviews for jobs that include a significant management or business aspect. One estimation problem is "How many gas stations are there in the United States?" It has been so widely reported that this problem was posed by Microsoft that it seems almost certain to be apocryphal; nevertheless, it is a good example.

These problems are usually not difficult compared with the more common brainteasers. You're not expected to know the actual statistic or fact. Instead, you are expected to do a rough order of magnitude calculation based on facts you do know. Because everything is an estimate anyway, try to adjust or round your figures so that any large numbers you use are powers (or at least multiples) of ten — this will significantly simplify your arithmetic.

Taking the gas station problem as an example, your calculation might go like this: "It takes me about six minutes to fill up my car. I go to the gas station about once a week, and there are usually two other cars there. If I assume this is average for Americans, each gas station services about 30 cars an hour. Suppose a gas station were open 12 hours a day, 7 days a week. That would be 84 hours a week. In reality, a gas station is probably open more than 12 hours a day, so I'll say the average gas station is open 100 hours a week. That means it services 3,000 cars a week. There's somewhere upwards of 250 million people in the United States. Not everyone has a car, so suppose there are 100 million cars on the road. If every car goes to the gas station once a week, like mine does, and each station sees 3,000 cars a week, there would have to be about 33,000 gas stations in the United States." This figure is probably off by a lot, but it's likely within an order of magnitude (that is, there are more than 3,300 gas stations and fewer than 330,000). It's much more important that you are able to form a framework for the estimation and rapidly work through the calculations than that you accurately estimate the statistic. For more practice, try estimating the number of kindergarten teachers in your state, the circumference of the earth, and the weight of a ferry boat.

Brainteaser Problems

Brainteasers draw from a much broader and more diverse body of knowledge than programming and technical problems, so a comprehensive review isn't possible here. The following brainteasers will hone your problem-solving skills in preparation for an interview.

Count Open Lockers

Suppose you are in a hallway lined with 100 closed lockers. You begin by opening all 100 lockers. Next, you close every second locker. Then you go to every third locker and close it if it is open or open it if it is closed (call this *toggling* the locker). You continue toggling every *n*th locker on pass number *n*. After your hundredth pass of the hallway, in which you toggle only locker number 100, how many lockers are open?

In a hall with *k* lockers, how many lockers remain open after pass *k*?

This problem is designed to seem overwhelming. You don't have time to draw a diagram of 100 lockers and count 100 passes through them. Even if you did, solving the problem that way wouldn't illustrate any skill or intuition, so there must be some trick that can be used to determine how many doors will be open. You just have to figure out what that trick is.

It's unlikely that you're going to be able to intuit the solution to this problem by just staring at it. What can you do? Although it's not practical to solve the entire problem by brute force, solving a few lockers in this manner is reasonable. Perhaps you'll notice some patterns you can apply to the larger problem.

Start by choosing an arbitrary locker, 12, and determining whether it will end open or closed. On which passes will you toggle locker 12? Obviously on the first pass, when you toggle every locker, and on the twelfth pass when you start with 12. You don't need to consider any pass after 12 because those will all start farther down the hall. This leaves passes 2 through 11. You can count these out: 2, 4, 6, 8, 10, **12** (you toggle on pass 2); 3, 6, 9, **12** (on 3); 4, 8, **12** (on 4); 5, 10, 15 (not on 5); 6, **12** (on 6); 7, 14 (not on 7), and so on. Somewhere in the middle of this process, you will probably notice that you toggle locker 12 only when the number of the pass you're on is a factor of 12. If you think about this, it makes sense: When counting by *n*, you hit 12 only when some integer number of *n*'s add to 12, which is another way of saying that *n* is a factor of 12. Though it seems simple in retrospect, this probably wasn't obvious before you worked out an example.

The factors of 12 are 1, 2, 3, 4, 6, and 12. Correspondingly, the operations on the locker door are open, close, open, close, open, close. So locker 12 will end closed. The solution seems to have something to do with factors. Primes are numbers with unique factor properties. Perhaps it would be instructive to investigate a prime numbered locker. You might select 17 as a representative prime. The factors are 1 and 17, so the operations are open, close. It ends closed just like 12. Apparently primes are not necessarily different from nonprimes for the purposes of this problem.

What generalizations can you make about whether a locker ends open or closed? All lockers start closed and alternate between being open and closed. So lockers are closed after the second, fourth, sixth, and so on, times they are toggled — in other words, if a locker is toggled an even number of times, then it ends closed; otherwise, it ends open. You know that a locker is toggled once for every factor of the locker number, so you can say that a locker ends open only if it has an odd number of factors.

The task has now been reduced to finding how many numbers between 1 and 100 have an odd number of factors. The two you've examined (and most others, if you try a few more examples) have even numbers of factors. Why is that? If a number i is a factor of n, what does that mean? It means that i times some other number j is equal to n. Of course, because multiplication is commutative ($i \times j = j \times i$), that means that j is a factor of n, too, so the number of factors is usually even because factors tend to come in pairs. If you can find the numbers that have unpaired factors, you will know which lockers will be open. Multiplication is a binary operation, so two numbers will always be involved, but what if they are both the same number (that is, $i = j$)? In that case, a single number would effectively form both halves of the pair and there would be an odd number of factors. When this is the case, $i \times i = n$. Therefore, n would have to be a perfect square. Try a perfect square to check this solution. For example, for 16, the factors are 1, 2, 4, 8, 16; operations are open, close, open, close, open—as expected, it ends open.

Based on this reasoning, you can conclude that only lockers with numbers that are perfect squares end open. The perfect squares between 1 and 100 (inclusive) are 1, 4, 9, 16, 25, 36, 49, 64, 81, and 100. So 10 lockers would remain open.

Similarly, for the general case of k lockers, the number of open lockers is the number of perfect squares between 1 and k, inclusive. How can you best count these? The perfect squares themselves are inconvenient to count because they're unevenly spaced. However, the square roots of the perfect squares greater than zero are the positive integers. These are very easy to count: The last number in the list of square roots gives the number of items in each list. For example, the square roots of 1, 4, 9, 16, and 25 are 1, 2, 3, 4, and 5; the last number in the list of square roots is the square root of the largest perfect square and is equal to the number of perfect squares. You need to find the square root of the largest perfect square less than or equal to k.

This task is trivial when k is a perfect square, but most of the time it won't be. In these cases, the square root of k will be a noninteger. If you round this square root down to the nearest integer, then its square is the largest perfect square less than k—just what you were looking for. The operation of rounding to the largest integer less than or equal to a given number is often called *floor*. Thus, in the general case of k lockers, there will be *floor(sqrt(k))* lockers remaining open.

The key to solving this problem is trying strategies to solve parts of the problem even when it isn't clear how these parts will contribute to the overall solution. Although some attempts, such as the investigation of prime numbered lockers, may not be fruitful, others are likely to lead to greater insight about how to attack the problem, such as the strategy of calculating the result for a single locker. Even in the worst case, where none of the things you try lead you closer to the final solution, you show the interviewer that you aren't intimidated by difficult problems with no clear solution and that you are willing to keep trying different approaches until you find one that works.

Three Switches

You are standing in a hallway next to three light switches, all of which are off. Each switch operates a different incandescent light bulb in the room at the end of the hall. You cannot see the lights from where the switches are. Determine which light corresponds to each switch. You may go into the room with the lights only once.

The crux of this problem comes quickly to the fore: There are only two possible positions for each switch (on or off) but there are three lights to identify. You can easily identify one light, by setting one switch differently than the other two, but this leaves you no way to distinguish the two left in the same position.

When confronted with a seemingly impossible task, you should go back to basics. The two key objects in this problem seem to be the switches and the lights. What do you know about switches and light bulbs? Switches make or break an electrical connection. When a switch is on, current flows through it. A light bulb consists of a resistive filament inside an evacuated glass bulb. When current flows through the filament, it consumes power, producing light and heat.

How can these properties help you solve the problem? Which of them can you detect or measure? The properties of a switch don't seem too useful. It's much easier to look at the switch to see whether it's off or on than to measure current. The light bulbs sound a little more promising. You can detect light by looking at the bulbs, and you can detect heat by touching them. Whether there is light coming from a bulb is determined entirely by its switch — when the switch is on, there is light; when it's off, there isn't. What about heat? It takes some time for a light to heat up after it's been switched on, and some time for it to cool after it's switched off, so you could use heat to determine whether a bulb had *been* on, even if it were off when you walked into the room.

You can determine which switch goes with each bulb by turning the first switch on and the second and third off. After ten minutes, turn the first switch off, leave the second off, and turn the third on. When you go into the room, the hot dark bulb corresponds to the first switch, the cold dark bulb to the second, and the lit bulb to the third.

Although there's nothing truly outlandish about this question — it's not just a stupid play on words, for instance — it is arguably a trick question. The solution involves coming up with something somewhat outside the definition of the problem. Some interviewers believe that questions like this will help them identify people who can "think outside the box" and develop nontraditional, innovative solutions to difficult problems. In the authors' opinion, these problems are cheap shots that don't prove much of anything. Nevertheless, these problems do appear in interviews, and you should be prepared for them.

Bridge Crossing

A party of four travelers comes to a rickety bridge at night. The bridge can hold the weight of at most two of the travelers at a time, and it cannot be crossed without using a flashlight. The travelers have one flashlight among them. Each traveler walks at a different speed: The first can cross the bridge in 1 minute, the second in 2 minutes, the third in 5 minutes, and the fourth takes 10 minutes to cross the bridge. If two travelers cross together, they walk at the speed of the slower traveler.

What is the least amount of time in which all the travelers can cross from one side of the bridge to the other?

Because there is only one flashlight, each trip to the far side of the bridge (except the last trip) must be followed by a trip coming back. Each of these trips consists of either one or two travelers crossing the bridge. To get a net movement of travelers to the far side of the bridge, you probably want to have two travelers on each outbound trip and one on each inbound trip. This strategy gives you a total of five trips, three outbound and two inbound. Your task is to assign travelers to the trips so that you minimize the total time for the five trips. For clarity, you can refer to each traveler by the number of minutes it takes him to cross the bridge.

Number 1 can cross the bridge at least twice as fast as any of the other travelers, so you can minimize the time of the return trips by always having 1 bring the flashlight back. This suggests a strategy whereby 1 escorts each of the other travelers across the bridge one by one.

One possible arrangement of trips using this strategy is illustrated in Figure 12-1. The order in which 1 escorts the other travelers doesn't change the total time: The three outbound trips have times of 2, 5, and 10 minutes, and the two inbound trips are 1 minute each, for a total of 19 minutes.

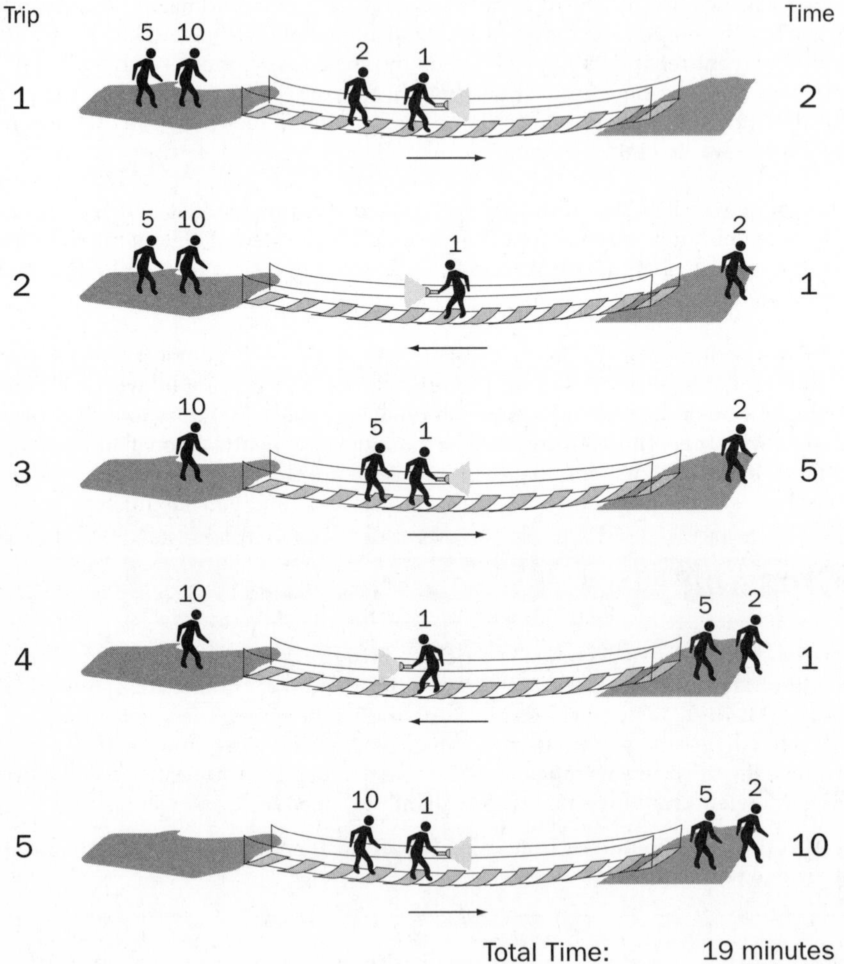

Figure 12-1

This solution is logical, obvious, and doesn't take long to discover. In short, it can't possibly be the best solution to an interview problem. Your interviewer would tell you that you can do better than 19 minutes, but even without that hint you should guess you arrived at the preceding solution too easily.

This puts you in an uncomfortable, but unfortunately not unusual, position. You know your answer is wrong, yet based on the assumptions you made, it's the only reasonable answer. It's easy to get frustrated at this point. You may wonder if this is a trick question: Perhaps you're supposed to throw the flashlight back or have the second pair use a lantern. No such tricks are necessary here. A more-efficient arrangement of trips exists. Because the only solution that seems logical is wrong, you must have made a false assumption.

Consider your assumptions, checking each one to see if it might be false. First among your assumptions was that outbound and inbound trips must alternate. This seems correct—there's no way to have an outbound trip followed by another outbound trip because the flashlight would be on the wrong side of the bridge.

Next, you assumed that there would be two travelers on each outbound trip and one on each return trip. This seems logical, but it's harder to prove. Putting two travelers on an inbound trip seems terribly counterproductive; after all, you're trying to get them to the far side of the bridge. An outbound trip with only one traveler is potentially more worthwhile, but coupled with the requisite return trip all it really accomplishes is exchanging the positions of two travelers. Exchanging two travelers might be useful, but it will probably waste too much time to be worth it. Because this possibility doesn't look promising, try looking for a false assumption elsewhere and reconsider this one if necessary.

You also assumed that 1 should always bring the flashlight back. What basis do you have for this assumption? It minimizes the time for the return trips, but the goal is to minimize total time, not return trip time. Perhaps the best overall solution does not involve minimized return trip times. The assumption that 1 should always return the flashlight seems hard to support, so it probably merits further examination.

If you're not going to have 1 make all the return trips, then how will you arrange the trips? You might try a process of elimination. You obviously can't have 10 make a return trip, because then he'd have at least three trips, which would take 30 minutes. Even without getting the remaining travelers across, this is already worse than your previous solution. Similarly, if 5 makes a return trip then you have two trips that are at least 5 minutes, plus one that takes 10 minutes (when 10 crosses). Just those three trips total 20 minutes, so you won't find a better solution by having 5 make a return trip.

You might also try analyzing some of the individual trips from your previous solution. Because 1 escorted everyone else, there was a trip with 1 and 10. In a sense, when you send 1 with 10, 1's speed is wasted on that trip because the crossing still takes 10 minutes. Looking at that from a different perspective, any trip that includes 10 *always* takes 10 minutes, no matter which other traveler goes along. Therefore, if you're going to have to spend 10 minutes on a trip, you might as well take advantage of it and get another slow traveler across. This reasoning indicates that 10 should cross with 5, rather than with 1.

Using this strategy, you might begin by sending 10 and 5 across. However, one of them has to bring the flashlight back, which you already know isn't the right solution. You'll want to already have someone faster than 5 waiting on the far side. Try starting by sending 1 and 2 across. Then have 1 bring the flashlight back. Now that there's someone reasonably fast (2) on the far side, you can send 5 and 10 across together. Then 2 returns the flashlight. Finally, 1 and 2 cross the bridge again. This scheme is illustrated in Figure 12-2.

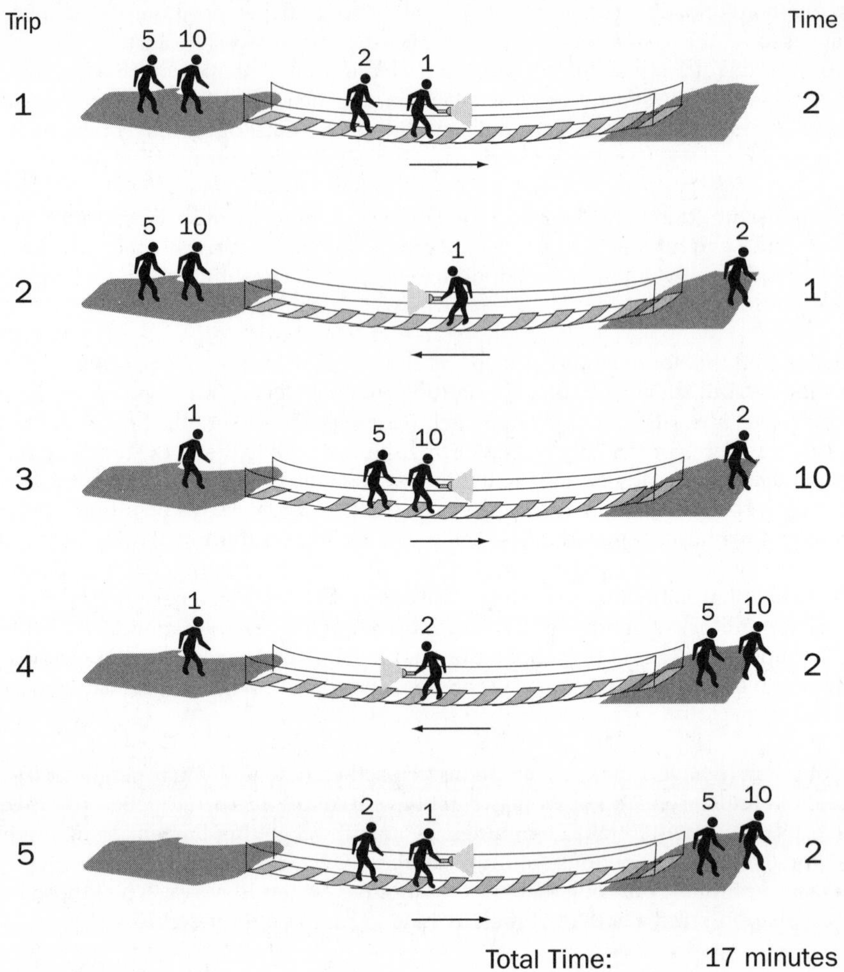

Figure 12-2

The times for the respective trips under this strategy are 2, 1, 10, 2, and 2, for a total of 17 minutes. Identifying the false assumption improved your solution by 2 minutes.

This problem is a slightly unusual example of a class of problems involving optimizing the process of moving a group of items a few at a time from one place to another. More commonly, the goal is to minimize the total number of trips, and there are often restrictions on which items can be left together. This particular problem is difficult because it suggests a false assumption (that 1 should escort each of the other travelers) that seems so obvious you may not even realize you're making an assumption.

Heavy Marble

You have eight marbles and a two-pan balance. All the marbles weigh the same, except for one, which is heavier than all the others. The marbles are otherwise indistinguishable. You may make no assumptions about how much heavier the heavy marble is. What is the minimum number of weighings needed to be certain of identifying the heavy marble?

The first step in solving this problem is to realize that you can put more than one marble in each pan of the balance. If you have equal numbers of marbles in each pan, then the heavy marble must be in the group on the heavy side of the balance. This saves you from having to weigh each marble individually, and it enables you to eliminate many marbles in a single weighing.

Once you realize this, you are likely to devise a binary search-based strategy for finding the heavy marble. In this method, you begin by putting half of the marbles on each side of the balance. Then you eliminate the marbles from the light side of the balance and divide the marbles from the heavy side of the balance between the two pans. As shown in Figure 12-3, you continue this process until each pan holds only one marble, at which point the heavy marble is the only marble on the heavy side of the balance. Using this process you can always identify the heavy marble in three weighings.

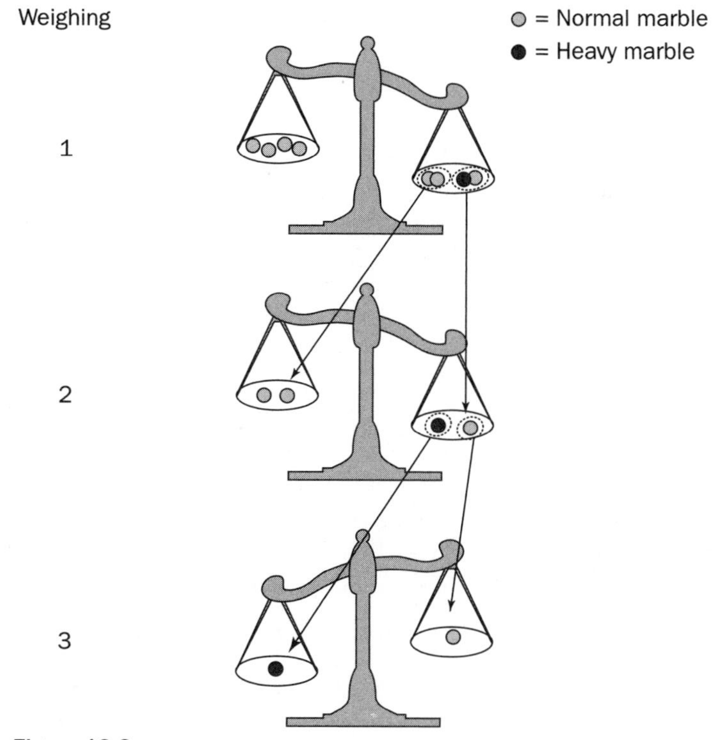

Figure 12-3

This may seem to be the correct answer. The solution wasn't completely obvious, and it's an improvement over weighing the marbles one by one. If you're telling yourself that this seemed too easy, you're right. The method described so far is a good start, but it's not the best you can do.

How can you find the heavy marble in fewer than three weighings? Obviously, you'll have to eliminate more than half the marbles at each weighing, but how can you do that?

Try looking at this problem from an information flow perspective. Information about the marbles comes from the balance, and you use this information to identify the heavy marble. The more information you derive from each weighing, the more efficient your search for the marble will be. Think about how you get information from the balance: You place marbles on it and then look at the result. What are all the possible results? The left pan side could be heavier, the right side could be heavier, or both sides could weigh exactly the same. So there are three possible results, but so far you've been using only two of them. In effect, you're only using ⅔ of the information that each weighing provides. Perhaps if you alter your method so that you use all of the information from each weighing you will be able to find the heavy marble in fewer weighings.

Using the binary search strategy, the heavy marble is always in one of the two pans, so there will always be a heavy side of the balance. In other words, you can't take advantage of all the information the balance can provide if the heavy marble is always on the balance. What if you divided the marbles into three equal-sized groups, and weighed two of the groups on the balance? Just as before, if either side of the balance is heavier, you know that the heavy marble is in the group on that side. But now it's also possible that the two groups of marbles on the balance will weigh the same — in this case, the heavy marble must be in the third group that's not on the balance. Because you divided the marbles into three groups, keeping just the group with the heavy marble eliminates ⅔ of the marbles instead of half of them. This seems promising.

There's still a minor wrinkle to work out before you can apply this process to the problem at hand. Eight isn't evenly divisible by three, so you can't divide the eight marbles into three equal groups. Why do you need the same number of marbles in each group? You need the same number of marbles so that when you put the groups on the balance the result doesn't have anything to do with differing numbers of marbles on each side. Really, you need only two of the groups to be the same size. You'll still want all three groups to be approximately the same size so you can eliminate approximately ⅔ of the marbles after each weighing no matter which pile has the heavy marble.

Now you can apply the three-group technique to the problem you were given. Begin by dividing the marbles into two groups of three, which you put on the balance, and one group of two, which you leave off. If the two sides weigh the same, the heavy marble is in the group of two, and you can find it with one more weighing, for a total of two weighings. On the other hand, if either side of the balance is heavier, the heavy marble must be in that group of three. You can eliminate all the other marbles, and place one marble from this group on either side of the balance, leaving the third marble aside. If one side is heavier, it contains the heavy marble; if neither side is heavier, the heavy marble is the one you didn't place on the balance. This is also a total of two weighings, so you can always find the heavy marble in a group of eight using two weighings. An example of this process is illustrated in Figure 12-4.

Generalize your solution. What is the minimum number of weighings to find a heavy marble among *n* marbles?

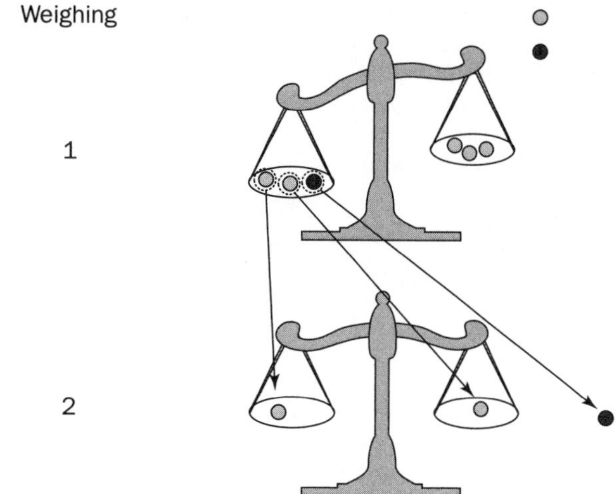

Figure 12-4

This is the part where the interviewer determines whether you hit on the preceding solution by luck or because you really understand it. Think about what happens after each weighing. You eliminate ⅔ of the marbles and keep ⅓. After each weighing you have ⅓ as many marbles as you did before. When you get down to one marble, you've found the heavy marble.

Based on this reasoning, you can reformulate the question as, "How many times do you have to divide the number of marbles by 3 before you end up with 1?" If you start with 3 marbles, you divide by 3 once to get 1, so it takes one weighing. If you start with 9 marbles you divide by 3 twice, so it takes two weighings. Similarly, 27 marbles require three weighings. What mathematical operation can you use to represent this "How many times do you divide by 3 to get to 1" process?

Because multiplication and division are inverse operations, the number of times you have to divide the number of marbles by 3 before you end up with 1 is the same as the number of times you have to multiply by 3 (starting at 1) before you get to the number of marbles. Repeated multiplication is expressed using exponents. If you want to express multiplying by 3 twice, you can write 3^2, which is equal to 9. When you multiply twice by 3 you get 9—it takes two weighings to find the heavy marble among 9 marbles. In more general terms, it takes *i* weighings to find the heavy marble from among *n* marbles, where $3^i = n$. You know the value of *n* and want to calculate *i*, so you need to solve this for *i*. You can solve for *i* using logarithms, the inverse operation of exponentiation. If you take $\log_3$ of both sides of the preceding equation you get $i = \log_3 n$.

This works fine as long as *n* is a power of 3. However, if *n* isn't a power of 3, then this equation calculates a noninteger value for *i*, which doesn't make much sense, given that it's extremely difficult to perform a fractional weighing. For example, if $n = 8$, as in the previous part of the problem, $\log_3 8$ is some number between 1 and 2 (1.893 . . . to be a little more precise). From your previous experience, you know it actually takes two weighings when you have eight marbles. This seems to indicate that if you calculate a fractional number of weighings you should round it up to the nearest integer.

Does this make sense? Try applying it to $n = 10$ and see whether you can justify always rounding up. $\log_3 9$ is 2, so $\log_3 10$ will be a little more than two, or three if you round up to the nearest integer. Is that the correct number of weighings for 10 marbles? For 10 marbles, you would start out with two groups of 3 and one group of 4. If the heavy marble were in either of the groups of 3, you could find it with just one more weighing, but if it turned out to be in the group of 4 you might need as many as two more weighings for a total of 3, just as you calculated. In this case the fractional weighing seems to represent a weighing that you might need to make under some circumstances (if the heavy marble happens to be in the larger group) but not others. Because you're trying to calculate the number of weighings needed to guarantee you'll find the heavy marble, you have to count that fractional weighing as a full weighing even though you won't always perform it, so it makes sense to always round up to the nearest integer. In programming, the function that rounds up to the nearest integer is often called *ceiling,* so you might express the minimum number of weighings needed to guarantee you'll find the heavy marble among *n* marbles as ceiling($\log_3(n)$).

For the group of 4 (out of the total of 10 marbles), you would divide the 4 marbles into two groups of 1 and one group of 2. If the heavy marble happened to be in the group of 2, you would need one more weighing (the third weighing) to determine which was the heavy marble. A fractional weighing may also represent a weighing that will always be performed but won't eliminate a full $2/3$ of the remaining marbles. For example, when $n = 8$, the fractional weighing represents the weighing needed to determine which marble is heavier in the case where the heavy marble is known to be in the group of two after the first weighing. In any case, it must be counted as a full weighing, so rounding up is appropriate.

This is another example of a problem designed such that the wrong solution occurs first to most intelligent, logically thinking people. Most people find it quite difficult to come up with the idea of using three groups, but relatively easy to solve the problem after that leap. It's not an accident that this problem begins by asking you to solve the case of eight marbles. As a power of 2, it works very cleanly for the incorrect solution, but because it's not a power (or multiple, for that matter) of 3 it's a little messy for the correct solution. People generally get the correct answer more quickly when asked to solve the problem for nine marbles. Look out for details like this that may steer your thinking in a particular (and often incorrect) direction.

This problem is a relatively easy example of a whole class of tricky problems involving weighing items with a two-pan balance. For more practice with these, you might want to try working out the solution to the preceding problem for a group of marbles in which one marble has a different weight, but you don't know whether it's heavier or lighter.

Summary

You'll probably encounter a brainteaser or two during the interview process, even if they're not directly related to your programming skills. Many interviewers use these kinds of problems to see your thought processes at work and determine how well you can think "outside the box."

Brainteasers come in many different forms, but the obvious answer is almost invariably wrong in all cases. Start by verifying your assumptions to make sure you're solving the right problem. Don't be intimidated by the problem—break it into pieces, simplify the problem, and solve specific cases in order to find the general solution. Beware of simple problems, as they're trickier than they seem. If you don't have all the facts you need, make reasonable estimates based on prior knowledge and common sense.

No matter what you're doing, think out loud and explain to the interviewer what you're doing and the reasoning behind your decisions. Focus on the problem and keep working; it's your thought processes that count the most here, not the answer itself.

13

Graphical and Spatial Puzzles

Many brainteasers are graphical or involve spatial thinking. All the techniques you've used on nongraphical puzzles are still applicable, but with these problems you have another very powerful technique available to you: diagrams.

Draw It First

The importance of drawing diagrams cannot be overstated. Consider that while humans have only been using written language and mathematics for a few thousand years, we've been evolving to analyze visual problems (for example, can that rhinoceros catch me before I get to that tree?) for millions of years. We are generally much better suited to solving problems presented in pictures than those presented in text or numbers.

Whenever possible, draw a picture.

In some cases, the actors in these brainteasers are static, but more often they are changing or in motion. When this is the case, don't draw just one picture, draw many. Make a diagram for each moment in time for which you have information. You can often gain insight by observing how the situation changes between each of your diagrams.

If the problem involves motion or change, draw multiple pictures of different points in time.

Most problems are two-dimensional. Even when a problem involves three-dimensional objects, the objects are often constrained to the same plane, allowing you to simplify the problem to two dimensions. It's much easier to diagram two dimensions than three, so don't work in three dimensions unless you have to.

If the problem is fundamentally a three-dimensional problem, you should assess your relative abilities with drawing and visualization before proceeding. If you're not very good at drawing, your diagram of a three-dimensional problem may do more to confuse than elucidate. On the other hand, if you're a good artist or drafter, but have trouble with visualization, you may be better off with a diagram. Whatever approach you take, try to attack spatial problems spatially, not with computation or symbolic mathematics.

Visualization may be more appropriate than diagramming for three-dimensional problems, but in either case, attack the problem spatially.

Graphical and Spatial Problems

Diagramming and visualization are the keys to solving the brainteasers that follow.

Boat and Dock

You are sitting in a small boat, holding the end of a rope. The other end of the rope is tied to the top of a nearby pier, such that it is higher above the water than your end of the rope. You pull on the rope, causing your boat to move toward the pier, stopping directly underneath the pier. As you pull on the rope, which of the following is faster: the speed the boat moves across the water or the speed the rope moves through your hands?

You should begin this problem by drawing a diagram, both to ensure you understand the scenario and to get you started on the solution. The edge of the pier, the water, and the rope form the legs of a right triangle, as shown in Figure 13-1. To facilitate further discussion, these segments are labeled A, B, and C, respectively.

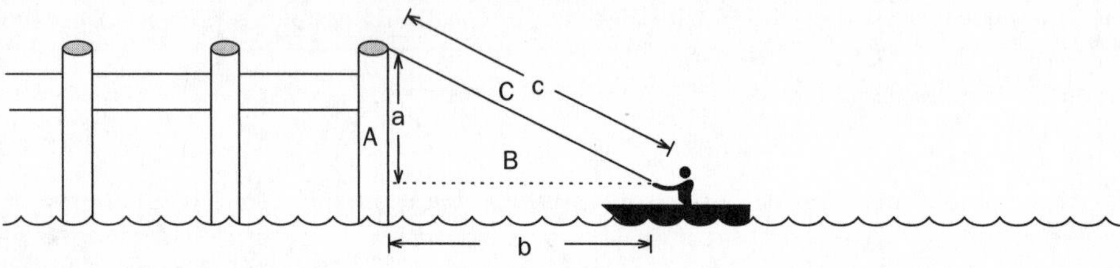

Figure 13-1

Here you have something familiar, but with an unusual twist. You've probably worked with right triangles ad nauseum in your math classes, but those are static figures — this triangle is collapsing. Be wary of this difference. Although it seems minor, it may be enough to make the wrong answer seem intuitively correct.

Given your experience with right triangles, you may decide to attack this problem mathematically. You need to determine whether side B or side C is shortened more quickly as the boat moves. Put another way, for a given change in the length of B, what is the change in the length of C? How might you calculate this? A derivative gives you the ratio of rates of change between two variables. If you calculated the derivative of C with respect to B and it were greater than 1, you would know that the rope was moving faster; conversely, if it were less than 1, the boat must have moved faster.

This is a good point at which to stop and consider where you've been and where you're going. You can set up an equation relating B and C using the Pythagorean theorem. It looks as if this method will eventually lead you to the correct answer. If you're good at math and comfortable with calculus, this may even be the best way to proceed. The apparent need for calculus, however, should serve as a warning that you may be missing an easier way to solve the problem.

Try going back to the original diagram and taking a more-graphical approach. What other diagrams might you draw? Because you don't know the boat's initial distance from the pier or how high the pier is, all diagrams of the boat in motion are effectively equivalent. What about when the boat stops under the pier, as shown in Figure 13-2? That would be different; for one thing, you would no longer have a triangle because the rope would be hanging down the side of the pier.

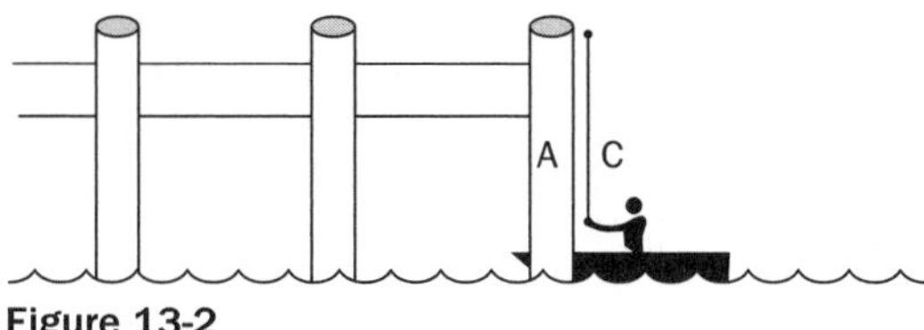

Figure 13-2

How far does the boat travel, and how much rope is hauled in between the times shown in the two figures? Because you aren't given any numbers, call the initial lengths of sides A, B, and C lowercase a, b, and c, respectively. When the boat is under the pier, side B has a length of 0, so the boat has moved through a distance of b. The rope, on the other hand, started with a length of c. In the second diagram, a length of rope equal to a is still out of the boat, so the total amount hauled in is $c - a$.

Because these distances were covered in the same time, the greater distance must have been covered at a higher speed. Which is greater, then, $c - a$, or b? Recall from geometry that the sum of the lengths of two sides of a triangle must always be greater than the length of the third. For example, $a + b > c$. Subtracting a, $b > c - a$. The boat traveled a greater distance, so it was moving faster across the water than the speed of the rope through your hands.

> *If you think about this, it makes intuitive sense. Suppose one side were longer than the other two put together. There would be no way to arrange the sides such that they met at three vertices because the shorter two sides would be too short to span the distance from one end of the long side to the other.*

For the mathematically curious, we'll pick up the calculus where we left it, to show that the solution can be determined using that method. From the Pythagorean theorem, $C^2 = A^2 + B^2$. This can be used to calculate the derivative of C with respect to B:

$$
\begin{aligned}
C &= \sqrt{A^2 + B^2} \\
\frac{dC}{dB} &= \frac{1}{2}\left(A^2 + B^2\right)^{-\frac{1}{2}}(2B) \\
&= \frac{B}{\sqrt{A^2 + B^2}}
\end{aligned}
$$

B is positive, so when A = 0, the final expression is equal to 1. When A is greater than 0, as in this problem, the denominator is greater than the numerator and the expression is less than 1. This means that for a given infinitesimal change in B, there is a smaller change in C, so the boat is moving faster.

In case you've been out of a math class for too long, the numerator is the expression above the fraction bar and the denominator is the expression below it.

This problem belongs to a curious class of puzzles that seem to be more difficult when you know more math. They are particularly devilish in interviews. Because you expect difficult questions and you may be a little nervous, you're unlikely to stop and ask yourself whether there's an easier way.

One of the nastiest examples of this type of problem involves two locomotives, heading toward each other at 10 mph. When they are exactly 30 miles apart, a bird sitting on the front of one locomotive flies off toward the other, traveling at 60 mph. When it reaches the other locomotive, it immediately turns around and flies back to the first. The bird continues like this until, sadly, it is smashed between the two locomotives as they collide. When asked how far the bird traveled, many calculus students will spend hours trying to set up and sum impossibly difficult infinite series. Most younger students who have never heard of an infinite series will instead determine that it took the locomotives 1.5 hours to close the 30 mile gap, and that in that time a bird traveling 60 mph would have traveled 90 miles.

Counting Cubes

Imagine a cubic array made up of a 3×3×3 arrangement of smaller cubes: The cubic array is three cubes wide, three cubes high, and three cubes deep. It may help to picture a Rubik's Cube, as shown in Figure 13-3.

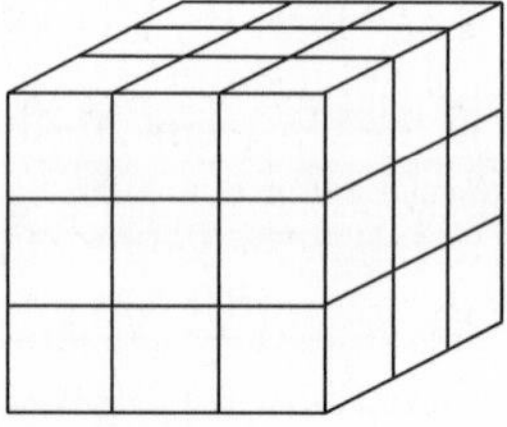

Figure 13-3

How many of the cubes are on the surface of the cubic array?

This is a spatial visualization problem. Different people find different techniques useful in visualization, so this discussion presents a variety of approaches. The hope is that you will find at least one of them useful. You can try to draw a diagram, but because the problem is in three dimensions, you may find your diagram more confusing than helpful.

One way you might try to solve this problem is by counting the cubes on each face of the array. A cube has six faces. Each face of the cubic array has nine cubes (3 × 3), so you might conclude that there are 6×9 = 54 cubes on the surface. There are only 3×3×3 = 27 cubes total, so it's obviously not possible for twice that many to be on the surface. The fallacy in this method is that some cubes are on more than one face—for example, the corner cubes are on three faces. Rather than try to make complicated adjustments for cubes that are on more than one face, you should look for an easier solution.

A better way to attack this problem is to count the cubes in layers. The array is three cubes high, so there are three layers. All the cubes on the top layer are on the surface (nine cubes). All the cubes of the middle layer except for the center cube are on the surface (eight cubes). Finally, all the cubes on the bottom layer are on the surface (nine cubes). This gives a total of 9 + 8 + 9 = 26 cubes on the surface.

The preceding method works, but perhaps a better way to find the solution is to count the cubes that are not on the surface and then subtract this number from the total number of cubes. Vivid, specific objects are often easier to visualize than vague concepts—you may want to imagine the cubes on the surface to be translucent red, and the nonsurface cubes to be bright blue. It is hoped that you can visualize that there is only one bright blue cube surrounded by a shell of red cubes. Because this is the only cube that isn't on the surface, there must be 27 – 1 = 26 cubes on the surface.

Now imagine that you have a 4×4×4 cubic array of cubes. How many cubes are on the surface of this array?

As the number of cubes increases, the accounting necessary for the layer approach becomes more complicated, so try to solve this by visualizing and counting the cubes that are not on the surface. The nonsurface cubes form a smaller cubic array within the larger array. How many cubes are in this smaller array? Your initial impulse may be that there are four cubes in the array; if so, consider whether it's possible to arrange four cubes into a cubic array (it isn't). The correct answer is that the non-surface cubes form a 2×2×2 array of eight cubes. There are a total of 4×4×4 = 64 cubes, so there are 64 – 8 = 56 cubes on the surface.

Generalize your solution to an $n \times n \times n$ cubic array of cubes. In terms of n, how many cubes are on the surface?

Now that you can't explicitly count the cubes, the problem starts to get a little more interesting. You know that there are n^3 cubes total. If you can calculate the number of cubes that aren't on the surface, you'll also be able to calculate the number that are. Try to visualize the situation, mentally coloring the surface cubes red and the interior cubes blue. What does it look like? You should be able to see a cubic array of blue cubes surrounded by a one-cube-thick shell of red cubes. If you can determine the size of the smaller array, you can calculate the number of cubes it contains. Because the smaller array fits entirely within the larger one, it must be fewer than n cubes across, but how many fewer?

Visualize a single line of cubes running all the way through the array. The line would be n cubes long. Because the shell of red surface cubes is one cube thick, both the first and last cubes would be red, and all the other cubes would be blue. This means there would be $n - 2$ blue cubes in the row, so the array of interior cubes is $n - 2$ cubes across. It's a cubic array, so its height and depth are the same as its width. Therefore, you can calculate that there are $(n - 2)^3$ cubes that are not on the surface. Subtracting this from the total number of cubes gives you $n^3 - (n - 2)^3$ cubes on the surface. Test this formula using the cases you've already worked out by hand: $3^3 - (3 - 2)^3 = 26$; $4^3 - (4 - 2)^3 = 56$. It looks as if you've got the answer for this part, but you're not done yet.

> **A cube is an object that measures the same distance across in three perpendicular directions in a three-dimensional space. A four-dimensional hypercube is an object that measures the same distance across in four perpendicular directions in a four-dimensional space. Calculate the number of 4D hypercubes on the surface of an $n \times n \times n \times n$ hypercubic array of 4D hypercubes.**

The fun really starts here. This started out as a visualization problem, but taking it to four dimensions makes it very difficult for most people to visualize. Visualization can still be helpful, though. You might (or might not) find the following device useful.

People often represent time as a fourth dimension. The easiest way to visualize time in a concrete fashion is to imagine a strip of film from a movie. Each frame in the filmstrip represents a different time, or a different location along the fourth dimension. In order to fully represent four dimensions, you have to imagine that each frame consists of a full three-dimensional space, not two-dimensional pictures as in a real filmstrip. If you can visualize this, you can visualize four dimensions.

Because a hypercube measures the same distance in each direction, the filmstrip representing the hypercubic array in this problem is n frames long. In each of the frames you see an $n \times n \times n$ array of cubes^3, just as in the previous part of the problem. This means there are $n \times n^3 = n^4$ hypercubes total. In terms of color, the arrays you see in the middle frames of the filmstrip look just like the array from the previous part of the problem—a red shell surrounding a blue core. All the cubes in the first and last frames are on the surface in the fourth dimension because they are at the ends of the filmstrip. All the cubes in these frames are red. In other words, there are $n - 2$ frames that have blue cubes, and each of these frames looks like the array from the previous part of the problem. Multiplying the number of frames with blue cubes by the number of blue cubes in each frame gives $(n - 2)(n - 2)^3 = (n - 2)$, the total number of blue hypercubes. Subtracting from the previous result yields $n^4 - (n - 2)^4$ hypercubes on the surface of the hypercubic array.

The frames are actually hypercubes because their existence in the frame gives them a duration of one frame, or a width of one unit in the time (fourth) dimension. However, it may be easier to think of them as normal 3D cubes when trying to visualize a single frame.

> **Generalize your solution to i dimensions. How many hypercubes are there on the surface of an $n \times n \times n \times \ldots \times n$ (i dimensions) hypercubic array of i dimensional hypercubes?**

You're almost there. At this point you may find it helpful to extend the device you've been using for visualization into many dimensions, or you may find it easier to dispense with visualization and solve the problem using patterns and mathematics. The following discussion examines both methods.

Visualizing a filmstrip gave you four dimensions, but there's no reason to limit yourself to a single filmstrip. If you imagine lining up n filmstrips side by side, you have five dimensions: three in each frame, one given by the frame number, and one more given by the filmstrip that holds the frame. Each of these filmstrips would look just like the filmstrip from the four-dimensional case, except for the rightmost and leftmost filmstrips. These two filmstrips would be surface filmstrips in the fifth dimension, so all of the cubes in each of their frames would be red. You can further extend this to six dimensions by imagining a stack of multiple layers of filmstrips. Beyond six dimensions, it again becomes difficult to visualize the situation (you might try thinking of different tables, each holding stacks of layers of filmstrips), but the device has served its purpose in illustrating that dimensions are an arbitrary construction — there is nothing special about objects with more than three dimensions. Each dimension you add gives you n copies of what you were visualizing before. Of these, two of the copies are always entirely on the surface, leaving $n - 2$ copies in which there are blue interior cubes. This means that with each additional dimension, the total number of hypercubes increases by a factor of n and the number of nonsurface hypercubes increases by a factor of $n - 2$. You have one of each of these factors for each dimension, giving you a final result of $n^i - (n - 2)^i$ hypercubes on the surface of the array.

Alternatively, you might take a pattern-based approach and note that you raised both parts of the expression to the power of 3 in the three-dimensional case and to the power of 4 in the four-dimensional case. From this you might deduce that the exponent represents the number of dimensions in the problem. You might check this by trying the one- and two-dimensional cases (a line and a square), where you would find that your proposed solution appears to work. Thinking about it mathematically, when you have n hypercubes in each of i directions, it seems reasonable that you would have a total of n^i hypercubes; for the same reason, raising $(n - 2)$ to the ith power also seems to make sense. This isn't a proof, but it should be enough to make you confident that $n^i - (n - 2)^i$ is the right answer.

It's interesting to look at the progression of the parts of this problem. The first part of the problem is quite easy. Taken by itself, the last part of the problem would seem almost impossible. Each part of the problem is only a little more difficult than the preceding, and each part helps you gain new insight, so by the time you reach the final part it doesn't seem so insurmountable. It's good to remember this technique. Solving simpler, easier, more specific cases can give you insight into the solution of a more difficult, general problem, even if you aren't led through the process explicitly as you were here.

The Fox and the Duck

A duck, pursued by a fox, escapes to the center of a perfectly circular pond. The fox cannot swim, and the duck cannot take flight from the water (it's a deficient duck). The fox is four times faster than the duck. Assuming the fox and duck pursue optimum strategies, is it possible for the duck to reach the edge of the pond and fly away without being eaten? If so, how?

The most obvious strategy for the duck is to swim directly away from where the fox is standing. The duck has to swim a distance of r to the edge of the pond. The fox, meanwhile, has to run around half the circumference of the pond, a distance of Πr. Because the fox moves four times faster than the duck, and $\Pi r < 4r$, it's apparent that any duck pursuing this strategy would soon be fox food.

Think about what this result tells you. Does it prove that the duck can't escape? No; it just shows that the duck can't escape using this strategy. If there weren't anything else to this problem, it would be a trivial geometry exercise — not worth asking in an interview — so this result suggests the duck *can* escape, you just don't know how.

Instead of focusing on the duck, try thinking about the fox's strategy. The fox will run around the perimeter of the pond to stay as close to the duck as possible. Because the shortest distance from any point in the circle to the edge lies along a radius, the fox will try to stay on the same radius as the duck.

How can the duck make life most difficult for the fox? If the duck swims back and forth along a radius, the fox can just sit on that radius. The duck could try swimming back and forth across the center point of the pond, which would keep the fox running as the duck's radius repeatedly switched from one side of the pond to the other. However, consider that each time the duck crosses the center point, he returns to the problem's initial configuration: He is in the center and the fox is at the edge. The duck won't make much progress that way.

Another possibility would involve the duck swimming in a circle concentric with the pond, so the fox would have to keep running around the pond to stay on the duck's radius. When the duck is near the edge of the pond, the fox has no trouble staying on the same radius as the duck because they are covering approximately equal distances and the fox is four times faster. However, as the duck moves closer to the center of the pond, the circumference of its circle becomes smaller and smaller. At a distance of $\frac{1}{4}r$ from the center of the pond, the duck's circle is exactly four times smaller than the circumference of the pond, so the fox is just barely able to stay on the same radius as the duck. At any distance less than $\frac{1}{4}r$ from the center, the fox has to cover more than four times the distance that the duck does to move between two radii. That means that as the duck circles, the fox will start to lag behind.

This strategy seems to give the duck a way to put some distance between it and the fox. If the duck swims long enough, eventually the fox will lag so far behind that the radius the duck is on will be 180↓ from the fox; in other words, the point on the shore closest to the duck will be farthest from the fox. Perhaps this head start would be enough that the duck could make a radial beeline for the shore and get there ahead of the fox. How can the head start be maximized? When the duck's circle has a radius of $\frac{1}{4}$r the fox just keeps pace with it, so at a radius of $\frac{1}{4}r$ minus some infinitesimal amount E, the duck would just barely pull ahead. Eventually, when it got 180↓ ahead of the fox, it would be $\frac{3}{4}r$ + E from the nearest point on the shore. The fox, however, would be half the circumference of the pond from that point: ΠrE. In this case, the fox would have to cover more than four times the distance that the duck does ($3r < \Pi r$), so the duck would be able to make it to land and fly away, as shown in Figure 13-4.

You might want to try to work out the solution to a similar problem on your own: This time, the fox is chasing a rabbit. They are inside a circular pen from which they cannot escape. If the rabbit can run at the same speed as the fox, is it possible for the fox to catch the rabbit?

Burning Fuses

You are given two fuses and a lighter. When lit, each fuse takes exactly one hour to burn from one end to the other. The fuses do not burn at a constant rate, though, and they are not identical. In other words, you may make no assumptions about the relationship between the length of a section of fuse and the time it has taken or will take to burn. Two equal lengths of fuse will not necessarily take the same time to burn. Using only the fuses and the lighter, measure a period of exactly 45 minutes.

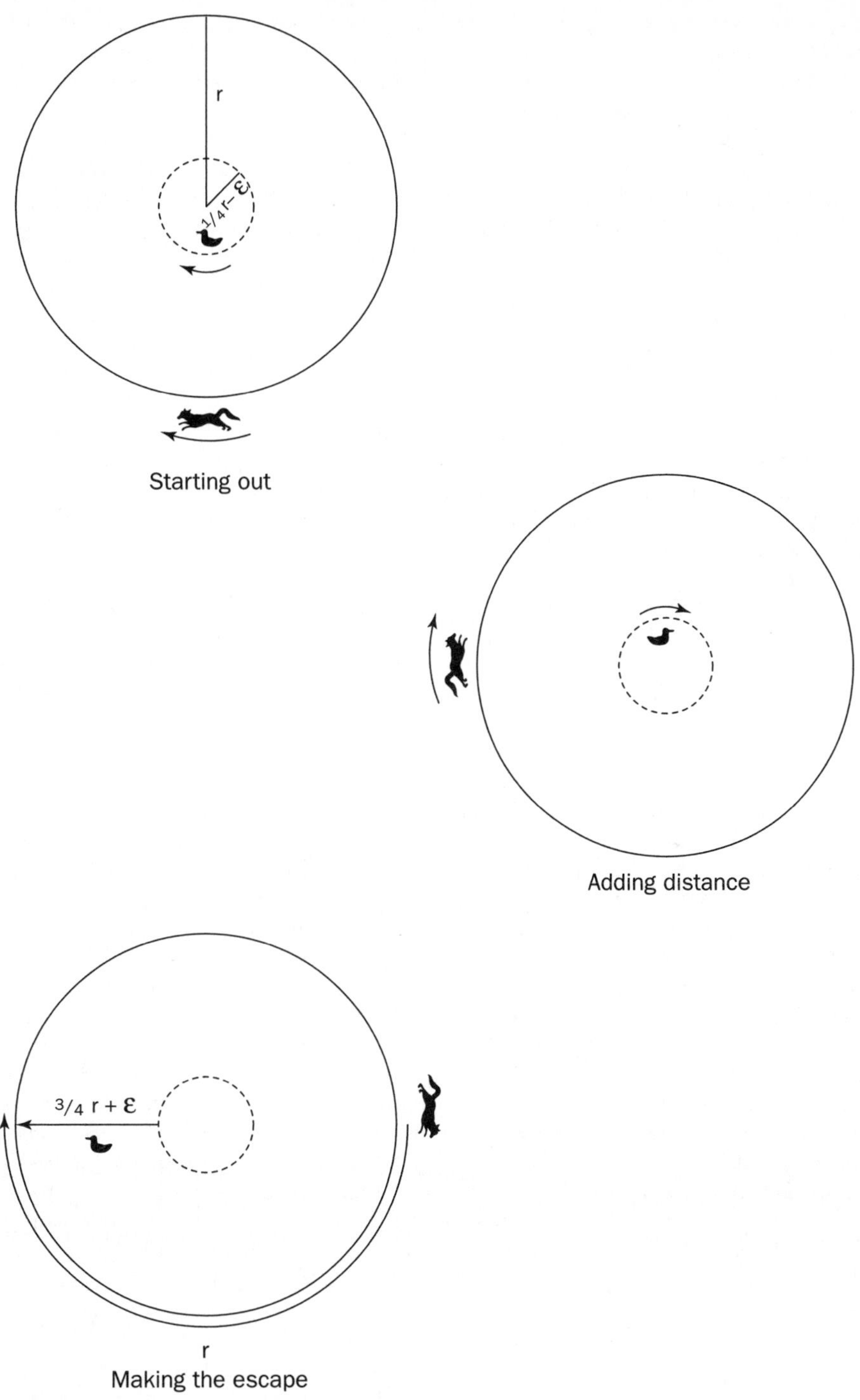
r
1/4 r – ε
Starting out
Adding distance
3/4 r + ε
r
Making the escape

Figure 13-4

One of the difficult parts of this problem is keeping firmly in mind that the length of a piece of fuse has nothing to do with the time it will take to burn. Although this is stated explicitly in the problem, constant rates and relationships between time and distance are so familiar that it can be easy to fall into the trap of trying to somehow measure a physical length of fuse. In fact, because the burn rate is unknown and variable, the only useful measure is time. Mindful of this, you can begin to solve the problem.

The materials and actions available to you are fairly circumscribed in this problem. In such a case, it can be useful to begin by considering all possible actions, and then identify which of these possible actions might be useful.

There are two locations where you can light the fuses: at an end or somewhere that is not an end (in the middle). If you light one of the fuses at an end, it will burn through in 60 minutes. That's longer than the total length of time you need to measure, so it probably isn't directly useful. If you light a fuse in the middle, you will end up with two flames, each burning toward a different end of the fuse. If you were extremely lucky, you might light the exact center (in burn time; it might not be the physical center) of the fuse, in which case both flames would extinguish simultaneously after 30 minutes. It's much more likely that you would miss the center of the fuse, giving you one flame that went out sometime before 30 minutes and a second that continued burning for some time after. This doesn't seem like a very reliable way to make a measurement.

When you lit the fuse in the middle, you got a different burn time than when you lit the end. Why is this? Lighting the middle of the fuse created two flames, so you were burning in two places at once. How else might you use two flames? You've seen that lighting the middle of the fuse is problematic because you don't really know where (in time) you're lighting. That leaves the ends of the fuse. If you light both ends of the fuse, the flames will burn toward each other until they meet and extinguish each other after exactly 30 minutes. This could be useful.

So far, you can measure exactly 30 minutes using one fuse. If you could figure out how to measure 15 minutes with the other fuse, you could add the two times to solve the problem. What would you need to measure 15 minutes? Either a 15-minute length of fuse, burning at one end, or a 30-minute length of fuse, burning at both ends, would do the trick. Because you're starting with a 60-minute length of fuse, this means you need to remove either 45 or 30 minutes from the fuse. Again, this must be done by burning because cutting the fuse would involve making a physical (distance) measurement, which would be meaningless. Forty-five minutes could be removed by burning from both ends for 22.5 minutes or one end for 45 minutes. Measuring 22.5 minutes seems an even harder problem than the one you were given; if you knew how to measure 45 minutes you'd have solved the problem, so this possibility doesn't look particularly fruitful. The other option is removing 30 minutes of fuse, which could be done by burning from both ends for 15 minutes or one end for 30 minutes. The need to measure 15 minutes returns you to the task at hand, but you do know how to measure 30 minutes: exactly 30 minutes elapse from lighting both ends of the first fuse until the flames go out. If you light one end of the second fuse at the same moment you light both ends of the first, then you'll be left with 30 minutes of fuse on the second fuse when the first fuse is gone. You can light the other end (the one that isn't already burning) of this second fuse as soon as the first goes out. The two flames burning on the 30-minute length of fuse will extinguish each other after exactly 15 minutes, giving you a total of 30 + 15 = 45 minutes.

Escaping the Train

Two boys walking in the woods decided to take a shortcut through a railroad tunnel. When they had walked ⅔ of the way through the tunnel, their worst fears were realized. A train was coming in the opposite direction, nearing the tunnel entrance. The boys panicked and each ran for a different end of the tunnel. Both boys ran at the same speed, 10 miles per hour. Each boy escaped from the tunnel just at the instant that the train would have squashed him into the rails. Assuming the train's speed was constant, and both boys were capable of instantaneous reaction and acceleration, how fast was the train going?

At first, this seems like a classic algebraic word problem, straight out of a high school homework set (or middle school, if you were an overachiever). When you begin to set up your *x*'s and *y*'s, however, you'll realize you're missing a lot of the information you would expect to have in a standard algebra rate problem. Specifically, although you know the boys' speeds, you don't have any information about distances or times. Perhaps this will be more challenging than it first appeared.

A good way to get started is by drawing a diagram using the information you've been given. Call the boys Abner and Brent (A and B to their friends). At the moment the problem begins, when the boys have just noticed the train, the train is an unknown distance from the tunnel, heading toward them. A and B are both in the same place, ⅓ of the tunnel length from the entrance closest to the train. A is running toward the train and B away from it, as shown in Figure 13-5.

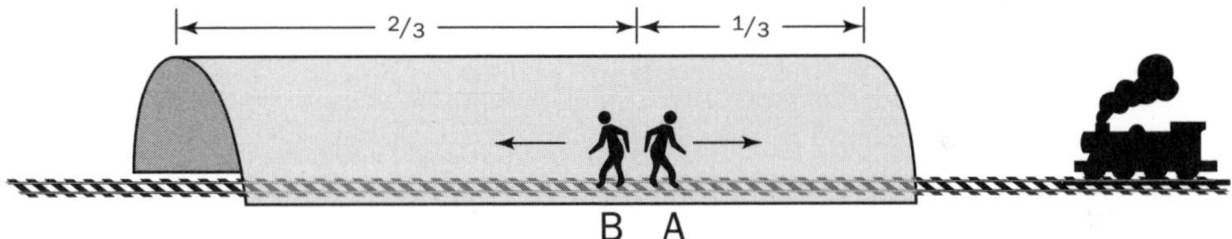

Figure 13-5

The only additional information you have is that both boys just barely escape. Try drawing diagrams of the moments of their escapes. A is running toward the train and has only ⅓ of the tunnel to cover, so he'll escape before B. Because he reaches the end of the tunnel at the last possible instant, he and the train must be at the end of the tunnel at the same time. Where would B be at this time? A and B run at the same speed; A moves ⅓ of the length of the tunnel before escaping, so B must also have run ⅓ of the length of the tunnel. That would put him ⅓ of the way from the end of the tunnel he's headed for, as shown in Figure 13-6.

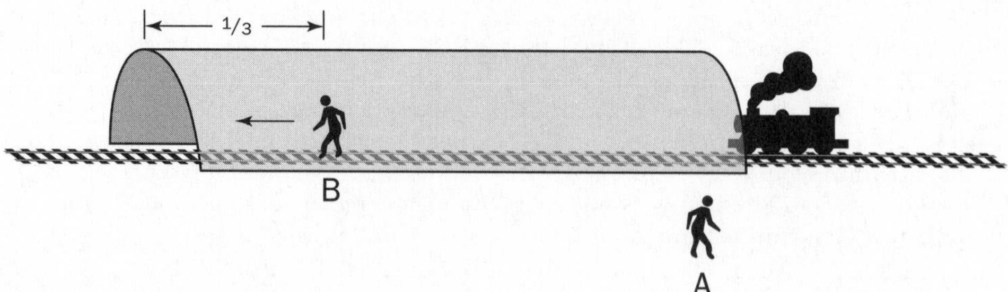

Figure 13-6

Now diagram B's escape. The train has come all the way through the tunnel, and both it and B are right at the end of the tunnel. (A is somewhere outside the other end of the tunnel, counting his blessings.) This situation is illustrated in Figure 13-7.

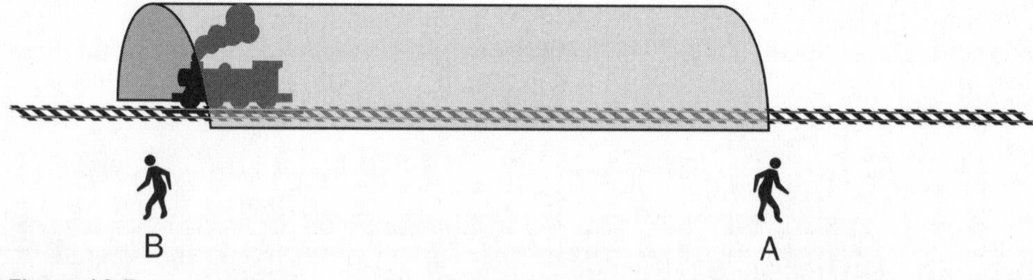

Figure 13-7

None of these diagrams seem particularly illuminating on their own. Because you're trying to determine the speed of the train, you should look at how it moves — how its position changes between your three diagrams. Between the first and second diagrams, A and B each run ⅓ of the length of the tunnel, while the train moves an unknown distance. No help there. Between the second and third diagrams, B again runs ⅓ of the tunnel length, while the train runs through the whole tunnel. Therefore, the train covers three times more distance than B in the same amount of time. This means the train must be three times as fast as B. B can travel 10 miles per hour, so the train moves at 30 miles per hour.

Summary

Many brainteasers are graphical in nature and serve to test your spatial thinking. You'll still want to apply the general brainteaser guidelines from the previous chapter to these kinds of questions, but often the correct answer will only be evident when you try to visualize the problem.

Don't underestimate the power of diagrams.

Knowledge-Based Questions

Knowledge-based questions vary greatly in frequency from interview to interview. Some interviewers will not ask knowledge-based questions, while others will focus solely on them. Interviewers often ask these questions when there is no whiteboard or paper available, such as at lunch, or when they are satisfied with your coding ability and want to test your general computer knowledge. These questions enable the interviewer to assess your background and determine your computer proficiency.

Preparation

Knowledge-based questions generally come from two sources: what you said on your résumé and your answers to questions earlier in the interview.

It's a very good idea to review your résumé prior to your interview and make sure you're prepared to answer questions about *every* item on the résumé, no matter how small. Some interviewers will even go through your résumé and ask you general questions about each item — "What is *X*?" and "What have you done with *X*?" For example, if you put SOAP on your resume, be prepared for the questions "What is SOAP?" and "What have you done with SOAP?" If you can't intelligently answer either question, you should remove the SOAP reference from your résumé.

Be prepared to answer questions about everything on your résumé.

In a similar vein, be careful with what you say during the interview. The interviewer may want some more in-depth explanation of technologies and techniques you mentioned, just to ascertain how deep your knowledge really goes. Sometimes the questioning is quite innocent. If you say you "started programming in Java several years ago," don't be surprised if the interviewer asks you what version of Java you started with. If all you did initially was read a book about Java 1.0.2 (which was the first public release of Java, now quite ancient) and didn't do any real programming until Java 1.2 was released, don't say you started with Java 1.0.2. If you do, you won't have a satisfactory answer for a question like *"What new feature in Java 1.1 did you like the best?"* — a reasonable question given all the changes to the language that were introduced with version 1.1 (inner classes, reflection, serialization, database classes, and so on). Be as truthful and accurate about your background as you can be so that your earlier answers don't trip you up later.

Problems

It would be impossible for us to cover every conceivable area of computer knowledge that could appear on a résumé or in an interview. Instead, this chapter provides a representative sample of knowledge-based questions. These questions focus on system-level issues, trade-offs between various ways of programming, and advanced features of languages. All these topic areas make sense from the interviewer's perspective. A candidate who claims to know a lot about computers but who isn't aware of basic system-level issues such as virtual memory and disk cache certainly doesn't seem very knowledgeable. Furthermore, many job assignments are not of the variety "Solve this problem by implementing this algorithm in this language," but may be more along the lines of "We have this problem that we need solved." A candidate who understands the trade-offs between various solutions and when to use each one is always preferred to a candidate who does not understand these differences. Finally, these questions enable the interviewer to assess experience and filter out résumé padding. It's unlikely that an experienced developer would have problems answering questions about advanced features in a language that she had used in development for some time. However, an inexperienced programmer or a resume padder might stumble. These questions can help interviewers separate the wheat from the chaff.

Interviewers prefer specific answers to general answers. For example, suppose you are asked, "What is AJAX?" One general answer is, "It stands for *asynchronous JavaScript and XML.*" While this answer is technically correct, it doesn't demonstrate that you really understand what AJAX programming is about and why it has become so popular. A better answer would be "AJAX, which is short for asynchronous JavaScript and XML, is an architectural style for building interactive Web applications in which simple tasks such as input validation are performed on the client via JavaScript and data exchanges with the server occur in the background over HTTP, with XML being the preferred format for returning data to the client for processing. Applications built using AJAX don't suffer the frustrating time lags that conventional Web applications do and are much more responsive to user input." It seems pretty clear which answer is better.

Offer specific and thorough responses.

One final note: The answers presented here are researched answers that result from many people thinking about a question and coming up with the best answer. As a candidate hearing a question for the first time, you are not expected to replicate such detailed solutions. Consider these answers to be the goal, and try to get as close to these solutions as possible.

C++ versus Java

What are the differences between C++ and Java?

C++ and Java are syntactically very similar. Java's designers intended this to make it easy for C++ developers to learn Java. Apart from this area of similarity, Java and C++ differ in a variety of ways, largely because of their different design goals. Security, portability, and rapid development were of paramount importance in the design of Java, whereas C++ is more concerned with performance and backward compatibility with C. Java is compiled to virtual machine byte-code and requires a virtual machine to run; C++ is compiled to native machine code. This usually makes C++ faster, but it gives Java greater potential for portability and security.

C++ is a superset of C and maintains features such as programmer-controlled memory management, pointers, and a preprocessor for full backward compatibility with C. In contrast, Java eliminates these and other bug-prone features. Java replaces programmer memory deallocations with garbage collection. Java further dispenses with C++ features such as operator overloading and multiple inheritance. These choices are seen by some to make Java a better choice for rapid development and for projects where portability and security are more important than performance.

A limited form of multiple inheritance can be simulated in Java using interfaces.

In Java, all objects are passed by reference, whereas in C++, the default behavior is to pass objects by value. Java does not perform automatic type casting as C++ does, though newer Java features such as generics and autoboxing now handle many common cases. In Java, all methods are virtual, meaning the implementation for a method is selected according to the type of the object as opposed to the type of the reference. In C++, methods must be explicitly declared as virtual. Java has defined sizes for primitive data types, while type sizes are implementation-dependent in C++ (and C).

In situations where there is legacy C code and a great need for performance, C++ has certain benefits, especially when low-level system access is required. In situations where portability, security, and speed of development are emphasized, Java (or a similar language such as C#) may be a better choice.

Friend Classes

Discuss friend classes in C++ and give an example of when you would use one.

The `friend` keyword is applied to either a function or a class. It gives the `friend` function or `friend` class access to the private members of the class in which the declaration occurs. Some programmers feel this feature violates the principles of object-oriented programming because it allows a class to operate on another class's private members. This violation can, in turn, lead to unexpected bugs when a change in the internal implementation of a class causes problems with the friend class that accesses it.

In some cases, however, the benefits of a `friend` class outweigh its drawbacks. For example, suppose you implemented a sophisticated dynamic array class. Imagine that you wanted a separate class to iterate through your array. The iterator class would probably need access to the dynamic array class's private members to function correctly. It would make sense to declare the iterator as a `friend` to the array class. The workings of the two classes are inextricably tied together already, so it probably doesn't make sense to enforce a meaningless separation between the two.

Note that while Java and C# do not support the concept of `friend` classes, they do support `nested` classes, and `nested` classes have access to their enclosing class' private data and methods. `nested` classes can therefore take the place of `friend` classes in many instances.

Inheritance

Assume you have the class hierarchy shown in Figure 14-1.

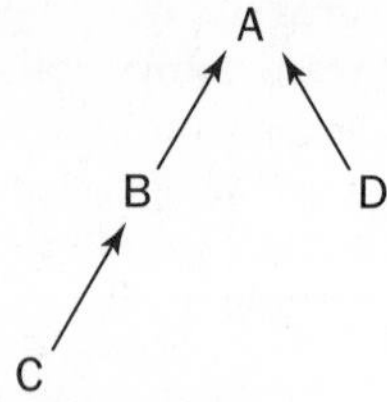

Figure 14-1

You are given a method that takes a B as an argument. Which of the classes can you pass to the method?

Clearly, you can pass B because that's exactly what the method takes. You can't possibly pass D because it may have totally different characteristics than B. A is the parent class of B. Consider that a child class is required to implement all of the methods of the parent, but the parent does not necessarily have all of the methods of a child. Thus, the parent class, A, cannot be passed to the method. C is the child class of B and is guaranteed to have all of the methods of B, so you can pass C to the method.

A hash table does one thing well. It can store and retrieve data quickly (in O(1) or constant time). However, its uses beyond this are limited.

Garbage Collection

Discuss what garbage collection is and explain different ways it can be implemented.

Garbage collection is the process by which a program automatically finds and reclaims memory that is no longer used or no longer accessible by an application. This reclamation occurs without programmer assistance. C#, Java, Lisp, and Perl are examples of languages with garbage-collection facilities.

Garbage collection provides several advantages over having a programmer explicitly deallocate memory. It eliminates bugs due to dangling pointers and memory leaks. It also promotes greater simplicity in program and interface design because the complicated mechanisms traditionally used to ensure that memory is properly freed (such as "smart pointers" in C++) are unnecessary. In addition, because programmers don't have to worry about memory deallocation, program development proceeds at a more rapid pace.

Garbage collection is not without its disadvantages, however. Garbage-collected programs often run more slowly because of the overhead needed for the system to determine when to deallocate and reclaim memory no longer needed. In addition, the system will occasionally over-allocate memory and may not free memory at the best possible time.

One method of garbage collection is to use *reference counting*. This involves tracking how many variables reference an object. Initially, there will be one reference to a piece of memory. The reference count will increase if the variable referencing it is copied. When a variable referencing an object changes value or goes out of scope, the object's reference count is decremented. If a reference count ever goes to 0, the memory associated with the object is freed: If no one is keeping a reference to the object, then the object (and hence its memory) is no longer needed.

Reference counting is simple and relatively fast. However, it doesn't handle circular references. Consider what happens in the case of a circularly linked list with nothing external pointing to it. Every element in the list has a nonzero reference count, yet the memory isn't referenced by any object outside the list itself. Thus, the memory could safely be deallocated, but reference-based garbage collection won't free it.

A second method of garbage collection is known as *mark and sweep*. In the first pass, the memory manager will mark all objects that can be accessed by any thread in the program. In the second pass, all unmarked objects are deallocated, or swept away.

Mark and sweep handles circular references, but it's also less efficient. The garbage collector runs at different points in an application's execution and may cause the application to pause while the garbage collecting occurs.

Network Performance

What are the two major issues in networking performance?

Any network can be measured by two major characteristics: latency and bandwidth. *Latency* refers to how long it takes a given bit of information to get through the network. *Bandwidth* refers to the rate at which data moves through the network once communication is established. The perfect network would have infinite bandwidth and no latency.

A pipe is a good analog for a network. The time it takes for a molecule of water to go through the whole pipe is determined by the length; this is analogous to the latency. The width of the pipe determines the bandwidth: how much water can pass in a given time.

Latency and bandwidth problems are often encountered when searching the Web. If you wait a long time for a page to display and then it appears quickly, this indicates good bandwidth but high latency. On the other hand, if a page starts loading right away but takes a long time to load, that is a symptom of a low-latency, low-bandwidth connection.

Cryptography

Discuss the differences between symmetric key cryptography and public key cryptography. Give an example of when you would use each.

Symmetric key cryptography, also called *shared key cryptography*, involves two people using the same key to encrypt and decrypt information. *Public key cryptography* makes use of two different keys: a public key for encryption and a private key for decryption. Symmetric key cryptography has the advantage that it's much faster than public key cryptography. It is also generally easier to implement, less likely to involve patented algorithms, and usually requires less processing power. On the downside, the two parties sending messages must agree on the same private key before securely transmitting information. This is often inconvenient or even impossible. If the two parties are geographically separated, then a secure means of communication is needed for one to tell the other what the key will be. In a pure symmetric key scenario, secure communication is generally not available. If it were, there would be little need for encryption to create another secure channel.

Public key cryptography has the advantage that the public key, used for encryption, does not need to be kept secret for encrypted messages to remain secure. This means public keys can be transmitted over insecure channels. Often, people use public key cryptography to establish a shared session key and then communicate via symmetric key cryptography using the shared session key. This solution provides the convenience of public key cryptography with the performance of shared key cryptography.

Both public key and symmetric key cryptography are used to get secure information from the Web. First your browser establishes a shared session key with the Web site using public key cryptography. Then you communicate with the Web site using symmetric key cryptography to actually obtain the private information.

New Cryptography Algorithms

If you discover a new cryptography algorithm, should you use it immediately?

This is not a trick question, but goes to the heart of modern cryptography. Basically, no algorithm stays secret for long, and almost every algorithm has at least minor bugs in it or in its implementation. It's virtually impossible to hide an algorithm given the number of people who develop it and know about it and the advanced techniques used by today's best crackers. If your security is based on the secrecy of your algorithm, you have what is called *security by obscurity,* which is effectively no security at all. It's very likely that a determined cracker could discover your algorithm. This can render your security worse than useless because you think you have security when in fact you have none.

Thus, it's best to make any algorithm public from the beginning and flush out the bugs, rather than keep it secret and encounter a lot of security problems when it is discovered. Only keys should be kept secret. If, after extensive public review and discussion, your algorithm is accepted as secure, then you can probably securely use the algorithm.

Hash Tables versus Binary Search Trees

Compare and contrast a hash table and a binary search tree. If you were designing the address book data structure for a personal digital assistant (PDA) with limited memory, which one would you use?

A binary search tree can insert and retrieve in O(log(n)). This is fast, though not as fast as a hash table's O(1). A binary search tree, however, also maintains its data in sorted order.

In a PDA, you want to keep as much memory as possible available for data storage. If you use an unordered data structure such as a hash table, you need additional memory to sort the values, as you undoubtedly want to display the values in alphabetical order. Therefore, if you use a hash table, you have to set aside memory for sorting that could otherwise be used as storage space.

If you use a binary search tree, you won't have to waste memory or processing time on sorting records for display. Although binary tree operations are slower than hash table operations, a device like this is likely to have no more than about 10,000 entries, so a binary search tree's O(log(*n*)) lookup will undoubtedly be fast enough. For these reasons, a binary search tree is better suited for this kind of task than a hash table.

Summary

Knowledge-based questions are an easy way for interviewers to assess your familiarity and experience with the programming languages and techniques they expect you to know based on the requirements for the job and what's in your résumé. Be sure you have a good grasp of the fundamental knowledge you'll need for the job for which you're applying.

Nontechnical Questions

Most technical interviews include some nontechnical questions. Some of these questions are asked early in the interview process to determine whether your experience, education, and goals make you appropriate for the job in question. There's no point in proceeding with the technical interviews if you're not the kind of candidate they had in mind. Others are asked after the technical interviews are over, to help the company prepare an offer that is acceptable to both parties. While you won't get an offer on the strength of your nontechnical answers alone, a poor performance on nontechnical issues can lose you an offer you otherwise might have had, so don't assume that the nontechnical questions are unimportant.

Nontechnical questions are important! Treat them that way.

Despite what you might think, nontechnical questions are often challenging in and of themselves, because they have no right or wrong answers. Answers are unique to each person, and different interviewers may expect different answers. Many books have been written about how to interview well, including how to answer nontechnical questions effectively. Rather than rehash what these books say, this chapter focuses on a few nontechnical questions that are particularly common in programming interviews.

Why Nontechnical Questions?

Nontechnical questions are generally designed to assess a candidate's experience and ability to fit in with other employees. Experience includes your work history and knowledge base. Even if you answer all of the technical questions perfectly, for example, you may not seem like the ideal candidate if the job isn't consistent with your previous experience.

Be careful when answering questions about your experience because the questions may indicate that the interviewer has doubts about your capability to do the job. It's important for you to allay any fears that your experience is lacking. For example, suppose you're asked the question, "Have you ever used Linux?" Your interviewer has seen your résumé, so he or she probably has a pretty good idea that you haven't. In effect, the interviewer is really saying, "We're using Linux — will you be able to do the job even though you've never used it?" Don't answer "No." Instead, emphasize a similar strength. For example, you could respond, "I haven't used Linux specifically, but I have done Unix development." Pay attention to the job description when it's explained to you. Emphasize any similar and relevant experience that makes you a strong candidate.

Fit is the other key theme of nontechnical questions. Fit refers to how well you will adapt to the organization and become a contributing member. Most people think this just means being a nice person, but that is only half the picture. It's also important to be good at working with others. For example, suppose you say something like, "At my last job, I designed and implemented a system to move our HR information gathering to the Web all by myself." This may sound like a positive comment about yourself, but it can set off alarms about whether you can and will work with other people. Therefore, it's important to emphasize the team concept. Describe how you want to be part of a great team and a contributing team player. Everyone likes hearing the word team — *everyone*.

Most nontechnical questions are designed to ensure that you have relevant experience and can fit in with the existing team.

Of course, some nontechnical questions are very practical. If the job is located in the San Francisco area and you reside elsewhere, relocation (or telecommuting) needs to be discussed.

Questions

When reading the sample questions and following discussions, try to come up with a sample answer yourself. Think of how you would respond to such a question and what points you would want to emphasize in different situations. It's much easier to think of an answer now than when you're in front of an interviewer. Don't be afraid to refine your response if you find that it isn't effective. Finally, make sure that every response positions you as a valuable employee.

"What Do You Want to Do?"

Always pay attention to who is asking this question. If it's a human-resource representative scheduling interviews, be honest and tell him what you want to do. The HR rep will generally use this information to set up interviews with appropriate groups.

If you're asked this question by a more-technical interviewer, watch out! If you answer this question poorly, you won't get an offer. These interviewers ask this question partly because they want to find out your goals and ambitions. If you want to do something different from the job that is available, your interviewer will probably decide that you should look for a different job. If you want the job, make sure you indicate that you're interested in doing it, sound sincere, and give a reason. For example, you could say, "I've always been interested in systems-level programming and really enjoy it, so I'm hoping to join a large company and do systems-level work." Or, you could say, "I want to do Web programming so I can show my work to my friends. I'm hoping to do this at a start-up where I can use my Web server experience and watch the company grow."

Sometimes, you may not be sure what specific kind of job you're interviewing for. In these cases, you can always fall back on describing the company you're applying to as the ideal company for you. Mention that you're hoping to do development that's exciting and provides a lot of opportunity to contribute and learn. You can say that you see the work as just one part of the package; other important parts are the team and the company. This sort of response shows that you have your act together and prevents you from talking your way out of a job.

There is a fine line between sounding enthusiastic and seeming dateless and desperate. No one wants an employee who has been rejected by everyone else. Make sure your answer never sounds like you'd be happy to take any sort of job the company would be willing to offer. This sort of response virtually guarantees nothing more than a "thank you for coming in" letter.

It's also possible that you know exactly what you want to do and wouldn't accept any other kind of job. If so, don't talk yourself up for a job you'd never accept anyway. This approach may prevent you from getting some job offers, but they aren't jobs that you want anyway. One advantage to expressing exactly what you want to do is that even if you don't begin the day interviewing with an interesting group, you may end the day interviewing with such a group.

One final note on answering this question: It's a good opportunity to mention that you want to work with a great team — don't pass it up. Make sure that being a member of a great team comes across as one of your priorities.

"What Is Your Favorite Programming Language?"

This may seem like a technical question, and there are certainly technical aspects to it. You want to give specific, technical reasons why you like any language that you mention, but there is also a hidden nontechnical agenda in this question. Many people develop almost religious attachment to certain languages, computers, or operating systems. These people can be difficult to work with because they often insist on using their favorites even when they are ill-suited to the problem at hand. You should be careful to avoid coming across as such a person. Acknowledge that there are some tasks for which your favorite language is a poor choice. Mention that you are familiar with a range of languages and that you believe that no one language is a universal solution. It's important to pick the best tool for the job.

This advice holds for other "favorites" questions, such as "What is your favorite kind of computer?" or "What is your favorite operating system?"

"What Is Your Work Style?"

This question usually indicates that the company you're interviewing with has an unorthodox work style. For example, it may be a start-up requiring long hours in cramped conditions or a larger company that's just beginning a new project. Or perhaps they're fervent believers in the two-person team programming model. In any case, know what your work style is and make sure it's compatible with the company.

"Tell Me About Your Experience."

This question is one that everyone should practice and have an answer for. We cannot overemphasize this! Make sure your answer highlights specific achievements and be enthusiastic as you talk about your projects. Enthusiasm is extremely important!

Talk not only about the factual aspects of your previous assignments, but also about what you learned. Talk about what went right, but also what went wrong. Describe positive and negative experiences and what you learned from each of them. Keep your response to around 30–60 seconds, depending on your experience. Again, be sure to practice this ahead of time.

"What Are Your Career Goals?"

This question gives you a chance to explain why you want this job (apart from the money) and how you see it fitting into your overall career. This is similar to the question about what you want to do. The employer is concerned that you may not want to do the job. In this case, it is because the job may not fit into your career goals. It's certainly okay to be confused about what you want to do — many people are. Try to have at least a general idea of where you see yourself going. Your answer might be as simple as, "I'm hoping to work in development for a while and work on some great projects. Then, I'm looking to go into project management. Beyond that, it's hard to say." This answer shows motivation and convinces the employer that you'll succeed on the job.

"Why Are You Looking to Change Jobs?"

Interviewers generally want to know what you don't like to do. Clearly, you don't like your last job or you would probably still be there. In addition, there's a fear that you may be trying to cover a weakness that caused you to leave your last job. Therefore, try to answer this question by citing either a change in environment, a factor out of your control, or a weakness that the interviewer already knows. For example, to cite a change in environment you could say, "I've worked in a large company for five years and experienced the software development process for a mature product. I no longer want to be a number in a large company. I want to join a start-up and be a key person from the ground up and watch something grow." Or, you could answer, "I worked at a start-up that didn't have its act together. Now I want to work at a company that does."

To cite a factor out of your control, you could say, "My current company has given up on the project I've been working on and they're trying to relocate me to something that I don't find interesting." Or, you could respond, "My company was acquired and the whole atmosphere has changed since then."

It's also generally acceptable to cite a weakness that the interviewer already knows. You could say, "My last job required extensive systems-level programming. I was way behind everyone else on that topic, and I don't find that sort of work very exciting. I'm much more interested in doing Web programming, which I do have experience in."

One final note: Even though money is often a good reason to change jobs, be careful about citing it as a prime reason. This raises the possibility that your current employer doesn't offer you more money because you're not that valuable and you're hoping someone else won't notice this fact.

"How Much Money Do You Want to Make?"

This question may appear in any context. It's most common, though, either at the initial screening or when the company has decided to make you an offer. If it's asked at the beginning, the employer may want to know if it's even worth talking to you, given your salary expectations, or the employer may genuinely have no idea what the position should pay. It is generally considered wise to put this question off as long as possible. It is not in your interest to discuss numbers until you've convinced the potential employer of your value. If you can't escape this question in the early stages of an interview, try to give a range of salaries with the amount that you want at the low end. This gives you good bargaining room later.

If you're asked the question near the end of the process, this can only indicate good things. If the interviewer has no interest in hiring you at this point, he won't bother asking this question. Generally, larger companies have less latitude in compensation packages than smaller companies. If you're asked this question, it probably indicates the company is willing to negotiate. It's important to realize companies are often unaware of how to make a competitive offer. This is your chance to tell them how to do exactly that.

First, it's important to do your homework ahead of time when answering this question. If you find that people with similar jobs in your area are making $40,000–$55,000 a year, you're probably not going to make $80,000 a year. Second, never undersell yourself. If you're looking for an annual salary of $70,000, don't tell an employer that you're looking for around $60,000 a year with the hope that the employer will, for some reason, offer more. This response makes it almost impossible for the employer to make a good offer. Third, consider carefully what you want in a total compensation package. You may be graduating from college and want a signing bonus to offset the costs of finding an apartment, moving, and placing deposits. Or, you may be looking to join a start-up offering generous stock options and slightly lower salaries. In any case, it's important to figure out exactly what you're looking for in terms of bonuses, benefits, stock options, and salary.

In general, try not to tip your hand too early when answering this question. The person with more information generally does better in a negotiation. Instead of answering a question about salary directly, ask what range the interviewer is prepared to offer. There are four possible answers to your question.

First, the range may be about what you expected. In this case, you can usually gain a slightly higher salary by following these rules: First, try not to act too excited — stay cool. Next, say that you had a similar but slightly higher range in mind, setting your minimum at the maximum of the offered range. For example, if the employer says, "We're expecting to pay $40,000 to $45,000," you should respond, "That seems about right. I'm looking to make $45,000 to $50,000 and hoping for the high end of that range." Finally, negotiate in a professional manner until you agree on a number with the interviewer; you'll probably receive an offer between $43,000 and $48,000.

The second possibility is that the negotiator starts with a range higher than you expected. This is great!

In the third case, the negotiator may not answer your question. He or she may give a response like "We have a wide range of salaries depending on the applicant. What were you expecting?" This response is actually quite favorable because it indicates that he or she probably has the authority to pay you a competitive salary. The response shows that the negotiator is willing to negotiate, but it also indicates that you may be subject to some hardball negotiating skills. Bearing in mind that negotiation will follow, respond with one number, the high end of your range. This gives you room to negotiate and still receive a favorable offer. For example, if you're expecting between $55,000 and $60,000, say, "I'm expecting $60,000 a year." Presenting it like this leaves the other negotiator less room to lowball you than if you give a range. Avoid weaker expressions like "I'm hoping for . . ." or "I'd really like . . . " The negotiator may accept your number, or may try to negotiate a slightly lower salary. If you remain professional and negotiate carefully, your final salary should fall within your desired range. Alternatively, the negotiator may respond by telling you that the company has a substantially lower range in mind. In this case, your response should be the same as in option four, which is described next.

The fourth option is that the offer may be less than you expected. In these cases, here are some tactics to try to increase the offer. First, re-emphasize your skills and state the salary range you were expecting. For example, if you were offered a salary of $35,000 but were expecting $50,000, you may say, "I have to admit I'm a little disappointed with that offer. Given my extensive experience with Web development and the contributions I can make to this company, I'm expecting a salary of $50,000." The negotiator may need time to get back to you, which is perfectly fine. If the negotiator doesn't increase the offer after hearing your range, he or she will often cite one of the following three reasons:

1. That amount wasn't budgeted.
2. Similar employees at the company don't make that much.
3. Your experience doesn't warrant such a salary.

None of these is an acceptable reason. First, the budget may be a constraint on the company, but it shouldn't be a constraint on your salary. If the company really wants you, it will find the money and a way around this artificial barrier. If the company truly can't find the money, it's such a cash-strapped, close-to-death organization that you probably don't want to work there anyway.

Second, it doesn't matter what the company pays other employees. That's between the company and those employees. Other employees shouldn't determine your compensation. You can respond by saying, "I wasn't aware that my compensation would be tied to other employees' compensations. I'm looking for a package that is commensurate with my skills of *X* and believe that $*Y* is such a package."

Finally, if you've done your homework, you know your experience and skills do warrant such a salary and the company is trying to lowball you. Simply re-emphasize your skills and explain that, after doing your research, you know your desired salary is indeed the competitive market salary. The company may realize it is out of touch with the market and increase its offer.

If the negotiator does not increase the offer but you still want the job, you have two last-ditch tactics. First, you can say that you're tempted to take the job, but that you'd like a salary review in six months to discuss your performance and compensation. You generally have a much stronger hand before you join a company, so you shouldn't expect miracles. Most negotiators, however, will grant this request. Make sure you get it in writing if you go this route. Second, try to negotiate other parts of the package. For example, you may be able to get additional vacation days, flex hours, or a sign-on bonus.

Here are a few final thoughts on the salary issue. Some people are embarrassed or shy about talking about salary. You should realize that you're already looking to engage in a business relationship, and salary is just one more part of the picture. No employer expects you to work for free, and there's no reason you should act as if compensation isn't important.

Many negotiators will cite factors such as benefits or work style to draw you to a company. These factors may be important reasons to join a company, and you'd certainly want all of the benefits spelled out. These perks, though, are generally not negotiable. Don't bother discussing non-negotiable factors in a negotiation, and don't get sidetracked if your negotiator mentions them.

"What Is Your Salary History?"

This is a different question from what you are expecting to make. In this case, the negotiator wants to know your previous salary — most likely to use this as a guide to determine your offer. If this question is raised (unless you were very happy with your previous salary), politely answer that you expect compensation appropriate for the new job and responsibilities and that the compensation that you received for a different set of tasks isn't relevant. In addition, resist any temptation to inflate your old salary because you may be asked to back up any claim with pay stubs or other proof.

"Why Should We Hire You?"

This question is obnoxious, rude, and belittling. It implies that there's no obvious reason why you're qualified for the job. Clearly, you have skills and experience that make you qualified; otherwise, the interviewer wouldn't be talking to you. In these instances, avoid becoming defensive and reciting your résumé to list your qualifications. Instead, keep things positive by talking about why you want to work at the company and why the job is a good match for your skills. This response shows you can handle criticism and may deflect your interviewer.

"Do You Have Any Questions for Me?"

Conventional wisdom has always said to ask a question because it shows enthusiasm. Nothing spoils a good interview, though, like asking a stupid question right at the end. Asking a contrived question just because you feel you should won't count in your favor. A thoughtful and articulate question can tell you a lot about the company and impress your interviewer. Often, your interviewer doesn't tell you what he or she does. This is a good time to ask. It lets you know more about what you would potentially be doing and shows genuine interest in the person. In addition, if the interviewer mentioned anything during the interview that sounded interesting, ask for more detail about it. This can yield further insight into your potential future employer. Finally, if you don't have questions, you can make a joke of it. You could say, "Gee, I know that I'm supposed to ask a question, but the people I interviewed with this morning answered all my questions. I guess you're off the hook!"

Summary

Nontechnical questions are just as important as the technical ones. While good answers to nontechnical questions won't get you hired if you bomb the technical part of the interview, bad answers can definitely preclude a job offer. Treat these questions with the respect they deserve.

Conclusion

At this point you should be feeling much more comfortable with programming interviews and have a good idea of what to expect when you apply for your next (or first!) job. Being prepared is half the battle, and will give you an edge over the candidates who are nervous and uncomfortable with the technical interview process.

Don't stop preparing once you put down this book. Here are some suggestions for what to do next:

- **Keep your brain nimble** — Puzzles are always good ways to train your mind to think outside the box.
- **Read about programming** — Try to stay current with the latest ideas and trends in computing.
- **Visit technical interview sites** — A Web search with the phrase "technical interview questions" will list a number of sites with questions similar to those found in this book. (Answers aren't usually provided, but even if they are it's better to work through the problems yourself.)

Finally, don't stop learning when you get that job. Keep developing your problem-solving skills; they can help at every stage of your career.

Get On the Mailing List!

Be sure to visit `http://www.piexposed.com` and join the *Programming Interviews Exposed* mailing list to get updates to the book and additional interview tips and articles.

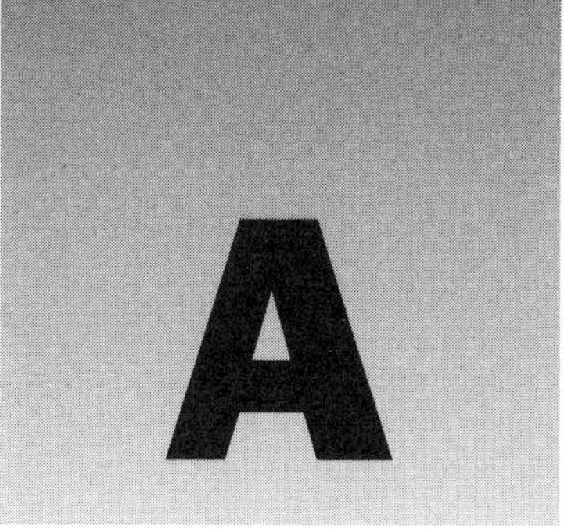

Résumés

Whether you have a contact in industry, are going through a company's recruiting process, or are using a headhunter, everyone will ask to see your résumé. Your résumé convinces people that you have relevant skills and talents and are worth consideration as a candidate. A good résumé is a necessary — but not sufficient — requirement for getting hired. If the person who reads your résumé doesn't find the relevant information they're looking for, they'll drop you for consideration and move on to the next job candidate. This is why it's so important that your résumé doesn't sell you short. This appendix examines and improves some typical developers' résumés to illustrate the techniques you can use to get your résumé in shape.

The Technical Résumé

Technical résumés are written differently than the nontechnical résumés described in most résumé books. Nontechnical jobs generally have some latitude in terms of necessary skills, but technical jobs usually require a very specific skill set. Employers aren't interested in talking to candidates who don't have the necessary skills for the job. This means that technical résumés generally require more specific information than nontechnical résumés.

A Poor Example

The example in this section starts with an extreme case of a very poor résumé from a junior developer. Although it is hoped that no real résumé would ever be this bad, the steps taken to improve such an extreme case are made clear and are relevant to almost anyone's résumé. Figure A-1 shows the sample résumé before improvements.

George David Lee

Current Address:
18 CandleStick Drive #234
San Mateo, CA 94403
650-914-3810
george@windblown.com

Permanent Address:
19 Juniata Dr.
Gladwyne, PA 19035
610-221-9999
george@my_isp.com

Objective: I am looking to join a growing and dynamic company. I am specifically interested in working for a company which provides interesting work and career opportunity. I am also interested in an organization which provides the opportunity for me to grow as an employee and learn new skills. Finally, I am interested in companies in the high-tech space that are looking to hire people.

Information:

- **Citizenship:** United States of America
- **Birthdate:** April 18, 1975
- **Place of Birth:** Denver, Colorado, USA
- **Hometown:** Philadelphia, Pennsylvania, USA
- **Social Security Number:** 445-626-5599
- **Marital Status:** Divorced

Work History:

June 2002-Present, Programmer

Windblown Technologies, Inc., San Francisco, California

I was part of a large group that moved old legacy applications to newer systems and used lots of new technologies and languages to do this. The advantages to our clients was that new computers are cheaper than old computers and they don't break as much. This way, it makes sense for them to have us do this. I did a portion of the programming on the new machines, but also had to work with the old machines. Our clients were able to see substantial cost savings as a result of our project. The group got quite good at moving these things and I was part of six projects in my time here. Another big project involved a lot of web stuff where I had to use a database and some other neat technologies. I am leaving because our current projects have not been very intresting and I feel like I am no longer learning anything here.

Reference: Henry Rogers
Windblown Technologies, Inc.
1818 Smith St. Suite #299
San Francisco, CA 94115
415-999-8845
henry@windblown.com

May 2002-June2002

BananaSoft Inc. Developer of apps., San Francisco, California

This job didn't really work out and I left really soon. All I did was work on some HTML programming which was never used.

No Reference

Figure A-1

January 2001-May2002
F=MA computing corp. Engineer, Palo Alto, California
My role here was to work with a group of people on our main project. This project centered around developing a piece of software that allowed you to figure out dependencies between clients and servers. The advantages of this device are that you can more quickly debug and maintain legacy client/server devices. This was an exciting and interesting position. The reason that I left was because my boss left and the company brought in a different boss who didn't know what he was doing.
Reference: Angelina Diaz
1919 44th St.
Palo Alto, CA 94405
650-668-9955
Angelina.diaz@fma.com
June 2001 – December 2001
I did not have a job during this time because I spent it traveling around Europe after college. I traveled through:

- England
- France
- Germany
- Czech Republic
- Ireland
- Italy
- Spain

September 1997 – June 2001
UCLA Housing and Dining Student Food Server, Los Angeles, California
My responsibilities included preparing dinner for over 500 students in the Walker Dining Commons. I started out as a card swiper for the first year. Later, I started to cook food and spend one year as a pasta chef. After working as a Pasta chef, I spend the last two years overseeing the salad production. I left this job because I graduated from college.
Reference: Harry Wong
UCLA Housing and Dining
1818 Bruin Dr.
Los Angeles, CA 91611
310-557-9988 extension 7788
hwong@dining.ucla.edu

June 2000-September 2000 and June 1999 – September 1999
AGI Communications, Intern, Santa Ana, California
Learned how to work in a large company and be part of a dynamic organization. Worked on a project for the human resources department which they eventually scrapped even after I had worked on it for two summers.
Reference: Rajiv Kumar
AGI Communications
1313 Mayflower St. Suite #202

Figure A-1 *(continued)*

Santa Ana, CA 92610
rajiv@agi.com
June 1997 – September 1997
Elm St. Ice cream shop, Senior Scooper, Bryn Mawr, Pennsylvania
My responsibilities included serving ice cream to customers, dealing with suppliers and locking up. After one month, I was promoted to senior scooper meaning that I got to assign people tasks.
Education:
University of California Los Angeles, Los Angeles, CA 1997-2001.
Bachelors of Science in Computer Systems Engineering, GPA 3.1 / 4.0
Member of Kappa Delta Phi Fraternity
Abraham Lincoln High School, Rosemont, PA 1993-1997, GPA 3.4/4.0

- Chess club president
- 11th grade essay contest award winner
- 3 Varsity letters in Soccer
- 2 Varsity letters in Wrestling

Hobbies:

- Partying
- Hiking
- Surfing
- Chess

Additional References are available upon request.

Figure A-1 ***(continued)***

Sell Yourself

Most of this résumé's problems result from a single fundamental error. Lee wrote his résumé to describe himself, not to get a job. Lee's résumé is much more an autobiography than it is a sales pitch for him and his skills. This is a very common problem. Many people believe their résumé should simply describe everything they've ever done. That way, a potential employer can carefully read all of the information and make an informed decision regarding whether to grant an interview. Unfortunately, it doesn't work this way. Employers spend very little time on each résumé they read. Your résumé must be a marketing tool that sells you and convinces an employer that you're valuable — quickly. When you keep this idea in mind, most of the other problems become self-evident.

Write your résumé to sell yourself.

Keep It Short

Lee's résumé has a number of other very common problems. One of the biggest is length. An interviewer may receive 50 résumés for an opening. From previous experience, he knows that the vast majority of the candidates are probably not appropriate for the job. The interviewer will have time to speak with only four or five of the candidates, so he must eliminate 90 percent of the applicants based on their résumés. Interviewers don't carefully read through each résumé; they quickly scan the résumé to determine whether they can find any reason to keep it. The one question going through the interviewer's mind is, "What can this person do for me now?" Your résumé has to look so good that the interviewer can't possibly risk passing on you. An interviewer won't wait very long to throw out a résumé. If he doesn't see anything he likes after 15 or 20 seconds of looking at the résumé's first page, the résumé won't make it any further.

Despite the need to make an impression, avoid the temptation to lie or add items you're unfamiliar with. Inflating your résumé can create a variety of problems. First, many interviewers will ask you about every item on your résumé; if you clearly aren't familiar with something, it calls your entire résumé into question. Second, if you claim knowledge of a wide variety of technologies outside your experience, an interviewer may not even have to talk to you to figure out that you're lying. Finally, if you throw in a grab bag of random buzzwords that don't follow any particular theme, you may appear to be a jack of all trades and master of none. The net result is that your résumé becomes a hindrance to your getting a job, as opposed to a tool that helps you.

Keep your résumé as short as possible. If you have less than five years of experience, one page is sufficient. More-experienced job hunters can use two pages. Under no circumstances should any résumé exceed three pages. Anything beyond that and you're writing a *curriculum vitae*, not a résumé, and CVs are not normally used by nonacademic job applicants in the United States. (International job applications may in fact require a fuller résumé, along the lines of a CV, so be sure to check and send the right kind of document.)

Keep your résumé short. Make every word count.

List the Right Information

Contentwise, Lee's résumé is not "buzzword compliant" — it doesn't mention technologies by name. This is a big problem, because many companies use automated systems that look for certain keywords in order to flag promising résumés. For example, when a position requires a "Java developer with XML experience," the system prints out all résumés with the words "Java" and "XML." Other companies file résumés by skills, but the result is the same. Because Lee's résumé is short on buzzwords, it is unlikely to even make it into the stack of résumés that an interviewer sees. He should list all software products, operating systems, languages, technologies, and methodologies that he's used. He should also list any other relevant topics he has experience with — for example, security algorithms or network protocols. Lee should then categorize his skills by topic, as shown in Figure A-2.

When you list specific products in your résumé, include version numbers to show that you're up to date with the latest-and-greatest technologies. Most version numbers are omitted from the examples shown here because they would be obsolete by the time you read this, but your résumé should be updated much more frequently than a book. Always keep your résumé updated with your most recent experiences; otherwise, don't bother using version numbers.

TECHNICAL SKILLS:

- Languages: C; C++; C#; Java; Perl; Visual Basic; JavaScript
- Internet Technology Experience: Extensive experience with Java servlets; JSP; mod_perl; XML and XSL; client/server architecture; HTML; CGI scripts; shell scripts; ASP; ASP.NET
- Operating Systems: UNIX (Linux, Solaris, HP-UX, FreeBSD); Macintosh; Windows XP, NT
- Databases: SQL; Oracle Products (Oracle RDMBS 10g, Oracle SQL*Plus, PL/SQL, PRO*C); MS SQL Server; IBM DB2; MySQL; JDBC; ODBC
- Graphics: OpenGL; extensive knowledge of scan-conversion routines

Figure A-2

Explicitly list your skills by name on your résumé.

Be Clear and Concise

Lee's résumé also needs to be formatted more cleanly. In its current form, it uses too many fonts, formats, and lines. This is generally annoying — some would say it makes his résumé look like a ransom note. It can also cause problems for an automated scanning system. Choose a standard font such as Times New Roman and stick with it throughout the résumé.

Lee's content is difficult to read, rambling and unfocused; it doesn't describe his contributions and doesn't sell him as a valuable employee. This is especially true regarding his work experience. First, Lee should reorganize his content into bulleted lists. These are faster to read than descriptions in paragraph form, and they make it easier for an interviewer to absorb more in less time. This increases the chances that his résumé will be one of the few that the interviewer decides to act on.

Lee's descriptions should be more focused. His descriptions don't clearly state exactly what he did. He describes what the team did and the general company focus, but not his role, which is the most important part of selling himself as a good candidate. He should also use action verbs such as *implemented, designed, programmed, monitored, administered,* and *architechted* to describe his contributions. These should describe specific actions, such as "designed database schema for Oracle 10g database and programmed database connectivity using Java threads and JDBC." When possible, he should quantify his tasks and describe the results of his work. For example, he could write "administered network of 20 Linux machines for Fortune 100 client, resulting in $1 million in revenues annually." This is a good sell job because it answers the question, "What can you do for me right now?" One caveat is to make sure that any metrics you give are impressive. If your metrics are not impressive, omit them.

Another part of focusing the content is to decide the order in which to list responsibilities for a certain job. Generally, you want to list responsibilities from most impressive to least impressive. However, make sure that you get the main point across first. For example, if you did both sales and development at a job, you may have some very impressive sales, some impressive development work, and a few less-impressive sales. If you want to emphasize that you were successful in sales, you should list all of your sales work first, followed by all of your development work. In addition, make sure your points follow a coherent order. This often means grouping items by topic area, even if it causes them to deviate slightly from a strict ranking by importance.

Many people have trouble selling themselves in their résumés. Often, this happens because they feel that they have to be modest and avoid boasting. As a result, many job applicants end up underselling themselves. Don't lie, but put the most impressive slant on whatever you have done. If you really have trouble saying nice things about yourself, ask a friend for help.

Present your experience in bulleted lists and cast it in the best possible light.

Relevant Information Only

Lee's résumé also includes irrelevant items that take up valuable space. One of the first items an interviewer reads about Lee is that he's a citizen of the United States and was born in Denver. Even though his citizenship or residence status may be important later in the game, when a job offer is about to be made, none of this information will convince an interviewer that he's the person for the job, and just wastes valuable space. (Again, international job applications are different and may require this kind of citizenship information.) Other irrelevant information includes his birthdate, hometown, Social Security number, marital status, hobbies, and travel history — information that doesn't make him a more attractive candidate.

Lee's use of the word "I" is unnecessary because the résumé is obviously about him. He shouldn't bother to mention references either. Interviewers won't check references until they're about to make an offer, so it's pointless to put them on your résumé. He doesn't even need to include "References are available upon request" because that's always implicit. Similarly, a résumé is not the place to mention why he left earlier jobs. This question is likely to come up in interviews, and it's a good idea to have a strong, positive response prepared, but it doesn't belong on a résumé. Lee's middle name should also be omitted unless he usually goes by George David.

Finally, omit any additional information that makes you a less-attractive candidate. For example, don't put something on your résumé such as "looking for half-time position until graduation in June, and then conversion to full time." Most interviewers would pass over someone like this and look for someone available full time instead. However, if the interviewer speaks with you and is impressed, it's a different story.

Lee needs to look at his résumé and focus all necessary information to make it as short and useful as possible. Every word must count. For example, he can start with his address information. It's not clear whether he should be contacted at his permanent or current address. He should give only one address, phone number, and e-mail address. Lee also lists too much information about his high school accomplishments. Old awards, accomplishments, or job tasks that are not relevant to your current job search should generally be omitted. Any job that occurred more than 10 years ago or is totally different from the job that you're seeking should be mentioned only briefly. For example, Lee goes into too much detail about his work at the ice cream shop and the dining hall. It's fine to mention this employment, but he won't get the job based on his responsibilities scooping ice cream. He should provide only relevant job data. Lee should also omit the job that he held for two months because it will only count against him. Finally, Lee's objective statement doesn't add anything. Everyone is looking for an "interesting" job with a "dynamic" company. His objective statement should briefly state what sort of job he wants, such as "software engineer" or "database programmer."

Include only relevant information.

Use Reverse Chronological Ordering

After improving the résumé's content, Lee needs to decide how to order his information most effectively. One obvious way to do this is chronologically. In this case, Lee would start out with his high school education, then his job at the ice cream shop, then college, and so forth. A reader could easily follow Lee's experience throughout his life. Even though this is a consistent ordering, it is a poor choice. Always put the most compelling reason for you to be considered for a job first, at the top of the résumé. Interviewers start reading résumés from the top, so you want to put your best stuff first, where it can convince the interviewer to read the rest of the résumé. After that first reason, continue to follow a clear and concise organization that spells out your qualifications. The end of the résumé is for the least-impressive information. Your most recent experiences are more relevant than your earliest experiences, so where you do use chronological ordering, put things in reverse order.

In Lee's case, his most impressive asset is undoubtedly his skills. He has a wide range of relevant skills. He should begin his résumé with these skills. Next, Lee should list either his work history or education. Early in your career you should generally put your education first, especially if you went to an impressive school. Later, put your experience first. In Lee's case, it's a toss-up as to whether to list his education or his work experience next. He's right on the cusp of when he should switch from listing education first to work history first. Lee did graduate from an impressive school not too long ago, and he has held several jobs since then, none of them for very long. Therefore, there's probably a slight advantage to listing his education before his work history. In Lee's case, his education is a single item. If he had more than one degree, he would put the most impressive one (usually a postgraduate or university degree) first.

Always Proofread

Lee also needs to proofread his résumé better. For example, he spelled "interesting" as "intresting" and used "spend" when he should have used "spent." Mistakes make you look careless and unprofessional. Many people stop reading a résumé as soon as they find a single mistake. At the very least, mistakes make you a weaker candidate. The only way to avoid mistakes is to proofread. Proofread over and over and over. Then, let the résumé sit for a while, come back to it, and proofread some more. It's also a good idea to ask a trusted friend to proofread for mistakes. While your friend is reading your résumé, find out if he or she thinks a section is unclear, has a recommendation on how to improve your résumé, or thinks you could do a better selling job. Your friend's reactions may give you a clue about how your résumé will appear to an interviewer.

One final matter concerns printing your résumé. Often, you will submit your résumé electronically and printing won't be an issue. If you print out your résumé, there's no need to use special paper or have your résumé professionally printed. Résumés are often photocopied, scanned, faxed, and written on, making fancy paper and printing a wasted expense. A laser printer and simple white paper will always suffice.

The Improved Example

Following all of the preceding recommendations, Lee's improved résumé appears in Figure A-3.

As you can see, this résumé is more likely to make the cut and get Lee opportunities to speak with interviewers. This résumé is based on the experiences and skills of the same person, but it looks almost entirely different.

George Lee
18 Candle Stick Drive #234
San Mateo, CA 94403
650-914-3810
george@my_isp.com

OBJECTIVE: Developer

TECHNICAL SKILLS:

- Languages: C; C++; C#; Java; Perl; Visual Basic; JavaScript
- Internet Technology Experience: Extensive experience with Java servlets; JSP; mod_perl; XML and XSL; Client/server architecture; HTML; CGI scripts; shell scripts; ASP; ASP.NET
- Systems: UNIX (Linux, Solaris, HP-UX, FreeBSD); Macintosh; Windows XP, NT
- Databases: SQL; Oracle Products (Oracle RDMBS 10g, Oracle SQL*Plus, PL/SQL, PRO*C); MS SQL Server; IBM DB2; MySQL; JDBC; ODBC
- Graphics: OpenGL; extensive knowledge of scan-conversion routines

EDUCATION:

University of California Los Angeles, Los Angeles, CA 1997-2001.
BS, Computer Systems Engineering GPA 3.1 / 4.0

EXPERIENCE:

6/02–Present **Developer and Consultant, Windblown Technologies, Inc., San Francisco, CA**

- Lead developer on four projects generating $1 million in revenues.
- Ported 100,000-line enterprise payroll application from PDP 11 to Sun Solaris.
- Designed database schema for Oracle 10g database; programmed database connectivity using Java threads and JDBC.
- Architected Web tracking application to monitor packages for shipping firm using JSP, JDBC, and an Oracle 10g database.
- Wrote front-end Java servlet code to allow an airline to securely communicate with its suppliers via the Internet.

1/01–5/02 **F=MA Computing Corp. Server-side Engineer, Palo Alto, CA**

- Improved on Internet order procurement performance by 25 percent using Apache, Perl CGI scripts, and Oracle.
- Developed TCP/IP stack tracer to find client/server dependencies.
- Created Web-based reporting system using Java servlets and IBM's DB2 database.
- Wrote Perl scripts to monitor mission-critical systems and notify administrators in case of failure.
- Ported DOS-based C client to Windows XP for automobile production monitoring.

Figure A-3 ***(continued)***

9/97–6/01	**UCLA Housing and Dining Student Food Server**
6/00–9/00	**AGI Communications, Santa Ana, CA, Developer** • Developed HR time tracking system
6/97–9/97	**Elm St. Ice Cream Shop, Bryn Mawr, PA, Ice Cream Scooper**

Figure A-3 ***(continued)***

Managers and Senior Developers

Although the same ideas that improved Lee's résumé will also improve a senior person's résumé, there are other issues to consider. Senior people generally have some management responsibility, and it's important that their résumés show they are capable of this task. For example, consider the résumé presented in Figure A-4 for a senior manager, Sam White. As you read through his résumé, try to see which of the techniques that benefited Lee's résumé could also be helpful for White.

White's résumé has the same major problem as Lee's first résumé. It is an autobiography, not a marketing tool. This structural problem is evident from the beginning, where he gives a brief timeline of his life over the past 30 years. Writing an autobiography is a common problem for senior people with impressive credentials such as White's. Many senior people mistakenly believe that if they describe their accomplishments, interviews will follow, but the only question going through an interviewer's mind is "What can you do for me now?", regardless of the applicant's seniority. In many ways, focus is even more important for a more-senior job because you need to make a greater impression in just as little time.

Many of the specific problems with this résumé are the same as with Lee's initial résumé. It's too long — White should cut his résumé to no more than two pages and strive for one and a half. White should also arrange his descriptions in bulleted lists so that they are easier to read.

However, White's main content problem is that his résumé doesn't sell him for the sort of job he's trying to get. White spends a lot of time describing various job tasks that are clearly junior tasks. Senior positions generally require some management and have less emphasis on technical skills. The ability to perform junior tasks won't get you an interview for a job that requires senior tasks. When applying for a senior position, stress your management skills and experience more than your technical skills or achievements in junior positions.

White also needs to show positive results from his past leadership. In this vein, it is necessary to both describe the experience and quantify the result. For example, White's résumé mentions "management and maintenance of Web development effort for both U.S. and Canadian sites." This is an impressive achievement, but the size of the undertaking is not clear; nor is it clear whether the project was a success. The description in White's résumé leaves open the possibility that the project was a total failure and he is being forced to resign in disgrace or that the project was trivial and consisted of posting a few documents to a Web server. White should quantify the results of his work whenever possible. For example, he could state, "Managed team of 7 in developing and maintaining U.S. and Canadian Web sites. Sites generate 33 million hits and $15 million annually."

Samuel Thomas White
3437 Pine St.
Skokie, IL 60077
813-665-9987
sam_white@mindcurrent.com

Statement:

Over the past 3 decades my career has evolved from a lab technician to Web project manager. During that time, I spent some time away and earned my Ph.D. in physics. I have taught college computer science off and on for over 18 years and published numerous journal publications. I have spent the past four years as a project manager overseeing a large Web application development.

At the present, I am actively pursuing MSCE certification to better architect the necessary solutions. I have completed introductory hands-on courses in Networking Fundamentals; Windows Server 2003, and SQL Server. I am taking continuing education courses in management and in other advanced technology topics. Last March, I attended my company's manager seminar conference.

Brief Computer History:

1977: Completed dissertation, moved to Chicago.

1977: I received my first personal computer. I wrote a program that implemented a rudimentary spreadsheet.

1979: I started to consult for a living. I was independent and worked primarily on assembly programming.

1980: Formed my company, Big Dipper Consulting. Worked on a variety of projects ranging from network debugging tools to graphics chip optimizations.

1994: My first trip on the Web with NCSA Mosaic. I knew that this would be big. I started out running simple static pages, then moved onto CGI scripting. I have been on the forefront of Web technologies and have fulfilled numerous consulting contracts and led many development efforts.

Work History:

CorePlus Corporation
7/1997 — Present Senior Web Manager

Responsibilities include: management and maintenance of Web development effort for both U.S. and Canadian sites, management for network redesign, establishing and implementing protocols, migrating from Windows NT to Solaris, leading security audit using cutting-edge tools and managing 12 employees, providing 24/7 access for both internal deployment

Figure A-4 *(continued)*

and overseas operations, establishing procedures to ensure constant monitoring during non-working hours in case of failures, upgrading all software as new software is released and determined to be stable, ordering computers for both everyday (email, Web), development and travel, establishing proper backup procedures, evaluating different vendors' software packages for current needs and anticipating future needs in both infrastructure and licenses.

Pile-ON Technologies
11/1995 — 8/1997 Senior Web Developer

Responsibilities included: designing a UNIX-based Web development environment, installing necessary software including web server, development tools and source control, integrating legacy applications on PDP 11 heirarchical database to work with CGI scripts that get and set the necessary information, selecting third-party screen scraping products to receive necessary information from legacy system, implementing security procedures to prevent denial of service, spoofing and other attacks, managing three junior developers and ensuring coordination and timeliness of efforts, verifying cross Web-browser compatibility for all Web design efforts, purchasing necessary infrastructure to ensure robustness against all possible problems, built in redundancy, hiring and building development team, reporting directly to the Senior VP of engineering, coordinating with customer support, upgrading network to include newest and fastest solutions, working with consultants to integrate new products.

Athnorn Inc.
6/1990 — 11/1995 Senior Engineer, MIS

Responsibilities began by working as a C++ developer working on client/server application and doing some system administration tasks such as ensuring network reliability and integration between onsite and offshore developers. Promoted to senior engineer after two years. Additional responsibilities included designing enterprise-wide source control system and development environment spanning multiple sites, enabling dial-up and telnet connections via a VPN, managing a team of 5 developers and coordinating with marketing to ensure timeliness and quality of product, worked with contractors to implement third-party development products, evaluated and selected various vendors solutions, traveled to Europe, Japan, and the Middle East to meet with clients and assess future needs and problems, worked on moving several products to UNIX based environment, designed system to allow synchronous development across multiple time zones, attended company management philosophy seminar, attained certification in advanced use of all products, ensured compliance with corporate standards, worked with customer support to respond to common problems.

Detroit Motor Company
Corp. of Engineers
1/1990 — 5/1990 Contract Programmer Analyst

Four-month contract position which involved substantial modifications and enhancements to existing database program. This included custom generation of reports, additional ways to add information to database, and integration with existing products to achieve common functionality and data change. Also created files which allowed for much

Figure A-4 ***(continued)***

faster uploading and downloading of information. Also provided help with the LAN and WAN, technical support and full documentation of existing system. Worked on integration with legacy applications as well.

Tornado Development Corp.
6/1988 — 10/1989 Contract Programmer

Responsible for planning, development and the administration of BSD File servers. Used Oracle and SQL to do a variety of tasks mostly having to do with order tracking and HR tasks such as payroll and employee benefits. Worked to provide technical support for all users on various types of platforms. Additionally installed and maintained a variety of common applications and was responsible for troubleshooting when problems occurred.

Garson and Brown, Attorneys at Law
6/1985-5/1988 Computer Engineer

Responsibilities include troubleshooting, maintenance, repair, and support of LAN/ WAN networks, often had to use telephone and troubleshoot problems with novice user, updated all company software including Novell, Windows and other third-party proprietary products, designed and installed LAN in office place, maintained LAN and was responsible for new users, provided all support and coordinated with vendors

Hummingbird Chip Designs
5/1980-6/1985 Chip Tester

Responsibilities included testing all chip designs thoroughly using a variety of third-party products that ensured reliability and yield, worked with consultants to attain knowledge using third-party testing products, wrote scripts that automated repetitive tasks, reported potential problems to developers, coordinated all yield test efforts, worked with customer service to verify customer problems, was a liaison between customer support and development

EDUCATION

Indiana University, Bloomington, IN, 1966-1970 BA in Physics

Junior Year Electronics Award Winner

Member of Lambda, Alpha, Nu Fraternity

Member of junior varsity fencing team

University of Wisconsin, Madison, Wisconsin, 1970-1977 PhD in Physics

Doctoral Thesis Work on Molecular Structure of Molybdenum compounds when exposed to intense laser bursts of varying intensity.

Figure A-4 ***(continued)***

Skills: Attended technical courses for Microsoft Windows 2003, Extensive experience with TCP/IP protocols, security protocols including SSL and PGP, HP Openview, Java, VB, VBScript, ActiveX, ASP, IIS, ASP.NET, Apache, Netscape Enterprise Server, FoxPro, SQL Relational databases including Oracle, Informix, Sybase, DB2 and SQL server, UNIX system administration (Irix and Linux), C, C++, C#, Network Architect, Shell Scripting, CGI scripting, HTML, DHTML, repairing printers

Hobbies:
Barbershop Quartet, Golf, Tennis, Frisbee
Horseback Riding, Walking, Swimming
Reading, Traveling, Cake Decorating
Other:
Conversant in Spanish
Citizen of the United States of America

References available upon request.

Figure A-4 ***(continued)***

White is looking for a job that is heavy on project management and lighter on skills. He should deemphasize his "flavor of the month" buzzwords and emphasize his experience. He may even want to eliminate his technology skills inventory to make sure the reader doesn't think he's trying to get a less-senior position.

White's revised résumé appears Figure A-5. Notice how the résumé explains his accomplishments much more clearly and does a much better sell job. White becomes someone who a company couldn't afford not to interview.

This revamped résumé is a much more effective marketing tool for White.

Sam White
3437 Pine St.
Skokie, IL 60077
813-665-9987
sam_white@mindcurrent.com

Objective: Senior Manager in Internet Development

Experience:

7/97–present **CorePlus Corporation, Director of Web Development, Santa Rosa, CA**

- Managed team of seven in developing and maintaining U.S. and Canadian Web sites. Sites generate 33 million hits and $15 million annually.

Figure A-5

- Led team of three system administrators to implement full network redundancy, perform a security audit, develop backup procedures, and upgrade hardware and software for an 800-computer Linux and Windows network.
- Evaluated all major systems purchases.
- Purchased $400,000 of software and professional services after evaluation of seven packages and three firms, leading to 20 percent faster customer service response times.
- Hired four developers and managed staff of seven with 100 percent retention.
- Selected contractors to migrate Web servers from Windows to Linux. Migration occurred one month ahead of schedule and 20 percent under budget.

11/95–8/97 **Pile-ON Technologies, Senior Web Developer, San Jose, CA**

- Designed UNIX Web development environment and supervised team of five in implementation of Web log visualization tools. Tools have generated $5,000,000.
- Evaluated and selected over $200,000 of software and services to supplement Web logs development efforts.
- Developed feature set for $7,000,000 product based on interviews with 20 clients.
- Wrote 100,000-line C++ libraries used by three products with similar database access patterns.
- Recruited and trained two junior developers.

6/90–11/95 **Athorn Inc., Lead Engineer, Fremont, CA**

- Coordinated five developers in on-time six-month project to develop client portion of client / server application to enable department store cash registers to update central databases in real time. Product has 50,000 users.
- Met with clients to determine future feature sets for cash register client.
- Implemented Virtual Private Network between San Francisco Bay Area office and New York City office.
- Installed and supported internal enterprise-wide source control used by 30 developers on 10 projects

6/88–10/89 **Contractor at many companies**

- Upgraded network systems at Detroit Motors, Inc.
- Installed and designed database applications for Tornado Development Corp.

6/85–5/88 **Garson and Brown, Attorneys at Law, Computer Engineer, Palo Alto, CA**

Figure A-5 ***(continued)***

5/80–6/85 **Hummingbird Chip Designs, QA Tester, San Jose, CA**

Education:

University of Wisconsin, Madison, Wisconsin, Ph.D. in Physics, 1970–1977

- Doctoral thesis work on molecular structure of molybdenum atoms when exposed to laser bursts of varying intensity.

Indiana University, Bloomington, Indiana, B.A. in Physics, 1970

Other:

- Fluent in Spanish

Figure A-5 *(continued)*

Sample Résumés

The two résumés presented so far cover many of the cases you're likely to encounter when you write your résumé. You may want to see more examples of good résumés for different sorts of people to get a feel for how to write an effective résumé. The remaining portion of this appendix presents three résumés of people with different experience searching for different kinds of technical jobs, as shown in Figures A-6, A-7, and A-8. As you look at the résumés, notice what content stands out and how this helps sell the person as a potentially valuable employee.

Jenny Ramirez
jenny_ramirez23@mit.edu
MIT University
PO BOX 4558
Cambridge, MA 02238
227-867-5309

EDUCATION:

9/2004–2007 **Massachusetts Institute of Technology, Cambridge, MA.**
BS, Electrical Engineering, 2007 (GPA 3.7/4.0)

- Specialist in databases and security
- National Merit Scholar, Phi Beta Kappa

EXPERIENCE:

6/2006–8/2006 **E-Commerce Developer, WebWorks Corporation, Huntington Beach, CA.**
Implemented search feature on Fortune 500 company's Internet storefront using ASP.NET and SQL Server. Designed sample projects, using Oracleand MS SQL Server to demonstrate performance trade-offs between

Figure A-6

the products to clients. Made initial contact with two companies that became clients and resulted in $80,000 in revenues. Wrote three proposals that were accepted and resulted in $200,000 in revenues.

6/2005–9/2005 **Web Software Developer, The Aircraft Tech., Renton, WA.**

- Designed, researched and implemented a database solution to improve tracking and reporting of employee accomplishments.
- Designed and implemented CGI scripts to dynamically report Web server statistics.

9/2005–12/2005 **Computer Instructor, MIT Computer Science Department**

1/2005–3/2005 **Deans Tutor, MIT School of Engineering**

TECHNICAL SKILLS:

- Languages: C, C++; C#; Java; ADA
- Internet Technology: Java servlets; ASP; ASP.NET; mod_perl; XML and XSL; HTML
- Systems: UNIX (HP-UX, Solaris); Windows XP, 98
- Database: SQL; MS SQL Server; SQL Anywhere

LANGUAGES:

Fluent in French, proficient in German

Figure A-6 ***(continued)***

Mike Shronsky

1814 Park Dr. #244
Albuquerque, NM 98872
352-664-8811
mikey_s227@warmmail.com

Objective: Software Engineer in Web Development

Work Experience:

5/2002–present **Warner Tractors Manufacturers, Albuquerque, NM, Software Engineer**

- Created AJAX interface to allow customers to compare various tractors.
- Wrote Java servlets to generate dynamic Web content from Oracle database.
- Implemented Perl CGI reporting scripts for CORBA system.

Figure A-7 ***(continued)***

- Wrote SQL queries and designed database schema for Oracle database.
- Researched and selected development environment of Linux, Apache, and Tomcat.

7/2000–4/2002 **Problems Solved, Inc., Albuquerque, NM, Programmer**

- Incorporated focus group input into redesign of order tracking UI to improve workflow efficiency by 20 percent.
- Wrote 160 pages of product documentation for order tracking application.
- Analyzed product performance by writing shell scripts.
- Wrote hundreds of Perl scripts to test various Web server responses for clients.

5/1998–7/2000 **Hernson and Walker Insurance Agents, Austin, TX, Systems Administrator**

Maintained network, ordered systems, and implemented data tracking system.

<u>Technical Skills:</u>

- Languages: Java, Perl, JavaScript
- Databases: Oracle, DB2, MySQL
- Systems: Windows XP, 98, NT, Unix (Solaris, Linux)
- Web Skills: CGI, JSP, Apache, IIS, Tomcat, Netscape Enterprise Web Server

<u>Education:</u> Harcum College, Ardmore, PA, 2002, BA in management

<u>Other:</u> Fluent in Russian

Figure A-7 ***(continued)***

Elaine Mackenzie
22 Mt. Rogers Rd.
Nashville, TN 37212
615-667-4491
macky52@yeehah.com

<u>Objective:</u> Technology Consulting

<u>Technical Skills:</u>

- Languages: C#, C++, Visual Basic, VBScript, JavaScript
- Operating Systems: Windows XP, Windows 2000, Windows NT
- Internet: ASP.NET, IIS, ColdFusion, HTML, DHTML, CSS, XML and XSL

Figure A-8

Experience:

9/02–present **Web Integrations Specialist, National Web Consulting, Inc., Nashville, TN**

- Lead consultant on three projects generating $900,000.
- Built Web front end in ASP.NET to interact with legacy databases and perform all Human Resources-related functions for a Fortune 100 client.
- Wrote ASP.NET code to interface with legacy hierarchical IBM database.
- Constructed Web user interface component on six different projects.
- Managed $300,000 project resulting in on-time and on-budget delivery.
- Landed three accounts, generating $720,000 in revenues.
- Formed partnerships with three third-party software vendors. Partnerships generated $1,500,000 through joint contracts.

8/98–9/02 **Information Systems Technology Specialist, Johnson & Warner, Systems Integration Division, Nashville, TN**

- Wrote 200,000 lines of C++ code and 150 pages of documentation and billed $1,200,000.
- Built order tracking system for Fortune 500 client, using ASP and SQL Server.
- Led design team that architected system layout for 25 Windows 2000 Web Servers using Resonate load balancing software.
- Landed two accounts generating $250,000 total.
- Sold $200,000 in follow-on services.
- Hired and trained two associate consultants.

Additional Information:

Fluent in Spanish and Czech

Education:

Foothill College, Los Altos Hills, CA, BA in Accounting, 1995

Figure A-8 ***(continued)***

Index

SYMBOLS

A

D

E

F

G

M

N

O

P

Q

R

S

T

U

V

W

Z